A ROUGH GUIDE

PHRASEBOOK

Compiled by Lexus

Credits

Compiled by Lexus with László Jotischky

Lexus Series Editor:	Sally Davies
Rough Guides Phrasebook Editor:	Jonathan Buckley
Rough Guides Series Editor:	Mark Ellingham

This first edition published in 1998 by Rough Guides Ltd, 1 Mercer Street, London WC2H 9QJ.

Distributed by the Penguin Group.

Penguin Books Ltd, 27 Wrights Lane, London W8 5TZ
Penguin Books USA Inc., 375 Hudson Street, New York 10014, USA
Penguin Books Australia Ltd, 487 Maroondah Highway, PO Box 257, Ringwood, Victoria 3134, Australia
Penguin Books Canada Ltd, Alcorn Avenue, Toronto, Ontario, Canada M4V 1E4
Penguin Books (NZ) Ltd, 182–190 Wairau Road, Auckland 10, New Zealand

Typeset in Rough Serif and Rough Sans to an original design by Henry Iles.
Printed by Cox & Wyman Ltd, Reading.

272 pp.

British Library Cataloguing in Publication Data
A catalogue for this book is available from the British Library.

ISBN 1-85828-304-3

CONTENTS

HELP US GET IT RIGHT
Lexus and Rough Guides have made great efforts to be accurate and informative in this Rough Guide Hungarian phrasebook. However, if you feel we have overlooked a useful word or phrase, or have any other comments to make about the book, please let us know. All contributors will be acknowledged and the best letters will be rewarded with a free Rough Guide phrasebook of your choice. Please write to 'Hungarian Phrasebook Update', at either Mercer Street (London) or Hudson Street (New York) – for full address see opposite. Alternatively you can email us at mail@roughguides.co.uk

Online information about Rough Guides can be found at our website www.roughguides.com

INTRODUCTION

The Rough Guide Hungarian phrasebook is a highly practical introduction to the contemporary language. Laid out in clear A-Z style, it uses key-word referencing to lead you straight to the words and phrases you want – so if you need to book a room, just look up 'room'. The Rough Guide gets straight to the point in every situation, in bars and shops, on trains and buses, and in hotels and banks.

The main part of the Rough Guide is a double dictionary: English-Hungarian, then Hungarian-English. Before that, there's a section called **The Basics**, which sets out the fundamental rules of the language and its pronunciation, with plenty of practical examples. You'll also find here other essentials like numbers, dates, telling the time and basic phrases.

To get you involved quickly in two-way communication, the Rough Guide includes dialogues featuring typical responses on key topics – such as renting a car and asking directions. Feature boxes fill you in on cultural pitfalls as well as the simple mechanics of how to make a phone call, what to do in an emergency, where to change money and more. Throughout this section, cross-references enable you to pinpoint key facts and phrases, while asterisked words indicate where further information can be found in The Basics.

In the **Hungarian-English** dictionary, we've given not just the phrases you're likely to hear (starting with a selection of slang and colloquialisms), but also all the signs, labels, instructions and other basic words you might come across in print or in public places.

Finally the Rough Guide rounds off with an extensive **Menu Reader**. Consisting of food and drink sections (each starting with a list of essential terms), it's indispensable, whether you're eating out, stopping for a quick drink or browsing through a local food market.

jó utat!
have a good trip!

The Basics

PRONUNCIATION

In this phrasebook, the Hungarian has been written in a system of imitated pronunciation so that it can be read as though it were English, bearing in mind the notes on pronunciation given below:

a	as in f**a**ther
ay	as in m**ay**
ch	as in **ch**urch
e, eh	as in b**e**d
ew	as in **dew**
g	always hard as in **g**oat
h, H	as in **h**ot, never silent
ī	as the 'i' sound in m**igh**t
J	as the 's' sound in mea**s**ure
nyuh	like the 'n' in o**n**ion, lightly sounded
o	as in **o**rdinary
oo	as in f**oo**t
ow	as in n**ow**
ts	as in ha**ts**
tyuh	like the 'tu' in **tu**ne, lightly sounded
uh	like the 'ur' in f**ur** without the r
y	as in **y**es
yuh	'y' as in **y**es, but lightly sounded, much less pronounced than 'y' above

Hungarian Pronunciation

a	'o' (as in h**o**t)
á	'a' (as in f**a**ther)
ai	'o-ee'
aj	'oy'
áj	'eye' sound, represented by ī
au	'ow'
c	'ts' (as in ha**ts**)
cs	'ch'
e	'e' (as in b**e**d) or eh (at end of word)
é	'ay'
ei	'eh-i'
ej	'ay'
g	'g' (as in **g**oat)
gy	'dj'
h	'h' (as in **h**ot)
ie	'i-eh'
ii	'i-i'
í	'ee'
j	'y' (as in **y**es)
ly	slight 'y' sound as in **y**es, but not as strongly pronounced, represented by yuh
ny	slight 'ni' sound as in o**ni**on, represented by nyuh
o	'o' (as in **o**rdinary)
ó	'aw' (as in **aw**e)
ö	'uh' (like the **ur** in f**ur** without the r)
ő	'ur'
s	'sh'
ssz	'ss'
sz	's'
szs	'sh'
ty	slight 'tu' as in **tu**ne, represented by tyuh

u	'oo' (as in **foo**t)
ú	'oo' (as in **foo**d)
ü	'ew' (as in **dew**)
ű	'ew' (as in **dew** but longer)
v	'v'
w	'v'
zs	's' as in mea**s**ure, represented by J

In Hungarian, the stress is always on the first syllable of a word. When two consonants occur together, they are always pronounced.

ABBREVIATIONS

adj	adjective
f	feminine
fam	familiar
m	masculine
pl	plural
pol	polite
sing	singular

THE HUNGARIAN ALPHABET

The Hungarian-English section and Menu Reader are in Hungarian alphabetical order which is as follows:

a/á, b, c, cs, d, e/é, f, g, gy, h, i/í, j, k, l, ly, m, n, ny, o/ó, ö/ő, p, r, s, sz, ty, u/ú, ü/ű, v, w, y, z, zs

GENERAL

One very special feature of Hungarian is that endings or suffixes are added to words where in the equivalent English separate words would be used. In Hungarian, for example, all prepositions and possessive adjectives are suffixes. In the Hungarian-English section of this book, suffixes have been listed as separate entries.

VOWEL HARMONY

Another special feature of the language is the concept of vowel harmony. There are two types of vowels in Hungarian, back vowels and front vowels:

back vowels		front vowels	
a	**á**	**e**	**é**
		i	**í**
o	**ó**	**ö**	**ő**
u	**ú**	**ü**	**ű**

If a word contains only back vowels, then it usually takes a back vowel suffix like **-ban** (in) or **-ra** (to). If a word contains only front vowels, it will take a front vowel suffix like **-ben** (in) or **-re** (to):

Miskolcra akarok menni
mishkoltsro okorok menni
I want to go to Miskolc

a repülőtérre akarok menni
o repewlur-tayrreh okorok menni
I want to go to the airport

Some Hungarian words contain both front and back vowels. The choice of the suffix is governed by the last vowel in the word.

The rules of vowel harmony also apply to foreign words and names (for example, **Roberttel, Bobbyval, Londonból, Leedsből, McDonaldhoz, pulóverben**).

When a suffix is added to a noun or other word that ends in one of the short vowels **a** or **e**, the **a** or **e** changes to **á** and **é** respectively:

szálloda
sallodo
hotel

szállodában
sallodabon
in a hotel

PREPOSITIONS

Whereas English prepositions (to, at, in etc) are separate words, in Hungarian prepositions are in the form of suffixes that are added to the end of a noun. The suffix used depends on whether the noun contains front or back vowels (see the rules of Vowel Harmony page 5). The main prepositional suffixes are as follows:

-ban/-ben in

az autóban
oz owtawbon
in the car

a hangversenyteremben
o hongversheh[nyuh]teremben
in the concert hall

-ban/-ben are used when referring to foreign countries, cities and place names:

Londonban lakom
londonbon lokom
I live in London

Firenzében lakom
firenzayben lokom
I live in Florence

-ba/-be in, into; to

az uszodába
oz oosodabo
into the swimming pool

az ékszerüzletbe
oz aykserewz-letbeh
into the jeweller's shop

menjünk fel a Várba
menyewnk fel o varbo
let's go up to the Royal Castle

-ba/-be are used to translate 'to' when referring to foreign countries and place names:

Londonba repülünk
londonbo repewlewnk
we're flying to London

-ból/-ből from; from inside; (from) out of

kiszállt az autóból
kis-alt oz owtawbawl
he got out of the car

kijött az üzletből
ki-yuht oz ewzletburl
he came out of the shop

-ból/-ből are used to translate 'from' when referring to foreign countries and place names:

Londonból
londonbawl
from London

Leedsből
leedshburl
from Leeds

-n/-on/-en/-ön on; in
Use -n when the noun ends in a vowel:

az utcán
oz oottsan
on the street

Use **-on** after back-vowel words:

az autóbuszon
oz owtawbooson
on the bus

Use **-en** after front-vowel words, unless the final vowel is **ö**, **ő**, **ü** or **ű**:

a repülőgépen
o repewlur-gaypen
on the plane

Use **-ön** after front-vowel words, if the final vowel is **ö**, **ő**, **ü**, or **ű**:

csütörtökön
chewtuhrtuhkuhn
on Thursday

-n/**-on**/**-en**/**-ön** are used to translate 'in' when referring to most Hungarian place names:

Magyarországon
modjororsagon
in Hungary

Budapesten
boodopeshten
in Budapest

-ra/re on, onto; to

szálljunk fel a vonatra/ repülőgépre
sal-yoonk fel o vonotro/repewlur-gaypreh
let's get on the train/plane

taxin megyek a repülőtérre
toksin medjek o repewlur-tayrreh
I am going to the airport in a cab

liften megyek fel a második emeletre
liften medjek fel o mashodik emeletreh
I am taking the lift to the second floor

-ra/**-re** are used to translate 'to' when referring to most Hungarian place names:

Magyarországra
modjoror-sagro
to Hungary

Budapestre
boodopeshtreh
to Budapest

-ról/-ről from, off

leszálltam a vonatról/ repülőgépről
lesalltom o vonotrawl/repewlur-gayprurl
I got off the train/plane

felemeltem a földről
felemeltem o fuhldrurl
I picked it up from the floor

-ról/-ről are used to translate 'from' when referring to most Hungarian place names:

Magyarországról
modjoror-sagrawl
from Hungary

Budapestről
boodopeshtrurl
from Budapest

-nál/-nél at, by

a szállodánál
o sallodanal
at the hotel

a kereszteződésnél
o kerestezur-dayshnayl
at the crossroads

az ablaknál van
oz obloknal von
it's by the window

-nál/-nél can also be added to someone's name to translate 'at someone's house':

Annánál
onnanal
at Anna's place

-hoz/-hez/-höz to; near to, beside

a garázshoz
o goraJhoz
to (just outside) the garage

az emléktárgy üzlethez
oz emlayktardj ewzlethez
to the souvenir shop

az emlékműhöz
oz emlaykmewhuhz
to the monument

-hoz/-hez/-höz also means 'to' when you are going to someone's house:

ma délután elmegyek Péterhez
mo daylootan elmedjek payterhez
I'll go to Peter's this afternoon

You also use -hoz/-hez/-höz to ask a taxi-driver to go to a particular place:

a Nemzeti Múzeumhoz szeretnék menni
o nemzeti moozeh-oomhoz seretnayk menni
I'd like to go to the National Museum

a Gellért sörözőhöz kérem
o gellayrt shuhruhzur-huhz kayrem
to the Gellért beer hall, please

-tól/-től from near, from just outside

a szállodától
o sallodatawl
from outside the hotel

a Hősök terétől
o hurshuhk terayturl
from near Heroes' Square

-nak/-nek to; for
add oda a kulcsot a recepciósnak
od odo o koolchot o retseptsi-awshnok
give the key to the receptionist

a fagylalt a hölgynek lesz
o fodjlolt o huhldjnek les
the ice cream is for the lady

In phrases like the above, Hungarians would avoid saying 'for her' because it's considered impolite, see Pronouns page 19.

But 'for' in the sense of 'paid for' is translated by the suffix -ért:

készpénzben fizetett a jegyért
kayspaynzben fizetett o yedjayrt
he paid cash for the ticket

'With'
'With' is translated by the suffixes -val/-vel if the noun ends in a vowel:

szeretnék egy szobát fürdőszobával
seretnayk edj sobat fewrdursobavol
I want a room with a bath

elment egy barátjával
elment edj boratyavol
he/she went out with a friend

elment egy nővel
elment edj nurvel
he/she went out with a woman

If the noun ends in a consonant, the consonant is doubled, and -al/-el are added to translate 'with':

kérek egy málnaszörpöt jéggel
kayrek edj malnosuhrpuht yayggel
I'd like a raspberry juice with ice

eheted a kezeddel
eheted o kezeddel
you may eat it with your hands

Other Prepositions

There are a few words corresponding to English prepositions that are not suffixes:

mögött	[muhguht]	behind
előtt	[elurt]	in front of
mellett	[mellet]	next to
alatt	[olot]	under
fölött	[fuhluht]	above
között	[kuhzuht]	between
felé	[felay]	towards

They are placed after the word they refer to:

a szálloda mögött
o sallodo muhguht
behind the hotel

a vendéglő mellett
o vendayglur mellet
next to the restaurant

PLURAL NOUNS

To form the plural of nouns ending in a vowel, add **-k**:

autó	**autók**
owtaw	owtawk
car	cars

When a noun ends in **a** or **e**, the **a** or **e** is changed to **á** and **é** respectively when the plural ending **-k** is added:

szálloda	**szállodák**
sallodo	sallodak
hotel	hotels
csempe	**csempék**
chempeh	chempayk
tile	tiles

To form the plural of a noun ending in a consonant, add the endings **-ak**, **-ek**, **-ok** or **-ök**, depending on whether the noun contains front or back vowels (see Vowel Harmony page 5):

ágy	[adj]	bed	**ágyak**	[adjok]	beds
üveg	[ewveg]	bottle	**üvegek**	[ewvegek]	bottles
diák	[diak]	student	**diákok**	[diakok]	students
ügynök	[ewdjnuhk]	agent	**ügynökök**	[ewdjnuhkuhk]	agents

Although the plural ending is invariably **-k**, there are a large number of irregular forms, where the plural changes the last syllable. Here are some common examples:

dolog	[dolog]	thing	**dolgok**	[dolgok]	things
étterem	[aytterem]	restaurant	**éttermek**	[ayttermek]	restaurants
falu	[foloo]	village	**falvak**	[folvok]	villages
férfi	[fayrfi]	man	**férfiak**	[fayrfiok]	men
híd	[heed]	bridge	**hidak**	[hidok]	bridges
kerék	[keraykl]	wheel	**kerekek**	[kerekek]	wheels
kéz	[kayz]	hand	**kezek**	[kezek]	hands
köröm	[kuhruhm]	nail	**körmök**	[kuhrmuhk]	nails
levél	[levayl]	letter; leaf	**levelek**	[levelek]	letters; leaves
pohár	[pohar]	glass	**poharak**	[pohorok]	glasses
sátor	[shator]	tent	**sátrak**	[shatrok]	tents
tér	[tayr]	square, place	**terek**	[terek]	squares, places
tó	[taw]	lake, pond	**tavak**	[tovok]	lakes, ponds

tükör	[tewkuhr]	mirror	**tükrök**	[tewkruhk]	mirrors
úr	[oor]	gentleman	**urak**	[oorok]	gentlemen
út	[oot]	way, road	**utak**	[ootok]	ways, roads
útlevél	[ootlevayl]	passport	**útlevelek**	[ootlevelek]	passports
ügyfél	[ewdjfayl]	client, customer	**ügyfelek**	[ewdjfelek]	clients, customers

Plural noun endings are not used with numbers:

egy busz	**két busz**	**három busz**	**száz busz**
edj boos	kayt boos	harom boos	saz boos
one bus	two buses	three buses	a hundred buses

ARTICLES

The indefinite article (a, an) is the same as the word for 'one' **egy**. It can often be omitted if the context is clear:

Tom diák
Tom diak
Tom is a student

The definite article (the) is **a** before a word beginning with a consonant:

a vonat
o vonot
the train

and **az** before a word beginning with a vowel:

az autóbusz
oz owtawboos
the bus

ADJECTIVES

Adjectives usually precede the word they describe, as in English:

magas épület
mogosh aypewlet
a tall building

szép kilátás
sayp kilatash
a beautiful view

Adjectives that directly precede the noun do not change in the plural:

a fiatal lányok
o fi-otol la-nyok
the young girls

In sentences like the following, when the adjective does not immediately precede the noun it refers to, the plural suffix **-k** (after vowels), or **-ak** or **-ek** (after consonants), is added to the adjective:

szépek ezek a festmények
saypek ezek o feshtmay-nyek
these paintings are beautiful

There are a few exceptions to these rules. Some adjectives have **-ok** as the plural ending:

nagy	**nagyok**
nodj	nodjok
big	

Adjectives which end in **ú**, **ű**, and **i**, take **-ak** or **-ek** rather than just **-k**:

gyönyörűek ezek a képek
djuh-nyuh-rewek ezek o kaypek
these pictures are wonderful

Comparatives

To form the comparative ('more ...', '...-er'), add the suffix **-bb** if the adjective ends in a vowel:

olcsó
olchaw
cheap, inexpensive

ez a szoba olcsóbb
ez o sobo olchawb
this room is cheaper

If the adjective ends in a consonant, add **-abb** if the final vowel is a back vowel or **-ebb** if the final vowel is a front vowel:

kényelmes
kay-nyelmesh
comfortable

az a szoba kényelmesebb
oz o sobo kay-nyelmesheb
that room is more comfortable

édes
aydesh
sweet

ez a bor édesebb
ez o bor aydesheb
this wine is sweeter

'Than' is expressed by **mint**:

itt melegebb az idő, mint Angliában
it melegeb oz idur mint ongliabon
the weather is warmer here than in England

or by using one of the endings **-nál** or **-nél**:

Budapest olcsóbb New Yorknál
boodopesht olchawb New Yorknal
Budapest is less expensive than New York

The following comparatives are irregular:

jó	**jobb**
yaw	yob
good	better
szép	**szebb**
sayp	seb
beautiful	more beautiful

Superlatives

The superlative ('most expensive', 'oldest' etc) is formed by adding **leg-** to the beginning of the comparative form:

ez a legrégibb templom Budapesten
ez o legraygib templom boodopeshten
this is the oldest church in Budapest

ez a legérdekesebb útvonal
ez o legayr-dekesheb ootvonol
this is the most interesting route

Two superlatives are irregular in that they do not end in **-bb**:

legfelső
legfelshur
the highest, the top

legalsó
legolshaw
the lowest, the bottom

ez a legfelső emelet
ez o legfelshur emelet
this is the top floor

ADVERBS

To form an adverb from an adjective, add **-n** if the adjective ends in a vowel, or **-en** or **-an** if it ends in a consonant. Use **-en** if the adjective contains front vowels and **-an** if the adjective contains back vowels (see Vowel Harmony page 5):

olcsó	[olchaw]	cheap	**olcsón**	[olchawn]	cheaply
szép	[sayp]	beautiful	**szépen**	[saypen]	beautifully
gyors	[djorsh]	quick	**gyorsan**	[djorshon]	quickly

Important exceptions to the above are:

jó	[yaw]	good	**jól**	[yawl]	well
rossz	[ross]	bad	**rosszul**	[rossool]	badly

DEMONSTRATIVES

Demonstrative adjectives are as follows:

ez a	[ez o]	this	**ezek a**	[ezek o]	these
az a	[oz o]	that	**azok a**	[ozok o]	those

Demonstrative pronouns are as follows:

ez	[ez]	this (one)	**ezek**	[ezek]	these
az	[oz]	that (one)	**azok**	[ozok]	those

Demonstratives and Suffixes

When demonstratives **ez** (this) and **az** (that) are the object of a sentence, the accusative suffix **-t** must be added (see below):

ezt akarom
ezt okorom
I want this one

azt szeretném látni
ozt seretnaym latni
I'd like to see that one

ezt a képeslapot kérem
ezt o kaypeshlopot kayrem
I want this card

azt az épületet érdemes megnézni
ozt oz aypewletet ayrdemesh megnayzni
that building is worth visiting

Prepositional suffixes are added to demonstrative adjectives as well as to the noun:

ez a ház
ez o haz
this house

ebben a házban
ebben o hazbon
in this house

az az üzlet
oz oz ewzlet
that shop

abban az üzletben
obbon oz ewzletben
in that shop

ACCUSATIVE

The object of a verb in Hungarian can be identified by the accusative ending **-t**. For example, in the sentence:

tegnap megnéztük a Várat
tegnop megnayztewk o varot
we visited the Castle yesterday

'the Castle' is the object of the verb.

If a noun ends in a vowel, you add **-t** to form the accusative. If a noun ends in the vowels **-a** or **-e**, these become **-át** or **-ét** respectively in the accusative form:

noun			accusative form	
söröző	[shuruhzur]	beer hall	**sörözőt**	[shuruhzurt]
szálloda	[sallodo]	hotel	**szállodát**	[sallodat]
este	[eshteh]	evening	**estét**	[eshtayt]

If a noun ends in a consonant, the accusative ending is **-at**, **-ot**, **-et** or **-öt**. The ending used depends on the last vowel in the word (see Vowel Harmony page 5). Sometimes the last syllable changes slightly in the accusative form:

noun			accusative form	
étterem	[aytterem]	restaurant	**éttermet**	[ayttermet]
retek	[retek]	radish	**retket**	[retket]
kenyér	[kenyayr]	bread	**kenyeret**	[kenyeret]
álom	[alom]	dream	**álmot**	[almot]
bor	[bor]	wine	**bort**	[bort]
tükör	[tewkuhr]	mirror	**tükröt**	[tewkruht]
sör	[shuhr]	beer	**sört**	[shuhrt]
nyár	[nyar]	summer	**nyarat**	[nyorot]
bokor	[bokor]	bush	**bokrot**	[bokrot]

gulyást rendeltem
gooyasht rendeltem
I ordered goulash

én majd kifizetem a számlát
ayn moyd kifizetem o samlat
I'll pay the bill

kérek egy pohár sört
kayrek edj pohar shuhrt
I'd like a glass of beer

When you have a group of words in the accusative, for example, 'a bottle of red wine', the accusative -t ending is added to the final word in the group:

rendeltem egy üveg vörös bort
rendeltem edj ewveg vuhruhsh bort
I ordered a bottle of red wine

When demonstratives are in the accusative, they also take the -t ending. See Demonstratives and Suffixes on the opposite page.

POSSESSIVES

Instead of possessive adjectives ('my', 'your' etc), Hungarian uses suffixes. The suffix used depends on whether the object possessed ends in a vowel or a consonant and whether its last vowel is a back or front vowel (see Vowel Harmony page 5). The possessive suffixes are as follows:

-m/-am/-om/-em/-öm	my
-d/-ad/-od/-ed/-öd	your (sing, fam)
-a/-e/-ja/-je	his; her; your (sing, pol)
-nk/-unk/-ünk	our
-(a)tok/-(o)tok/-(e)tek/-(ö)tök	your (pl, fam)
-uk/-ük/-juk/-jük	their; your (pl, pol)

back-vowel nouns ending in a consonant

vonat	[vonot]	train			
vonatom	[vonotom]	my train	**vonataim**	[vonoto-eem]	my trains
vonatod	[vonotod]	your train	**vonataid**	[vonoto-eed]	your trains
vonatja	[vonot-yo]	his/her train; your train	**vonatjai**	[vonot-yo-ee]	his/her trains; your trains
vonatunk	[vonotoonk]	our train	**vonataink**	[vonoto-eenk]	our trains
vonatotok	[vonototok]	your train	**vonataitok**	[vonoto-eetok]	your trains
vonatjuk	[vonot-yook]	their train; your train	**vonatjaik**	[vonot-yo-eek]	their trains; your trains

front-vowel nouns ending in a consonant

fivér	[fivayr]	brother			
fivérem	[fivayrem]	my brother	**fivéreim**	[fivayraym]	my brothers
fivéred	[fivayred]	your brother	**fivéreid**	[fivayrayd]	your brothers
fivére	[fivayreh]	his/her brother; your brother	**fivérei**	[fivayray]	his/her brothers; your brothers
fivérünk	[fivayrewnk]	our brother	**fivéreink**	[fivayraynk]	our brothers
fivéretek	[fivayretek]	your brother	**fivéreitek**	[fivayraytek]	your brothers
fivérük	[fivayrewk]	their brother; your brother	**fivéreik**	[fivayrayk]	their brothers; your brothers

nouns ending in a back vowel

szoba	[sobo]	room			
szobám	[sobam]	my room	**szobáim**	[soba-im]	my rooms
szobád	[sobad]	your room	**szobáid**	[soba-id]	your rooms
szobája	[sobī-o]	his/her room; your room	**szobái**	[soba-i]	his/her rooms; your room
szobánk	[sobank]	our room	**szobáink**	[soba-ink]	our rooms
szobátok	[sobatok]	your room	**szobáitok**	[soba-itok]	your rooms
szobájuk	[sobī-ook]	their room; your room	**szobáik**	[soba-ik]	their rooms; your rooms

nouns ending in a front vowel

gyűrű	[djewrew]	ring			
gyűrűm	[djewrewm]	my ring	**gyűrűim**	[djewrewim]	my rings
gyűrűd	[djewrewd]	your ring	**gyűrűid**	[djewrewid]	your rings
gyűrűje	[djewrew-yeh]	his/her ring; your ring	**gyűrűi**	[djewrewi]	his/her rings; your rings
gyűrűnk	[djewrewnk]	our ring	**gyűrűink**	[djewrewink]	our rings
gyűrűtök	[djewrewtuhk]	your ring	**gyűrűitek**	[djewrewitek]	your rings
gyűrűjük	[djewrew-yewk]	their ring; your ring	**gyűrűik**	[djewrewik]	their rings; your rings

In Hungarian, possessive endings are also used with prepositions to translate what in English would be a preposition plus a pronoun, in expressions such as 'with you', 'to them' (see pages 19–21).

Possessive Pronouns

These are as follows:

az enyém	[oz enyaym]	mine
az öné	[oz uhnay]	yours (sing, pol)
a tiéd	[o ti-ayd]	yours (sing, fam)
az övé	[oz uhvay]	his; hers
a miénk	[o mi-aynk]	ours
az önöké	[oz uhnuhkay]	yours (pl, pol)
a tiétek	[o ti-aytek]	yours (pl, fam)
az övék	[oz urvayk]	theirs

a kék táska az enyém, a fekete az övé
o kayk tashko oz eh-nyaym o feketeh oz uhvay
the blue bag is mine, the black one is hers

a tiétek tágasabb, mint a miénk
o ti-aytek tagoshobb mint o mi-aynk
yours is roomier than ours

az Önöké biztosan drágább volt, mint az övék
oz uhnuhkay biztoshon dragabb volt mint oz uhvayk
yours must have been more expensive than theirs

PERSONAL PRONOUNS

Subject Pronouns

én	[ayn]	I
te	[teh]	you (sing, fam)
ő	[ur]	he; she
Ön	[uhn]	you (sing, pol)
maga	[mogo]	you (sing, less pol)
mi	[mi]	we
ti	[ti]	you (pl, fam)
ők	[urk]	they
Önök	[uhnuk]	you (pl, pol)
maguk	[mogook]	you (pl, less pol)

Unlike English, pronouns are often omitted in Hungarian:

hová akar menni?
hova okor menni
where do you want to go?

még nem vagyok kész!
mayg nem vodjok kays
I am not ready yet!

but they may be retained for emphasis or for clarification:

én már kész vagyok, de ő még öltözködik
ayn mar kays vodjok deh ur mayg uhltuhzkuhdik
I am ready, but she's getting dressed

Te (pl: **ti**) is the familiar word for 'you' and is used between friends of both sexes, children, teenagers, and people who formally agree (often with a drink) to be on such terms. This has to be proposed by the older or higher-ranking person, or by the woman if across the gender line. **Te** should not generally be used when speaking to strangers or acquaintances; the only exception to this is that it is OK to use it when speaking to strangers of the same sex up to about 25 years of age.

The polite form **Ön** (pl: **Önök**) should be used when speaking to strangers, or people to whom respect is due on account of their age or position. For example, a student speaking to a professor would always use **Ön**. The polite forms **Ön/Önök** are used respectively with the third person singular and plural of the verb. Often you will not need to use either word because it's common to omit pronouns in Hungarian, but you must still use the third person of the verb or appropriate form of the possessive (see pages 15–17) to be polite.

Maga (pl: **maguk**) is not familiar, but, in most cases, it is not really polite either; it simply indicates that the speaker is not on familiar terms with the person addressed. To be on the safe side, you should use **Ön/Önök**. One situation in which **maga** would be acceptable is in an informal discussion between a man and a woman of more or less the same age, who aren't on familiar terms. **Ön** would not generally be used between two young people as it would be considered pompous; in this situation, you should use **maga** instead. The pronouns, **maga/maguk** are used respectively with the third person singular and plural of the verb.

The pronoun **ő** means both 'he' and 'she'. This is why it is used far less than in languages which distinguish between genders. Generally, whether 'he' or 'she' is meant will generally be obvious from the context in which it is used. But, if you need to differentiate between 'he' and 'she', for example, to translate a sentence such as: 'he wants red wine, but she wants an ice cream', you say:

az úr vörös bort akar, de a hölgy fagylaltot kér
oz oor vuhruhsh bort okor deh o huhldj fodjloltot kayr
(literally: the gentleman wants red wine, but the lady wants an ice cream)

Object Pronouns

engem	[engem]	me
téged	[tayged]	you (sing, fam)
őt	[uht]	him; her
önt	[uhnt]	you (sing, pol)
magát	[mogat]	you (sing, less pol)
minket	[minket]	us
titeket	[titeket]	you (pl, fam)
őket	[uhket]	them
Önöket	[uhnuhket]	you (pl, pol)
magukat	[mogookot]	you (pl, less pol)

As with subject pronouns, object pronouns may be omitted if the meaning is clear:

hol az útleved? – keresem
hol oz ootleved – kereshem
where's your passport? – I'm just looking for it

láttad Pétert? – én is őt keresem
lattod paytert – ayn ish urt kereshem
have you seen Peter? – I'm looking for him too

Pronouns and Prepositional Suffixes

Many of the prepositional suffixes, for example, **-val/-vel**, **-nak/-nek**, are used with possessive endings (see pages 15–17) to translate expressions using pronouns in English such as 'with me', 'to you' etc. The possessive part is added to the end of the preposition. Some of these are:

velem	[velem]	with me
veled	[veled]	with you (sing, fam)
vele	[veleh]	with him; with her; with it
velünk	[velewnk]	with us
veletek	[veletek]	with you (pl, fam)
velük	[velewk]	with them
nekem	[nekem]	for me; to me
neked	[neked]	for you; to you (sing, fam)
neki	[neki]	for him; to him; for her; to her; for it; to it
nekünk	[nekewnk]	for us; to us
nektek	[nektek]	for you; to you (pl, fam)
nekik	[nekik]	for them; to them
nálam	[nalom]	at my place
hozzá	[hozza]	to him
tőlük	[turlewk]	from them

With all the above forms, however, the third person singular and plural cannot be used for the polite form. For example:

vele megyek
veleh medjek
I'm going with him/her

can only mean 'I'm going with him/her' and not 'with you'. The polite versions of 'with you' are:

Önnel megyek
uhnnel medjek
I'm going with you (sing, pol)

Önökkel megyek
uhnukkel medjek
I'm going with you (pl, pol)

The polite forms for 'for you' and 'to you' are:

Önnek uhnnek for you (sing, pol)	**Önért** uhnayrt for you (pl, pol)
Önöknek uhnuhknek to you (sing, pol)	**Önökért** uhnuh-kayrt to you (pl, pol)

To translate 'behind me', 'in front of you' etc using prepositions like **mögött** (behind), **előtt** (in front of) and **mellett** (near), add the corresponding possessive ending to the preposition:

mögöttem állt (possessive suffix: -**em**) muhguhttem alt he stood behind me	**előtte** (possessive suffix: -**e**) elurtteh in front of him

melletünk
(possessive suffix -**ünk**)
melletewnk
next to us

VERBS

In the English-Hungarian and Hungarian-English sections of this book, verbs are given in the infinitive form ('to give', 'to do' etc), which in Hungarian ends in -**ni**. Verbs are conjugated using the third person singular of the present tense as the verb stem to which the appropriate person endings are added. Generally, the verb stem/third person singular is obtained by removing the final -**ni** from the infinitive:

adni	[odni]	to give	**ad**	[od]	he/she gives
állni	[alni]	to stand	**áll**	[al]	he/she stands
beszélni	[besaylni]	to speak	**beszél**	[besayl]	he/she speaks

Some common verbs whose stem/third person singular cannot be obtained by removing -**ni** from the infinitive are shown in the table below, including some verbs whose third person singular ends in -**ik**. The stem for these verbs is obtained by removing the -**ik** from the third person singular. In cases when the third person singular form is not used to form verb stem, the irregular verb stem is shown in brackets:

aludni	[oloodni]	to sleep	**alszik**	[olsik]	he/she sleeps
álmodni	[almodni]	to dream	**álmodik**	[almodik]	he/she dreams
dolgozni	[dolgozni]	to work	**dolgozik**	[dolgozik]	he/she works
ejteni	[ayteni]	to drop	**ejt**	[ayt]	he/she drops
emlékezni	[emlaykezni]	to remember	**emlékszik**	[emlayksik]	he/she remembers

enni	[enni]	to eat	**eszik**	[esik]	he/she eats
érteni	[ayrteni]	to understand	**ért**	[ayrt]	he/she understands
fázni	[fazni]	to be cold	**fázik**	[fazik]	he/she is cold
feküdni	[fekewdni]	to lie	**fekszik**	[feksik]	he/she lies (stem: **feksz**)*
hazudni	[hozoodni]	to lie, tell a lie	**hazudik**	[hazudik]	he/she tells a lie
inni	[inni]	to drink	**iszik**	[isik]	he/she drinks
jönni	[yuhnni]	to come	**jön**	[yuhn]	he/she comes (stem: **jöv**)*
menni	[menni]	to go	**megy**	[medj]	he/she goes (stem: **men**)*
mondani	[mondoni]	to say	**mond**	[mond]	he/she says
segíteni	[shegeeteni]	to help	**segít**	[shegeet]	he/she helps
tanítani	[toneetoni]	to teach	**tanít**	[toneet]	he/she teaches
tenni	[tenni]	to put; to do	**tesz**	[tes]	he/she puts; he/she does*
úszni	[oosni]	to swim	**úszik**	[oosik]	he/she swims
utazni	[ootozni]	to travel	**utazik**	[ootozik]	he/she travels
venni	[venni]	to take; to buy	**vesz**	[ves]	he/she takes; he/she buys*
vinni	[vinni]	to carry	**visz**	[vis]	he/she carries

* These verbs are irregular in that the stem changes for part of the conjugation:

jönnek	**mennek**	**tettem**	**vettem**
yuhnnek	mennek	tettem	vettem
they come	they go	I did	I took

Transitive and Intransitive Verb Forms

There are only two proper tenses in Hungarian, the present and the past. For each tense, Hungarian verbs have two conjugation patterns, known as transitive and intransitive. Transitive forms are used when the action of a verb has a specified object, for example, 'making' in 'I'm making breakfast' is a transitive verb in English. Intransitive forms are used in sentences like: 'I'm driving', 'I'm eating', when there is no specified object.

The transitive verb forms can only be used where the object of the verb is specifically defined:

látom a Hiltont (transitive)
latom o hiltont
I (can) see the Hilton Hotel

but:

látok egy magas épületet (intransitive)
latok edj mogosh aypewletet
I (can) see a tall building

Sometimes the object of a sentence (such as 'it' below) will be omitted because the use of the transitive verb form makes the meaning unambiguous:

megteszed nekem?
megtesed nekem
will you do it for me?

Present Tense

The verb endings used to form the present tense depend on whether the verb stem contains a back vowel or a front vowel (see Vowel Harmony page 5) and whether the third person singular of the intransitive verb ends in -ik. Here are some examples of conjugation patterns for both transitive and intransitive forms in the present tense:

verb stem with back vowel

transitive			intransitive	
látni	to see (stem: **lát**)			
látom	[latom]	I see	**látok**	[latok]
látod	[latod]	you see	**látsz**	[lats]
látja	[lat-yo]	he/she sees; you see	**lát**	[lat]
látjuk	[lat-yook]	we see	**látunk**	[latoonk]
látjátok	[lat-yatok]	you see	**láttok**	[lattok]
látják	[lat-yak]	they see; you see	**látnak**	[latnok]

verb stem with front vowel

transitive			intransitive	
rendelni to order (stem: **rendel**)				
rendelem	[rendelem]	I order; I'm ordering etc	**rendelek**	[rendelek]
rendeled	[rendeled]	you order	**rendelsz**	[rendels]
rendeli	[rendeli]	he/she orders; you order	**rendel**	[rendel]
rendeljük	[rendel-yewk]	we order	**rendelünk**	[rendelewnk]
rendelitek	[rendelitek]	you order	**rendeltek**	[rendeltek]
rendelik	[rendelik]	they order; you order	**rendelnek**	[rendelnek]

verb stem with front vowel ü

	intransitive	
ülni* to sit (stem: **ül**)		
I sit, I'm sitting etc	**ülök**	[ewluhk]
you sit	**ülsz**	[ewls]
he/she sits; you sit	**ül**	[ewl]
we sit	**ülünk**	[ewlewnk]
you sit	**ültök**	[ewltuhk]
they sit; you sit	**ülnek**	[ewlnek]

* The verb **ülni** and many verbs ending in **-ülni** only exist in the intransitive form.

verb stem with front vowel (3rd person singular ending in -ik)

transitive			intransitive	
inni to drink				
iszom	[isom]	I drink, I'm drinking etc	**iszom**	[isom]
iszod	[isod]	you drink	**iszol**	[isol]
issza	[isso]	he/she drinks; you drink	**iszik**	[isik]
isszuk	[issook]	we drink	**iszunk**	[isoonk]
isszátok	[issatok]	you drink	**isztok**	[istok]
isszák	[issak]	they drink; you drink	**isznak**	[isnok]

GRAMMAR

verb stem with back vowel (3rd person singular ending in -ik)

transitive			intransitive	
hazudni to lie, to tell a lie (stem: **hazudik**)				
hazudom	[hozoodom]	I'm lying, I lie etc	**hazudom**	[hozoodom]
hazudod	[hozoodod]	you're lying	**hazudol**	[hozoodol]
hazudja	[hozood-yo]	he/she's lying; you're lying	**hazudik**	[hozoodik]
hazudjuk	[hozood-yook]	we're lying	**hazudunk**	[hozoodoonk]
hazudjátok	[hozood-yatok]	you're lying	**hazudtok**	[hozoodtok]
hazudják	[hozood-yak]	they're lying; you're lying	**hazudnak**	[hozoodnok]

verb stem with front vowel (3rd person singular ending in -ik)

transitive			intransitive	
enni to eat				
eszem	[esem]	I eat	**eszem**	[esem]
eszed	[esed]	you eat	**eszel**	[esel]
eszi	[esi]	he/she eats; you eat	**eszik**	[esik]
esszük	[esh-sewk]	we eat	**eszünk**	[esewnk]
eszitek	[esitek]	you eat	**esztek**	[estek]
eszik	[esik]	they eat	**esznek**	[esnek]

Past Tense

The verb endings used to form the past tense depend on whether the verb stem contains a back vowel or a front vowel (see Vowel Harmony page 5) and whether the third person singular of the intransitive verb ends in **-ik**. Here are some examples of conjugation patterns for both transitive and intransitive forms in the past tense:

verb stem with back vowel

transitive			intransitive	
látni	to see (stem: **lát**)			
láttam	[lattom]	I saw	**láttam**	[lattom]
láttad	[lattod]	you saw	**láttál**	[lattal]
látta	[latto]	he/she saw; you saw	**látott**	[latot]
láttuk	[lattook]	we saw	**láttunk**	[lattoonk]
láttátok	[lattatok]	you saw	**láttatok**	[lattotok]
látták	[lattak]	they saw; you saw	**láttak**	[lattok]

verb stem with front vowel

transitive			intransitive	
rendelni to order (stem: **rendel**)				
rendeltem	[rendeltem]	I ordered, I was ordering etc	**rendeltem**	[rendeltem]
rendelted	[rendelted]	you ordered	**rendeltél**	[rendeltayl]
rendelte	[rendelteh]	he/she ordered; you ordered	**rendelt**	[rendelt]
rendeltük	[rendeltewk]	we ordered	**rendeltünk**	[rendeltewnk]
rendeltétek	[rendeltaytek]	you ordered	**rendeltetek**	[rendeltetek]
rendelték	[rendeltayk]	they ordered; you ordered	**rendeltek**	[rendeltek]

verb stem with front vowel ü

			intransitive	
ülni* to sit (stem: **ül**)				
		I sat, I was sitting etc	**ültem**	[ewltem]
		you sat	**ültél**	[ewltayl]
		he/she sat; you sat	**ült**	[ewlt]
		we sat	**ültünk**	[ewltewnk]
		you sat	**ültetek**	[ewltetek]
		they sat; you sat	**ültek**	[ewltek]

* The verb **ülni** and many verbs ending in **-ülni** only exist in the intransitive form.

verb stem with front vowel (3rd person singular ending in -ik)

transitive			intransitive	
inni to drink				
ittam	[ittom]	I drank, I was drinking etc	**ittam**	[ittom]
ittad	[ittod]	you drank	**ittál**	[ittal]
itta	[itto]	he/she drank; you drank	**ivott**	[ivot]
ittuk	[ittook]	we drank	**ittunk**	[ittoonk]
ittátok	[ittatok]	you drank	**ittatok**	[ittotok]
itták	[ittak]	they drank; you drank	**ittak**	[ittok]

verb stem with back vowel (3rd person singular ending in -ik)

transitive			intransitive	
hazudni to lie, to tell a lie				
hazudtam	[hozoodtom]	I lied, I was lying etc	**hazudtam**	[hozoodtom]
hazudtad	[hozoodtod]	you lied	**hazudtál**	[hozoodtal]
hazudta	[hozoodto]	he/she lied; you lied	**hazudott**	[hozoodot]
hazudtuk	[hozoodtook]	we lied	**hazudtunk**	[hozoodtoonk]
hazudtátok	[hozoodtoonk]	you lied	**hazudtatok**	[hozoodtotok]
hazudták	[hozoodtak]	they lied; you lied	**hazudtak**	[hozoodtok]

verb stem with front vowel (3rd person singular ending in -ik)

transitive	intransitive			
enni to eat				
ettem	[ettem]	I ate, I was eating etc	**ettem**	[ettem]
etted	[etted]	you ate	**ettél**	[ettayl]
ette	[etteh]	he/she ate; you ate	**evett**	[evet]
ettük	[ettewk]	we ate	**ettünk**	[ettewnk]
ettétek	[ettaytek]	you ate	**ettetek**	[ettetek]
ették	[ettayk]	they ate	**ettek**	[ettek]

Some examples of the transitive and intransitive forms in the past tense:

fehér bort ittunk a vacsorához (intransitive)
fehayr bort ittoonk o vochorahoz
we drank white wine with our dinner

tegnap láttam Pétert Esztergomban (transitive)
tegnop lattom paytart estergombon
yesterday I saw Peter in Esztergom

Future Tense

If the context is obvious, the present tense is often used to express a future meaning:

jövök
yuhvuhk
I come

holnap megint jövök
holnop megint yuhvuhk
I'll come again tomorrow

An alternative way to express the future is to use the appropriate form of the verb **fog** followed by the infinitive:

transitive			intransitive	
fogom	[fogom]	I will	**fogok**	[fogok]
fogod	[fogod]	you will	**fogsz**	[fogs]
fogja	[fog-yo]	he/she will	**fog**	[fog]
fogjuk	[fog-yook]	we will	**fogunk**	[fogoonk]
fogjátok	[fog-yatok]	you will	**fogtok**	[fogtok]
fogják	[fog-yak]	they will	**fognak**	[fognok]

látni fogsz (intransitive)
latni fogs
you'll see

látni fogod a házam (transitive)
latni fogod o hazom
you'll see my house

látni fogsz egy házat (intransitive)
latni fogs edj hazot
you'll see a house

'To Be'

The verb **lenni** 'to be' is irregular:

vagyok	[vodjok]	I am	**voltam**	[voltom]	I was
vagy	[vodj]	you are	**voltál**	[voltal]	you were
van	[von]	he/she is	**volt**	[volt]	he/she was
vagyunk	[vodjoonk]	we are	**voltunk**	[voltoonk]	we were
vagytok	[vodjtok]	you are	**voltatok**	[voltotok]	you were
vannak	[vonnok]	they are	**voltak**	[voltok]	they were

leszek	[lesek]	I will be
leszel	[lesel]	you will be
lesz	[les]	he/she will be
leszünk	[lesewnk]	we will be
lesztek	[lestek]	you will be
lesznek	[lesnek]	they will be

The third person **van/vannak** is usually omitted in cases like the following:

a fiam orvos
o fi-om orvosh
my son is a doctor

nem elég hideg a bor
nem elayg hideg o bor
the wine is not chilled enough

ez a buszunk
ez o boosoonk
this is our bus

Van, however, is included in sentences like:

az útlevelem a fiókban van
oz ootlevelem o fi-awkbon von
my passport is in the drawer

a trafik az előcsarnokban van
o trofik oz elurchornokbon von
the tobacconist's is in the lobby

Van/vannak also mean 'there is/there are' or 'is there?/are there?':

van film a fényképezőgépben?
von film o fay[nyuh]kaypezur-gaypben
is there film in the camera?

a recepción vannak külföldi telefonkönyvek
o retseptsi-awn vonnok kewlfuhldi telefonkuh[nyuh]vek
there are foreign telephone books at the reception

Vannak may be used without a subject when it refers to people generally:

vannak a teremben
vonnok o teremben
there are people in the hall

vannak a fürdőszobában
vonnok o fewrdursobabon
there's somebody in the bathroom

'To Have'

There is no verb 'to have' in Hungarian. **Van/vannak** (there is/there are) and **nincs/ nincsenek** (there is no/there are no) are used with the possessive endings (see pages 15-17) and added to the noun:

van egy ötletem
von edj uhtletem
I have an idea (literally: there is an idea of mine)

jó öttetei vannak
yaw uhttetay vonnok
he has good ideas

van pénzed?
von paynzed
do you have (any) money?

nincs pénzem
ninch paynzem
I have no money

nincsenek terveink
ninchenek tervaynk
we have no plans

Negatives

To form the simple negative of a sentence, use the word **nem** 'no/not':

nem megyek moziba
nem medjek mozibo
I don't go to the cinema

nem akarunk még vacsorázni
nem okoroonk mayg vochorazni
we don't want to have dinner yet

az idegenvezető nem magyarázta meg
oz idegenvezetur nem modjorazto meg
the guide did not explain

nem volt drága a jegy
nem volt drago o yedj
the ticket was not expensive

In other types of negative sentence, Hungarian uses double negatives. In Hungarian, you do not say 'there isn't anybody', literally you say 'there isn't nobody'. No specific word exists in Hungarian for 'anybody' or 'anything', as both only occur in negative sentences.

Senki/semmi (nobody/nothing) are usually accompanied by the negative words **sem** or **sincs**:

senki sincs itthon
shenki shinch it-hon OR

nincs itthon senki
ninch it-hon shenki
there's nobody in

senki sem tud semmit
shenki shem tood shemmit
nobody knows anything

semmi baj
shemmi boy
nothing is the matter

semmit sem lehet tenni
shemmit shem lehet tenni OR

nem lehet tenni semmit
nem lehet tenni shemmit
nothing can be done

semmit sem találtam a zsebemben
shemmit shem tolaltom o Jebemben
I found nothing in my pocket

To translate 'there's no', use **nincs**, and for 'there are no', use **nincsenek**:

nincs hely a kocsiban
ninch heh^{yuh} o kochibon
there's no room in the carriage

nincsenek kiszolgálók az üzletben
ninchenek kisolgalawk oz ewzletben
there are no assistants in the shop

nincs itthon senki
ninch it-hon shenki
there's nobody in

'Have To', 'Must'

'Have to' or 'must' is expressed in Hungarian by the irregular verb **kell**, which only exists in the third person. It also has a past tense (**kellett**):

holnap egész nap dolgoznom kell
holnop egays nop dolgoznom kel
tomorrow I must work all day

holnap nem kell egész nap dolgoznom
holnop nem kel egays nop dolgoznom
I don't have to work all day tomorrow

The adjective **szabad** (free) is used to translate 'one must not' or 'you must not':

holnap nem szabad egész nap dolgoznom
holnop nem sobod egays nop dolgoznom
I must not work all day tomorrow, I'm not allowed to work all day tomorrow

The verb **kell** may also express the need or desire for something:

kell egy darab sütemény?
kel edj dorob sewtemay[nyuh]
do you want a piece of cake?

el kell mennem a sarki boltba
el kel mennem o shorki boltbo
I have to go to the corner shop

QUESTIONS

Questions can be asked by changing the intonation of a sentence. This is done by raising your voice on the final or penultimate syllable:

ez az Operaház
ez oz operohaz
this is the Opera House

ez az Opera*ház*?
ez oz operohaz
is this the Opera House?

Szabó úr itt van
sobaw oor it von
Mr Szabó is here

Szabó úr itt *van*?
sobaw oor it von
is Mr Szabó here?

The word **ugye** is used to translate 'isn't it?', 'wasn't it?', 'haven't you?' etc. It can occur either at the beginning or at the end of a question:

ugye nem haragszik, ha Ön mellé ülök?
oo-djeh nem horogsik ho uhn mellay ewluhk
you don't mind my sitting next to you, do you?

Interrogative (question) words are usually at the beginning of the sentence and they are always emphasized in speech:

merre van a postahivatal?
merreh von o poshto-hivotol
which way is it to the post office?

hol a fürdőszoba?
hol o fewrdursobo
where is the bathroom?

WORD ORDER

Hungarian word order is flexible; it depends on which part of the sentence you wish to emphasize, for example:

ez a busz a Várba megy
ez o boos o varbo medj
this bus goes to the Castle

a Várba megy ez a busz
o varbo medj ez o boos
this bus goes to the Castle (and not somewhere else)

megy ez a busz a Várba
medj ez o boos o varbo
this bus does go to the Castle (amongst other places)

a Várba ez a busz megy
o varbo ez o boos medj
this is the bus that goes to the Castle (and no other bus does)

IMPERSONAL CONSTRUCTIONS

Impersonal constructions may be formed using words like kell (it is necessary, one must) or lehet (it is possible to) or the expression azt mondják (they say that, it is said that):

nem kell készpénzben fizetni
nem kel kayspaynzben fizetni
it is not necessary to pay cash

mikor lehet látni?
mikor lehet latni
when can one see it?, when is it possible to see it?

azt mondják, ez nagyon jó vendéglő
ozt mond-yak ez nodjon jaw vendayglur
they say this is a very good restaurant

DATES

The word order for dates is:

year – month – day

1998. március 15. or 1998. március 15-e
the 15th March 1998

Dates are usually abbreviated in writing. If the month is shown as a number, Roman numerals are used:

1998.III.15.

1998 in full is written as follows:

ezerkilencszáz kilencvennyolc
ezerkilents-saz kilents-ven-nyolts
(one thousand – nine hundred – ninety-eight)

See Numbers page 37.

Dates are formed using the versions of the ordinal numbers below:

1st	elseje	[elseh-yeh]
2nd	másodika	[masodiko]
3rd	harmadika	[hormodiko]
4th	negyedike	[nedjeh-dikeh]
5th	ötödike	[uhtuh-dikeh]
6th	hatodika	[hotodiko]
7th	hetedike	[heteh-dikeh]
8th	nyolcadika	[nyoltsodiko]
9th	kilencedike	[kilentseh-dikeh]
10th	tizedike	[tizeh-dikeh]
11th	tizenegyedike	[tizenedjeh-dikeh]
12th	tizenkettedike	[tizen-ketteh-dikeh]
13th	tizenharmadika	[tizen-hormo-dikeh]
14th	tizennegyedike	[tizen-nedjeh-dikeh]
15th	tizenötödike	[tizen-uhtuh-dikeh]
16th	tizenhatodika	[tizen-hotodiko]
17th	tizenhetedike	[tizen-heteh-dikeh]
18th	tizennyolcadika	[tizen-nyoltsodiko]
19th	tizenkilencedike	[tizen-kilentseh-dikeh]
20th	huszadika	[hoosodiko]
21st	huszonegyedike	[hooso-nedjeh-dikeh]
22nd	huszonkettedike	[hooson-ketteh-dikeh]
23rd	huszonharmadika	[hooson-hormodiko]
24th	huszonnegyedike	[hooson-nedjeh-dikeh]
25th	huszonötödike	[hooson-uhtuh-dikeh]

26th	huszonhatodika	[hooson-hotodiko]
27th	huszonhetedike	[hooson-heteh-dikeh]
28th	huszonnyolcadika	[hooson-nyoltso-diko]
29th	huszonkilencedike	[hooson-kilentseh-dikeh]
30th	harmincadika	[hormints-adiko]
31st	harmincegyedike	[hormints-edjeh-dikeh]

január tizenötödike
yonoo-ar tizen-uhtuh-dikeh
the 15th January

január huszadika
yonoo-ar hoosodiko
the 20th January

Dates are usually abbreviated and you will see the number followed by **-a** or **-e** depending on the ending of the ordinal number:

2-a (abbreviation of **második**a)
2nd

31-e (abbreviation of **harmincegyedike**)
31st

The exception to this is '1st' which is **1-je** (abbreviation of **elseje**).

To say 'on' a date, change the ending to **-án** (if the ordinal ends in **-a**) or **-én** (if it ends in **-e**):

július másodikán
yooli-oos masodikan
on the 2nd July

július harmincegyedikén
yooli-oos hormints-edjeh-dikayn
on the 31st July

'On' a date can be abbreviated to **-án** or **-én**:

július 2-án
on the 2nd July

július 31-én
on the 31st July

The exception is the abbreviation for 'on the first' which is **1-jén**.

DAYS

Sunday	vasárnap	[vosharnop]
Monday	hétfő	[haytfur]
Tuesday	kedd	[ked]
Wednesday	szerda	[serdo]
Thursday	csütörtök	[chewturtuhk]
Friday	péntek	[payntek]
Saturday	szombat	[sombot]

MONTHS

January	január	[yonoo-ar]
February	február	[febroo-ar]
March	március	[martsi-oosh]
April	április	[aprilish]
May	május	[mī-oosh]
June	június	[yooni-oosh]
July	július	[yooli-oosh]
August	augusztus	[owgoostoosh]
September	szeptember	[september]
October	október	[oktawber]
November	november	[november]
December	december	[detsember]

TIME

what time is it?	hány óra van?	[ha^{nyuh} awro von]
one o'clock	egy óra	[ed-yuh awro]
two o'clock	két óra	[kayt awro]
ten o'clock	tíz óra	[teez awro]
five past one	öt perccel múlt egy	[uht pertsel moolt edj]
ten past two	tíz perccel múlt kettő	[teez pertsel moolt kettur]
quarter past one	negyed kettő	[nedjed kettur]
quarter past two	negyed három	[nedjed harom]
half past one	fél kettő	[fayl kettur]
half past ten	fél tizenegy	[fayl tizenedj]
twenty to ten	húsz perc múlva tíz	[hoos perts moolvo teez]
quarter to one	háromnegyed egy	[harom-nedjed edj]
quarter to ten	háromnegyed tíz	[harom-nedjed teez]
at eight o'clock	nyolc órakor	[nyolts awrukor]
at half past four	fél ötkor	[fayl uhtkor]
at quarter to ten	háromnegyed tízkor	[harom-nedjed teezkor]
at quarter past one	negyed kettőkor	[nedjed ketturkor]
noon	dél	[dayl]
midnight	éjfél	[ayfayl]
18.00	tizennyolc óra	[tizen-nyolts awro]
14.30	tizennégy harminc	[tizenedj harmints]

am	(up to 2am)	éjjel	[ay-yel]
	(2–4am)	hajnali	[hoynoli]
	(5–9am)	reggel	[reggel]
	(10am onwards)	délelőtt	[daylelurt]
pm	(1–5pm)	délután	[daylootan]
	(6–10pm)	este	[eshteh]
	(11pm onwards)	éjjel	[ay-yel]

1am	éjjel egy óra	[ay-yel edj awro]
2am	hajnali két óra	[hoynoli kayt awro]
8am	reggel nyolc óra	[nyolts awro]
10am	délelőtt tíz óra	[daylelurt teez awro]
1pm	délután egy óra	[daylootan edj awro]
6pm	este hat óra	[eshteh hot awro]
11pm	éjjel tizenegy óra	[ay-yel tizenedj awro]

at 8am	reggel nyolckor	[nyoltskor]
at 11am	délelőtt tizenegykor	[daylelurt tizenedjkor]
at noon	délben, déli tizenkettőkor	[daylben, dayli tizen-ketturkor]
at 4pm	délután négykor	[daylootan naydjkor]
at 8pm	este nyolckor	[eshteh nyoltskor]
at 11pm	éjjel tizenegykor	[ay-yel tizenedjkor]
at midnight	éjfélkor, éjjel tizenkettőkor	[ayfaylkor, ay-yel tizen-ketturkor]

In formal situations and in writing, times are written as follows using the word **órakor**:

este nyolc órakor
eshteh nyolts awrokor
at 8pm

hour	óra	[awro]
minute	perc	[perts]
one minute	egy perc	[edj perts]
two minutes	két perc	[kayt perts]
second	másodperc	[mashodperts]
quarter of an hour	negyedóra	[nedjeh-dawro]
half an hour	félóra	[faylawro]
three quarters of an hour	háromnegyedóra	[haromnedjeh-dawruh]

NUMBERS

0	nulla	[noollo]
1	egy	[edj]
2	kettő, két*	[kettur, kayt]
3	három	[harom]
4	négy	[naydj]
5	öt	[uht]
6	hat	[hot]
7	hét	[hayt]
8	nyolc	[nyolts]
9	kilenc	[kilents]
10	tíz	[teez]
11	tizenegy	[tizenedj]
12	tizenkettő, tizenkét*	[tizen-kettur, tizen-kayt]
13	tizenhárom	[tizen-harom]
14	tizennégy	[tizen-naydj]
15	tizenöt	[tizenuht]
16	tizenhat	[tizenhot]
17	tizenhét	[tizenhayt]
18	tizennyolc	[tizen-nyolts]
19	tizenkilenc	[tizen-kilents]
20	húsz	[hoos]
21	huszonegy	[hooson-edj]
22	huszonkettő, huszonkét	[hooson-kettur]
30	harminc	[hormints]
31	harmincegy	[hormints-edj]
32	harminckettő, harminckét*	[hormints-kettur]
40	negyven	[nedjven]
50	ötven	[uhtven]
60	hatvan	[hotvon]
70	hetven	[hetven]
80	nyolcvan	[nyoltsvon]
90	kilencven	[kilentsven]
100	száz	[saz]
110	száztíz	[sazteez]
200	kétszáz	[kaytsaz]
300	háromszáz	[haromsaz]
400	négyszáz	[naydjsaz]

500	ötszáz	[uhtsaz]
600	hatszáz	[hutsaz]
700	hétszáz	[haytsaz]
800	nyolcszáz	[nyolts-saz]
900	kilencszáz	[kilents-saz]
1,000	ezer	[ezer]
10,000	tízezer	[teezezer]
20,000	húszezer	[hoosezer]
100,000	százezer	[sazezer]
1,000,000	millió	[milli-aw]

* There are two words for the number two in Hungarian. **Kettő** is used on its own:

hány darab poggyásza van?
ha[nyuh] dorob pog-djaso von
how many pieces of luggage do you have?

kettő
kettur
two

Két is used when the number precedes the noun:

két bőröndöm van
kayt bur-ruhnduhm von
I have two suitcases

There are two words for the numbers 12, 22 and all numbers ending in 2; as above for 2, use the **-kettő** form when the number is used on its own.

Ordinals

1st	első	[elshur]
2nd	második	[mashodik]
3rd	harmadik	[harmodik]
4th	negyedik	[nedjeh-dik]
5th	ötödik	[uhtuh-dik]
6th	hatodik	[hotodik]
7th	hetedik	[heteh-dik]
8th	nyolcadik	[nyoltsodik]
9th	kilencedik	[kilentseh-dik]
10th	tizedik	[tizeh-dik]

Dates are formed using the ordinals as listed on pages 33–34.

BASIC PHRASES

yes
igen

no
nem

OK
jó
[yaw]

hello (to one person)
szervusz
[servoos]

(to more than one person)
szervusztok
[servoostok]

(answer on phone)
halló
[hollaw]

good morning
jó reggelt
[yaw]

good evening
jó estét kívánok
[yaw eshtayt keevanok]

good night
jó éjszakát
[yaw aysokat]

goodbye/see you!
viszontlátásra
[visontlatashro]

see you!
viszlát!
[vislat]

please
kérem
[kayrem]

yes, please
igen, kérek
[kayrek]

could you please ...?
lenne szíves ...?
[lenneh seevesh]

thank you
köszönöm
[kuhsuhnuhm]

thank you very much
köszönöm szépen
[saypen]

no, thank you
köszönöm, nem

don't mention it
nincs mit
[ninch]

how do you do?
örvendek
[urvendek]

how are you? (fam)
hogy vagy?
[hodj vodj]

(pol)
hogy van?
[von]

fine, thanks
köszönöm, jól?
[kuhsuhnuhm yawl]

nice to meet you
örvendek
[urvendek]

excuse me (to get past)
szabad?
[sobod]

(to get attention)
bocsánat, uram [bochanot oorom],
hölgyem [huhldjem]

excuse me/sorry
bocsánatot kérek
[kayrek]

sorry?/pardon me? (didn't understand/hear)
tessék?
[tesh-shayk]

I see/I understand
értem
[ayrtem]

I don't understand
nem értem

do you speak English?
tud Ön angolul?
[tood uhn ongolool]

I don't speak Hungarian
nem tudok magyarul
[toodok modjorool]

could you speak more slowly?
tudna egy kicsit lassabban beszélni
[toodno edj kichit lash-shobbon besaylni]

could you repeat that?
lesz szíves megismételni?
[les seevesh megish-maytelni]

CONVERSION TABLES

1 centimetre = 0.39 inches

1 inch = 2.54 cm

1 metre = 39.37 inches = 1.09 yards

1 foot = 30.48 cm

1 yard = 0.91 m

1 kilometre = 0.62 miles = 5/8 mile

1 mile = 1.61 km

km	1	2	3	4	5	10	20	30	40	50	100
miles	0.6	1.2	1.9	2.5	3.1	6.2	12.4	18.6	24.8	31.0	62.1

miles	1	2	3	4	5	10	20	30	40	50	100
km	1.6	3.2	4.8	6.4	8.0	16.1	32.2	48.3	64.4	80.5	161

1 gram = 0.035 ounces

g	100	250	500
oz	3.5	8.75	17.5

1 kilo = 1000 g = 2.2 pounds
1 oz = 28.35 g
1 lb = 0.45 kg

kg	0.5	1	2	3	4	5	6	7	8	9	10
lb	1.1	2.2	4.4	6.6	8.8	11.0	13.2	15.4	17.6	19.8	22.0

kg	20	30	40	50	60	70	80	90	100
lb	44	66	88	110	132	154	176	198	220

lb	0.5	1	2	3	4	5	6	7	8	9	10	20
kg	0.2	0.5	0.9	1.4	1.8	2.3	2.7	3.2	3.6	4.1	4.5	9.0

1 litre = 1.75 UK pints / 2.13 US pints

1 UK pint = 0.57 l
1 US pint = 0.47 l

1 UK gallon = 4.55 l
1 US gallon = 3.79 l

centigrade / Celsius

C = (F - 32) × 5/9

C	-5	0	5	10	15	18	20	25	30	36.8	38
F	23	32	41	50	59	65	68	77	86	98.4	100.4

Fahrenheit

F = (C × 9/5) + 32

F	23	32	40	50	60	65	70	80	85	98.4	101
C	-5	0	4	10	16	18	21	27	29	36.8	38.3

English-Hungarian

A

a, an* egy [edj]
about: about 20 körülbelül húsz [kurewlbelewl]
it's about 5 o'clock körülbelül öt óra van [awro von]
a film about Hungary Magyarországról szóló film [modjororsagrawl sawlaw]
above fölött [fuhluht]
abroad külföldön [kewlfuhlduhn]
absolutely (I agree) úgy van [oodj von]
absorbent cotton vatta [votto]
accelerator gázpedál
accept elfogadni [elfogodni]
accident baleset [boleshet]
there's been an accident baleset történt [turtaynt]

> Road accidents should be reported to the Hungária Biztosító insurance company in Budapest within 24 hours; if someone is injured the police must also be notified.

accommodation szállás [sallash]

> Guesthouses, inns and motels are categorized with one to three stars. Private guesthouses are often less expensive than hotels with the same star rating. Some guesthouses are purpose-built, with a restaurant on the premises, others are simply someone's house with a TV in the living room and a few rooms upstairs. There's no correlation between their appearance and title – some call themselves **panzió** (or **penzió**), others **fogadó**. The latter designation is also used for inns, which can be a guesthouse under another name or more of a motel. Places that actually describe themselves as motels are usually on the edge of town, or further out along the highway. Some coexist with bungalows and a campsite to form a tourist complex; quite a few are near a thermal bath or swimming pool, with restaurants and sports facilities too.
> Although the rating system bears some relation to price, local circumstances are more relevant. In some towns, a centrally located guesthouse might cost more than an older one- or two-star hotel; elsewhere they could be the best alternative to a pricey three-star establishment. Similarly, some motels are really cheap, and others on a par with hotels in better locations.
> see **hostel, hotel** and **private room**

accurate pontos [pontosh]
ache fájdalom [fīdolom]
my back aches fáj a hátam [fī o]
across: across the road az utca

másik oldalán [oz oottso mashik oldolan]

adapter (for voltage) adapter [odopter]

(plug) elosztó [elostaw]

address cím [tseem]

what's your address? mi a címe? [o tseemeh]

> Addresses usually begin with the name, followed by the postcode and city:
>
> Kovács Gábor úrnak
> 1028 Budapest
> Torockó u. 72. II./5.
> Magyarország
>
> The word **úrnak** means 'to Mr ...' (the word for 'Mr' is **úr**). The last two figures (II./5.) indicate the floor and the flat number.

address book notesz [not-es]

admission charge belépődíj [belaypurdee[yuh]]

adult felnőtt [felnurt]

advance: in advance előre [elur-reh]

aeroplane repülőgép [repewlurgayp]

after után [ootan]

after you tessék [tesh-shayk]

after lunch ebéd után

afternoon délután [daylootan]

in the afternoon délután

this afternoon ma délután [mo]

aftershave arcszesz [orts-ses]

aftersun cream napozó kenőcs [nopozaw kenurch]

afterwards utána [ootano]

again megint

against (next to) ... mellé

(opposed to) ... ellen

age kor

ago: a week ago egy héttel ezelőtt [edj hayttel ezelurt], egy hete [heteh]

an hour ago egy órával ezelőtt [awravol], egy órája [awra-yo]

agree: I agree rendben van [von]

AIDS 'AIDS'

air levegő [levegur]

by air repülőgépen [repewlurgaypen]

air-conditioning klímaszabályozás [kleemosoba-yozash]

airmail: by airmail légiposta [laygiposhto]

airmail envelope légiposta boríték [laygiposhto boreetayk]

airplane repülőgép [repewlurgayp]

airport repülőtér [repewlurtayr]

to the airport, please a repülőtérre, kérem [o repewlurtayrreh kayrem]

airport bus reptéri buszjárat [reptayri boos-yarot]

aisle seat folyosó melletti ülés [fo-yoshaw melletti ewlaysh]

alarm clock ébresztőóra [aybrestur-awro]

alcohol alkohol [olkohol]

alcoholic drink szeszesital [seseshitol]
all minden
all of it az egész [oz egays]
all of them mindegyik [mindedjik]
that's all, thanks köszönöm, ez minden [kuhsuhnuhm]
allergic: I'm allergic to ... allergiás vagyok a ...-ra [ollergi-ash vodjok o ...-ro]
allowed: are you allowed to ...? szabad ...? [sobod]
all right: it's all right rendben van [von]
I'm all right semmi bajom [shemmi boy-om]
are you all right? nem történt baja? [turtaynt boy-o]
almond mandula [mondoolo]
almost majdnem [moydnem]
alone egyedül [edjedewl]
alphabet ábécé [abaytsay]

a	o	í	ee	r	ayr
á	a	j	yay	s	esh
b	bay	k	ka	sz	ess
c	tsay	l	el	t	tay
cs	chay	ly	yuh	u	oo
d	day	m	em	ú	oo
e	eh	n	en	ü	ew
é	ay	ny	nyuh	ű	ew
f	ef	o	o	v	vay
g	gay	ó	aw	w	dooplo vay
gy	djay	ö	uh	y	ipsilon
h	ha	ő	ur	z	zay
i	ee	p	pay	zs	Jay

already már
also is [ish]
although bár
altogether együtt [edjewt]
always mindig
am*: I am vagyok [vodjok]
am*: at 8am reggel nyolckor
at 11am délelőtt tizenegykor [daylelurt]
amazing (surprising) csodálatos [chodalotosh]
(very good) remek
ambulance mentőautó [mentur-owtaw], mentők [menturk]
call an ambulance! hívják a mentőket! [heev-yak o menturket]

> Dial 104 for the ambulance service.

America Amerika [omeriko]
American amerikai [omeriko-ee]
I'm American amerikai vagyok [vodjok]
among között [kuhzuht]
amount összeg [uhsseg]
amp: a 13-amp fuse tizenhárom amperes biztosíték [tizenharom omperesh biztosheetayk]
and és [aysh]
angry dühös [dewhuhsh]
animal állat [allot]
ankle boka [boko]
anniversary (wedding) (házassági) évforduló [(hazosh-shagi) ayvfordoolaw]
annoy: this man's annoying me bosszant ez az ember [bossont ez oz]

annoying bosszantó [bossontaw]
another egy másik [edj mashik]
can we have another room? kaphatnánk egy másik szobát? [kop-hotnank edj mashik sobat]
another beer, please még egy sört kérek [mayg edj shurt kayrek]
antibiotics antibiotikum [ontibiotikoom]
antifreeze fagyásgátló [fodjashgatlaw]
antihistamine antihisztamin [ontihistomin]
antique: is it an antique? ez eredeti?
antique shop antik üzlet [ontik ewzlet]
antiseptic fertőtlenítő [ferturtleneetur]
any: do you have any ...? van ...? [von]
sorry, I don't have any sajnálom, nincs [shoynalom ninch]
anybody* akárki [okarki]
(somebody) valaki [voloki]
anybody can go akárki elmehet
does anybody speak English? beszél valaki angolul? [besayl voloki ongolool]
there wasn't anybody there nem volt ott senki [shenki]
anything* (whatever) bármi
(something) valami [volomi]
if you see anything ha bármit látsz [ho barmit lats]
can you see anything? látsz valamit? [volomit]

•••••• DIALOGUES ••••••

anything else? parancsol még valamit? [poronchol mayg]
nothing else, thanks köszönöm, semmi mást [kuhsuhnuhm shemmi masht]

would you like anything to drink? szeretne valamit inni? [seretneh]
I don't want anything, thanks köszönöm, semmit sem kérek [shemmit shem kayrek]

apart from ...-tól/-től eltekintve [-tawl/-turl eltekintveh]
apartment lakás [lokash]
apartment block (rented apartments) **bérház** [bayrhaz]
(privately-owned apartments) társasház [tarshosh-haz]
appendicitis vakbélgyulladás [vokbayldjoollodash]
appetizer előétel [eluraytel]
apple alma [olmo]
appointment (to be arranged) bejelentkezés [bayyelentkezaysh]
(already arranged) találkozó [tolalkozaw]

•••••• DIALOGUE ••••••

good morning, how can I help you? jó reggelt kívánok, miben segíthetek? [yaw reggelt keevanok miben shegeet-hetek]
I'd like to make an appointment be szeretnék jelentkezni [beh seretnayk yelentkezni]

what time would you like? milyen időpontra? [mi-yen idurpontro]
three o'clock három órára [awraro]
I'm afraid that's not possible, is four o'clock all right? sajnos, az lehetetlen, négy óra megfelel? [shoynosh oz lehetetlen naydj awro]
yes, that will be fine igen, nagyon jó [nodjon yaw]
the name was? milyen névre? [mi-yen nayvreh]

apricot barack [borotsk]
April április [aprilish]
are*: we are vagyunk [vodjoonk]
you are (sing, pol) van [von]
(sing, fam) vagy [vodj]
(pl, pol) vannak [vonnok]
(pl, fam) vagytok [vodjtok]
they are vannak [vonnok]
area terület [terewlet]
area code irányítószám [ira-nyeetawsam]
arm kar [kor]
arrange: will you arrange it for us? elintézné nekünk? [elintayznay nekewnk]
arrival érkezés [ayrkezaysh]
arrive érkezni [ayrkezni]
when do we arrive in Budapest? mikor érkezünk Budapestre? [mikor ayrkezewnk boodopeshtreh]
we arrived today ma érkeztünk [mo]
has my fax arrived yet? megérkezett a faxom? [megayrkezet o foksom]
art művészet [mewvayset]
art gallery képtár [kayptar], képcsarnok [kaypchornok]
artist (man/woman) művész/művésznő [mewvays/mewvaysnur]
as: as big as olyan nagy, mint [o-yon nadj]
as soon as possible mihelyt lehet [mi-hayt]
ashtray hamutartó [homoo-tortaw]
ask kérni [kayrni]
I didn't ask for this nem ezt kértem [ezt kayrtem]
could you ask him to ...? lenne szíves megkérni, hogy ...? [lenneh seevesh megkayrni hodj]
asleep: he/she is asleep alszik [olsik]
aspirin aszpirin [ospirin], kalmopirin [kolmopirin]
asthma asztma [os-mo]
astonishing elképesztő [elkaypestur]
at* ...-nál/-nél [-nal/-nayl]
(inside) ...-ban/-ben [-bon/-ben]
at the hotel (outside) a szállodánál [o sallodanal]
(inside) a szállodában [–bon]
at six o'clock hat órakor [awrokor]
at László's Lászlónál
ATM készpénz automata [kayspaynz owtomoto]
attractive vonzó [vonzaw]
aubergine padlizsán [podliJan]
August augusztus [owgoostoosh]
aunt nagynéni [nodjnayni]
Australia Ausztrália [owstrali-o]

Australian ausztráliai [owstrali-o-ee]
I'm Australian ausztráliai vagyok [vodjok]
Austria Ausztria [owstri-o]
Austrian osztrák [ostrak]
automatic (adj) automata [owtomoto]
(noun: car) automata sebességváltós kocsi [shebesh-shaygvaltawsh kochi]
autumn ősz [urs]
in the autumn ősszel [urssel]
avenue út [oot]
(main road) sugárút [shoogaroot]
average (not good) közepes [kuhzepesh]
on average átlagban [atlogbon]
awake: is he/she awake? ébren (van)? [aybren (von)]
away: go away! eredj innen! [ered^yuh]
is it far away? messze van innen? [messeh von]
awful rettenetes [rettenetesh]

B

baby csecsemő [chechemur]
baby food csecsemő táplálék [taplalayk]
baby's bottle cuclisüveg [tsootslish-ewveg]
baby-sitter 'baby-sitter'
back (of body) hát
(back part) hátsó rész [hatshaw rays]
at the back hátul [hatool]
can I have my money back? kérem vissza a pénzemet! [kayrem visso o paynzemet]
to come back visszajön [vissoy-uhn]
to go back visszamegy [visso-medj]
backache hátfájás [hatfa-yash]
bacon szalonna [solonno]
bad rossz [ross]
a bad headache súlyos fejfájás [shoo-yosh fayfa-yash]
badly rosszul [rossool]
bag zsák [Jak]
(handbag) kézitáska [kayzitashko]
(suitcase) bőrönd [bur-ruhnd]
baggage poggyász [podjas]
baggage checkroom csomagmegőrző [chomog-megurzur]
bakery pékség [paykshayg]
balcony erkély [erkay]
a room with a balcony erkélyes szoba [erkay-yesh sobo]
bald kopasz [kopos]
ball (large) labda [lobdo]
(small) golyó [go-yaw]
ballet balett [bolet]
ballpoint pen golyóstoll [go-yawshtol]
banana banán [bonan]
band (musical) együttes [edjewttesh]
bandage kötés [kuhtaysh]
Bandaid® ragtapasz [rogtopos], leukoplaszt [leh-ookoplast]
bank (money) bank [bonk]
see **money**

bank account bankszámla [bonksamlo]
bar bár
a bar of chocolate egy tábla csokoládé [edj tablo chokoladay]

> Bars vary tremendously. Those to be avoided at all costs, not only by women but also by men not looking for a fight, are the stand-up drink shops (**italbolt**). Buffets are only slightly better, especially those situated near or inside railway stations, or at main junctions of urban public transport. As a rule, the safest bets are coffee houses, bistros, hotel bars and bars in inner-city districts, summer restaurants with gardens and **cukrászda** [tsookrasdo] (pastry shops), all of which serve alcoholic drinks. see **beer**

barber's borbély [borbay[yuh]]
basket kosár [koshar]
(in shop) bevásárló kosár [bevasharlaw]
bath fürdő [fewrdur]
can I have a bath? megfürödhetném? [megfewruhd-hetnaym]
bathroom fürdőszoba [fewrdursobo]
with a private bathroom fürdőszobával [fewrdur-sobavol]
baths fürdő [fewrdur]
bath towel fürdőtörülköző [fewrdur-turewl-kuhzur]
bathtub fürdőkád [fewrdur-kad]
battery elem
(for car) akkumulátor [okkoomoolator]
be* lenni
beans bab [bob]
French beans ceruzabab [tseroozobob]
green beans zöldbab [zuhldbob]
broad beans szárazbab [sarozbob]
beard szakáll [sokal]
beautiful szép [sayp]
because mert
because of ... ... miatt [mi-ot]
bed ágy [adj]
I'm going to bed now lefekszem [lefeksem]
bed and breakfast szoba reggelivel [sobo]
see **hotel** and **private room**
bedroom hálószoba [halawsobo]
beef marhahús [morho-hoosh]
beer sör [shur]
two beers, please két pohár sört kérek [shurt kayrek]

> Bottled beer of the lager type (**világos** [vilagosh]) is the most common, although you might come across **barna sör** [borno shur] (brown ale) and **csapolt sör** [chopolt shur] (draught beer). Western brands like Tuborg, Wernesgrünner and Gold Fassel are imported or →

brewed under licence at Nagykanizsa, and the famous old Austro-Hungarian beer **Dreher** has made a comeback, displacing cheaper Hungarian brands such as **Kőbányai**, or imported Czech **Urquell** Pilsen. Other brands to try are **Arany Ászok**, a very cheap light beer, and **Pannonia Sör**, a pleasant hoppy beer from Pécs.
Beer halls (**söröző** [shuruhzur]) range from plush establishments sponsored by foreign breweries to humble stand-up joints where you order either a **pohár** (a small glass) or a **korsó** [korshaw] (a half-litre mug). It's useful to know that söröző is often just another name for restaurant.

before előtt [elurt]
begin kezdeni
  when does it begin? mikor kezdődik? [kezdurdik]
beginner kezdő [kezdur]
beginning kezdet
  at the beginning kezdetben
behind mögött [muhguht]
  behind me mögöttem
beige drapp [drop]
below alatt [olot]
belt öv [uhv]
bend (in road) kanyar [ko-nyor]
beside ... mellett
best legjobb [leg-yob]
better jobb [yob]
  are you feeling better? jobban van? [yobbon von]
between között [kuhzuht]
beyond túl [tool]
bicycle bicikli [bitsikli]
big nagy [nodj]
  too big túl nagy [tool]
  it's not big enough nem elég nagy [elayg]
bike shop kerékpár szaküzlet [keraykpar sokewzlet]
bikini 'bikini'
bill számla [samlo]
  (US) bankjegy [bonkyedj]
  could I have the bill, please? megkaphatnám a számlámat, kérem? [megkop-hotnam o samlamot kayrem]

Bills at all restaurants need to be carefully examined as those presented at the end of an elaborate dinner have been known to bear scant relationship to the prices indicated on the menu. This is especially true in cases where foreign visitors entertain chance acquaintances who recommend the eating place.
If your menu indicates that all prices are higher after 6 or 7pm, it's best to clarify how much higher in order to avoid getting stuck with a potential surcharge of 500-600 per cent. Say: '**mennyivel drágább este hat után?**' [men-nyivel dragab eshteh hot ootan] ('how much is the surcharge after 6pm?').
see **tip**

bin tartó [tortaw]
bin liners szemétláda bélelő [semaytlado baylelur]
bird madár [modar]
birthday születésnap [sewletay-shnop]
happy birthday! gratulálok születésnapjára! [grotoolalok sewletay-shnop-yaro]
biscuit keksz [keks]
bit: a little bit egy kicsit [edj kichit]
a big bit nagy darab [nodj dorob]
a bit of ... egy kis ... [edj kish]
a bit expensive egy kicsit drága
bite (by insect) csípés [cheepaysh]
(by dog) harapás [horopash]

Insect bites are the most common minor complaint; pharmacies stock **Vietnámi balzsam** (Vietnamese-made 'Tiger Balm' – the best bug repellent going) and bite ointment. Mosquitoes are also a nuisance, but the bug to beware of in forests is the **kullancs**, which bites and then burrows into the human skin, causing inflammation of the brain. The risk is fairly small, but if you get a bite which seems particularly painful, or are suffering from a high temperature and stiff neck following a bite, it's worth having it inspected as soon as possible.

bitter (taste etc) keserű [kesherew]
black fekete [feketeh]
black market fekete piac [pi-ots]
blanket takaró [tokoraw]
bleach fehérítő [fehayreetur]
bless you! egészségére! [egayshay-gayreh]
blind vak [vok]
blinds roló [rolaw]
Venetian blinds reluxa függöny [relookso fewgguh[nyuh]]
blister vízhólyag [veezhaw-yog]
blocked (pipe, sink) eldugult [eldoogoolt]
block of flats (rented flats) bérház [bayrhaz]
(privately-owned flats) társasház [tarshosh-haz]
blond (adj) szőke [surkeh]
blood vér [vayr]
high blood pressure magas vérnyomás [mogosh vayr-nyomash]
blouse blúz [blooz]
blow-dry légszárítás [laygsareetash]
I'd like a cut and blow-dry hajvágást és légszárítást szeretnék [hoyvagasht aysh laygsareetasht seretnayk]
blue kék [kayk]
blusher pirosító [pirosheetaw]
boarding pass beszálló kártya [besallaw kar-tyo]
boat hajó [hoy-aw]
body test [tesht]
boiled egg főtt tojás [furt to-yash]
boiler kazán [kozan]

bone csont [chont]
bonnet (of car) motorház fedő [fedur]
book (noun) könyv [kuhn^{yuh}v]
(verb) foglalni [foglolni]
I'd like to book a seat szeretnék jegyet venni [seretnayk yedjet]

•••••• DIALOGUE ••••••

I'd like to book a table for two szeretnék asztalt foglalni két személyre [seretnayk ostolt foglolni kayt semay^{yuh}reh]
what time would you like it booked for? mikorra szeretné? [mikorro seretnay]
half past seven fél nyolcra
that's fine rendben van [von]
and your name? szabad a nevét? [sobod o nevayt]

bookshop/bookstore könyvüzlet [kuh^{nyuh}vewzlet], könyvesbolt [kuh^{nyuh}veshbolt]
boot (footwear) csizma [chizmo]
(of car) csomagtartó [chomogtortaw]
border (of country) határ [hotar]
bored unatkozó [oonotkozaw]
I'm bored unatkozom [oonotkozom]
boring unalmas [oonolmosh]
born: I was born in ... ...-ban/ben születtem [–bon/ben sewlettem]
borrow kölcsönkérni [kuhlchuhnkayrni]
may I borrow ...? kölcsön kaphatnám ...? [kuhlchuhn kophotnam]
both mindkettő [mindkettur]
both of them mindketten
both of us mindkettőnk [mindketturnk]
bother: sorry to bother you elnézést a zavarásért [elnayzaysht o zovorashayrt]
bottle üveg [ewveg]
a bottle of red wine egy üveg vörös bor [edj ewveg vuruhsh]
bottle-opener üvegnyitó [ewveg-nyitaw]
bottom (of person, container) fenék [fenayk]
at the bottom of ... (hill) ... lábánál [labanal]
(street) ... végén [vaygayn]
box doboz
box office pénztár [paynztar]
boy fiú [fi-oo]
boyfriend barát [borat]
bra melltartó [melltortaw]
bracelet karperec [korperets]
brake (noun) fék [fayk]
(verb) fékezni [faykezni]
brandy konyak [ko-nyok]
bread kenyér [keh-nyayr]
white bread fehér kenyér [fehayr]
wholemeal bread barna kenyér [borno]
rye bread rozskenyér [roJkeh-nyayr]

Bread is supplied automatically in many restaurants. White bread remains the staple of the nation, but in many supermarkets, especially in Budapest, you →

can usually get a range of **barna** (wholemeal) and **rozs** (rye) breads. In bakeries and grocery stores as well as supermarkets, the most common type of bread is supplied in loaves of two kilograms, but these can be cut to smaller sizes on request.

break (verb) eltörni [elturni]
I've broken the ... eltörtem a ... [elturtem o]
I think I've broken my wrist azt hiszem, eltörtem a csuklómat [ozt hisem elturtem o chooklawmot]
break down defektet kapni [kopni]
I've broken down defektes a kocsim [defektesh o kochim]
breakdown defekt
breakdown service autómentő [owtawmentur]
breakfast reggeli
break-in betörés [beturaysh]
breast mell
bridge (over river) híd [heed]
brief (adj) rövid [ruhvid]
briefcase aktatáska [oktotashko]
bright (light etc) fényes [fay-nyesh]
bright red élénk vörös [aylaynk vuruhsh]
brilliant (idea) ragyogó [rodjogaw]
(person) kiváló tehetségű [kivalaw tehet-shaygew]
bring hozni
I'll bring it back later majd visszahozom [moyd visso-hozom]
Britain Nagy-Britannia [nodj-britonni-o]
British brit
brochure brosúra [broshooro]
broken törött [turuht]
brooch melltű [meltew]
brother fivér [fivayr]
brother-in-law sógor [shawgor]
brown barna [borno]
bruise zúzódás [zoozawdash]
brush kefe [kefeh]
(artist's) ecset [echet]
bucket vödör [vuhdur]
buffet car büfékocsi [bewfaykochi]
buggy (for child) gyerekkocsi [djerekkochi]
building épület [aypewlet]
bungalow földszintes lakóépület [fuhldsintesh lokaway-pewlet]
bunk ágy [adj]
bureau de change pénzváltás [paynzvaltash]
burglary betörés [beturaysh]
burn (noun) égési seb [aygayshi sheb]
(verb) égni [aygni]
burnt: this is burnt (food) ez odaégett [odo-ayget]
burst repedés [repedaysh]
a burst pipe csőrepedés [chur-repedaysh]
bus (autó)busz [(owtaw)boos]
what number bus is it to ...? melyik busz megy ...-ra/-re? [meh-yik boos medj ...-ro/-reh]
when is the next bus to ...?

mikor indul a következő busz ...-ra/-re? [indool o kuhvetkezur]
what time is the last bus? mikor megy az utolsó busz? [oz ootolshaw]

•••••• DIALOGUE ••••••

does this bus go to ...? megy ... ez a busz?
no, you need a number ... nem, oda a ... busz megy [odo]

> Buses are often the quickest way to travel between towns and, although bus fares are higher than rail fares, bus travel is still good value.
> Timetables are clearly displayed in bus stations (**autóbusz állomás** or **autóbusz pályaudvar**) in every Hungarian town. Arrive early to confirm the **kocsiállás** [kochi-allash] (departure bay) and to be sure of getting a seat. For long-distance services originating in Budapest or major towns, you can buy tickets with a seat booking up to half an hour before departure; after that you get them from the driver, and risk standing throughout the journey. Services in rural areas may be limited to one or two a day, and tickets are only available on board the bus.
> Express buses numbered in red halt only at main stops, while express buses whose number is accompanied by an 'E' run almost non-stop between bus terminuses.
> Public transport within towns is generally excellent, with buses, trolley buses (**trolibusz** [troliboos]) and trams (**villamos** [villamosh]) running from dawn until around 11pm. All forms of urban public transport, however, tend to be very crowded at all times.
> Tickets for all urban services are sold in strips at tobacconists and street stands, as well as at most major tram terminuses. Tickets should be punched on board the vehicle. Generally, the local fare for all transport is identical, so the same kind of ticket can be used on all types of city transport.

business üzlet [ewzlet]
bus station autóbusz állomás [owtawboos allomash], autóbusz pályaudvar [pa-yowdvor]
bus stop buszmegálló [boosmegallaw]
bust mellszobor [mellsobor]
busy (restaurant etc) tele van [teleh von]
(person) elfoglalt [elfoglolt]
I'm busy tomorrow holnap nem érek rá [holnop nem ayrek]
but de [deh]
butcher's hentes [hentesh]
butter vaj [voy]
button gomb
buy vásárolni [vasharolni]
(specific purchase) megvenni

where can I buy ...? hol kapok ...? [kopok]
by: by bus autóbuszon [owtawbooson]
by car autón [owtawn]
written by ... írta ... [eerto]
by the window az ablaknál [oz]
by the lake a tó mellett
by Thursday csütörtökre [-reh]
bye viszlát [vislat]

C

cabbage káposzta [kaposto]
café büfé [bewfay], falatozó [folotozaw]
see snack
cagoule viharkabát [vihorkobat]
cake sütemény [shewtemay[nyuh]]
(gâteau) torta [torto]
cake shop cukrászda [tsookrasdo]
call (noun: phone) hívás [heevash]
(verb: to phone) telefonálni [telefonalni]
what's it called? hogy hívják? [hodj heev-yak]
she's called ... ...-nak/-nek hívják [-nok/-nek]
please call the doctor legyen szíves, hívjon orvost [ledjen seevesh heev-yon orvosht]
please give me a call at 7.30am tomorrow legyen szíves, keltsen fel reggel fél nyolckor [keltshen fel reggel fayl nyoltskor]
please ask him to call me legyen szíves, kérje meg, hogy hívjon fel [kayr-yeh meg hodj heev-yon]
call back: I'll call back later később visszahívom [kayshurb visso-heevom]
call round: I'll call round tomorrow holnap átjövök [holnop at-yuhvuhk]
camcorder videokamera [videh-o-komero]
camera fényképezőgép [fay[nyuh]kaypezurgayp]
camera shop fotóüzlet [fotawewzlet]
camp (verb) táborozni [taborozni]
can we camp here? itt letáborozhatunk? [letaboroz-hotoonk]
camping gas 'camping' gáz
campsite tábor

Throughout Hungary campsites and bungalows share a single site. Rates for bungalows (also called **faház**, literally 'wooden houses') depend on amenities and size. The first-class bungalows – with well-equipped kitchens, hot water and a sitting room or terrace – are excellent, while the most primitive at least have clean bedding and don't leak. Campsites, usually signposted **kemping**, similarly range from deluxe to third-class. The most elaborate places boast a restaurant and shops (sometimes even →

a disco) and tend to be overcrowded; second- or third-class sites often have a nicer ambience. Fees are calculated on a basic ground rent, plus a charge per head and for any vehicle, plus, for non-students, an obligatory **kurtaxe** (local tax). While a few resorts and towns have semi-official free campsites (**szabad kemping**), camping rough is illegal.

can (tin) konzerv
  a can of beer egy doboz sör [edj doboz shur]
can: can you ...? tudsz ...? [toods]
  can I have ...? kérek ... [kayrek]
  I can't ... nem tudok ... [toodok]
Canada Kanada [konodo]
Canadian kanadai [konodo-ee]
  I'm Canadian kanadai vagyok [vodjok]
canal csatorna [chotorno]
cancel: I want to cancel my booking (seat reservation) töröltetni akarom a foglalásom [turuhltetni okorom a foglolasom]
  (tickets) vissza akarom váltani a jegyemet [visso okorom valtoni o yedjemet]
  I want to cancel my reservation (hotel) le akarom mondani a foglalásom [leh okorom mondoni o foglolasom]
candies cukorka [tsookorko]
candle gyertya [djer-tyo]
canoe kajak [ko-yok]
canoeing kajakozás [ko-yokozash]
can-opener konzervnyitó [konzerv-nyitaw]
cap (hat) sapka [shopko]
  (of bottle) kupak [koopok]
car autó [owtaw], kocsi [kochi]
  by car autóval [owtawvol], kocsival [kochivol]
carafe boroskancsó [boroshkonchaw]
  a carafe of house white, please egy kancsó házi fehérbort kérek [edj konchaw hazi fehayrbort kayrek]
caravan lakókocsi [lokawkochi]
caravan site lakókocsi parkoló [lokawkochi porkolaw]
card (birthday etc) lap [lop]
  here's my (business) card itt a névjegyem [o nayv-yedjem]
cardigan kardigán [kordigan]
cardphone kártyára működő telefon [kar-tyaro mewkuhdur]
careful gondos [gondosh]
  be careful! legyen óvatos! [ledjen awvotosh]
caretaker (man/woman) házmester/házmesterné [hazmeshter/hazmeshternay]
car park autópark [owtawpork]
Carpathian Mountains a Kárpátok
carpet szőnyeg [sur-nyeg]
car rental autóbérlés [owtawbayrlaysh]

Renting a car is easy provided you're 21 or older, and hold a valid national driving licence that's at least one year old. You can order a car through rental agencies in your own country, and from hotel reception desks or certain travel agencies within Hungary, using cash or credit cards. In Budapest these agencies are Cooptourist, Ibusz and Főtaxi; Ibusz, Volántourist and Cooptourist offices offer the same service in the provinces.
see **rent**

carriage (of train) vagon [vogon], vasúti kocsi [voshooti kochi]
carrier bag zacskó [zochkaw]
carrot sárgarépa [shargoraypo]
carry vinni
carry-cot csecsemőhordozó [chechemur-hordozaw]
carton karton [korton]
carwash autómosó [owtawmoshaw]
case (suitcase) táska [tashko]
cash (noun) készpénz [kayspaynz] (verb) beváltani [bevaltoni]
will you cash this for me? lesz szíves ezt beváltani? [les seevesh ezt]
cash desk pénztár [paynztar], kassza [kassa]
cash dispenser készpénz automata [kayspaynz owtomoto]
cassette kazetta [kozetto]
cassette recorder kazettás magnó [kozettash mognaw]
castle vár
casualty department baleseti osztály [bolesheti osta[yuh]]
cat macska [mochko]
catch (verb) elfogni
where do we catch the bus to ...? hol áll meg a busz ...-ra/-re? [o boos ...-ro/-reh]
cathedral székesegyház [saykeshedj-haz]
Catholic (adj) katolikus [kotolikoosh]
cauliflower karfiol [korfi-ol]
cave barlang [borlong]
ceiling mennyezet [men-nyezet]
celery zeller
cellar (for wine) borospince [boroshpintseh]
cemetery temető [temetur]
centigrade fok Celsius [tselzi-oosh]
centimetre centiméter [tsentimayter]
central központi [kuhzponti]
central heating központi fűtés [fewtaysh]
centre központ [kuhzpont]
how do we get to the city centre? hogy jutunk a belvárosba? [hodj yootoonk o belvaroshbo]
certainly hogyne [hodjneh]
certainly not dehogyis [dehodjish]
chair szék [sayk]
champagne pezsgő [peJgur]
change (noun: small change) apró(pénz) [opraw(paynz)]

(money back) visszajáró pénz [vissoy-araw paynz]
(verb: money) átváltani [atvaltoni]
can I change this for ...? átváltaná ezt ...-ra/-re? [atvaltona ezt ...-ro/-reh]
I don't have any change nincs aprópénzem [ninch oprawpaynzem]
can you give me change for a 1,000-forint note? fel tudna váltani egy ezrest? [toodno valtoni edj ezresht]

•••••• DIALOGUE ••••••

do we have to change (trains)? át kell szállni valahol? [sallni volohol]
yes, change at Hatvan/no, it's a direct train igen, Hatvanban/nem, ez közvetlen járat [hotvonbon/nem ez kuhzvetlen yarot]

changed: to get changed átöltözni [atuhltuhzni]
charge (noun) ár
(verb) felszámítani [felsameetoni]
charge card folyószámla kártya [fo-yawsamlo kar-tyo]
see **credit card**
cheap olcsó [olchaw]
do you have anything cheaper? ennél olcsóbb nincs? [ennayl olchawb ninch]
check (US: noun) csekk [chek]
(bill) számla [samlo]
could I have the check, please? megkaphatnám a számlámat, kérem? [megkop-hotnam o samlamot kayrem]
see **bill**
check (verb) ellenőrizni [ellenurrizni]
could you check the ...? lenne szíves megnézni ...? [lenneh seevesh megnayzni]
check in (verb: hotel) bejelentkezni [beh-yelentkezni]
(airport) jegyet kezeltetni [yedjet kezeltetni]
where do we have to check in? hol kell jegyet kezeltetni? [yedjet kezeltetni]
check-in jegykezelés [yedjkezelaysh]
cheek (on face) arc [orts]
cheerio! (to one person) szervusz! [servoos]
(to more than one person) szervusztok! [servoostok]
cheers! (toast: informal) egészségedre! [egayshaygedreh]
(formal) egészségére! [egayshay-gayreh]
(to more than one person) egészségünkre! [egayshaygewnkreh]
cheese sajt [shoyt]
chemist's drogéria [drogayri-o]
(dispensing) patika [potiko]
see **pharmacy**
cheque csekk [chek]
do you take cheques? csekket elfogad? [elfogod]
see **money** and **traveller's**

cheque
cheque book csekk-könyv [chek-kuh^{nyuh}v]
cheque card csekk kártya [chek-kar-tyo]
cherry cseresznye [cheres-nyeh]
chess sakk [shok]
chest mell(kas) [mell(kosh)]
chewing gum rágógumi [ragawgoomi]
chicken (meat) csirkehús [chirkehoosh]
chickenpox bárányhimlő [bara^{nyuh}himlur]
child gyermek [djermek], gyerek [djerek]
  children gyerekek [djerekek]
children's pool gyerekmedence [djerekmedentseh]
children's portion gyermekadag [djermekodog]
chilli pepper csilipaprika [chilipopriko]
chin áll [al]
Chinese kínai [keeno-ee]
chips hasábburgonya [hoshabburgo-nyo]
  (US) 'chips'
chocolate csokoládé [chokoladay]
  milk chocolate tejcsokoládé [tay–]
  plain chocolate keserű csokoládé [kesherew]
  hot chocolate meleg csokoládé
choose választani [valostoni]
Christian name keresztnév [kerestnayv]
Christmas Karácsony [koracho^{nyuh}]
Christmas Eve szenteste [senteshteh]
merry Christmas! kellemes karácsonyi ünnepeket! [kellemesh koracho-nyi ewnnepeket]
church templom

> Hungary's really important churches charge a small fee to see their crypts and treasures, and may prohibit sightseeing during services (**mise** or **istentisztelet**, or **Gottesdienst** in German). In small towns and villages, churches are usually kept locked except for worship in the early morning and/or evening (around 6–9pm). A small tip is in order if you rouse the verger to unlock the building during the day; he normally lives nearby in a house with a doorbell marked **plébánia csengője**.

cider almabor [olmobor]
cigar szivar [sivor]
cigarette cigaretta [tsigoretto]

> Cigarettes are sold in tobacconists (**dohánybolt**), supermarkets, bars and restaurants. Marlboro and Camel made under licence are cheaper than imports, but still more expensive than Hungarian brands like charcoal-filtered Helikon and Sopianae, or →

Symphonia and Munkás. **Tilos a dohányzás** (or **dohányozni tilos**) means 'no smoking', and applies to cinemas, the metro, all buses, trams and trolley buses.

cigarette lighter öngyújtó [uhndjoo^yuh^taw]
cinema mozi

Virtually all foreign films are dubbed in Hungary. Some larger cinemas in Budapest have retractable roofs and may go 'topless' on summer nights. There are a number of open-air cinemas in the country called **kertmozi**.

circle kör [kuhr]
(in theatre) emelet
city város [varosh]
city centre város központ [kuhzpont]
classical music komolyzene [komoyzeneh]
clean (adj) tiszta [tisto]
can you clean these for me? lenne szíves kitisztítani? [lenneh seevesh kitisteetoni]
cleaning solution (for contact lenses) tisztító oldat [tisteetaw oldot]
cleansing lotion kozmetikai arcbőrtisztító krém [kozmetiko-ee ortsbur-tisteetaw kraym]
clear világos [vilagosh]
clever okos [okosh]
cliff szikla [siklo]
climbing hegymászás [hedjmasash]
cling film nylon fólia ['nylon' fawli-o]
clinic klinika [kliniko]
cloakroom ruhatár [roo-hotar]
clock óra [awro]
close (verb) bezárni [bezarni]

•••••• DIALOGUE ••••••

what time do you close? hánykor zárnak? [ha^nyuh^kor zarnok]
we close at 7pm on weekdays and 6pm on Saturdays hétköznapokon hétkor, szombaton hatkor zárunk [haytkuhz-nopokon haytkor somboton hotkor zaroonk]
do you close for lunch? tartanak ebédszünetet? [tortonok ebaydsewnetet]
yes, between 1 and 3pm igen, egy és három között ebédszünet miatt zárva [edj aysh harom kuhzuht ebayd-syewnet mi-ot zarvo]

closed zárva [zarvo]
cloth (fabric) szövet [suhvet]
(for cleaning etc) törlőruha [turlur-roo-ho]
clothes ruha [roo-ho]
clothes line ruhaszárító kötél [roo-hosareetaw kuhtayl]
clothes peg ruhaszárító csipesz [chipes]
cloudy felhős [felhursh]
clutch kuplung [kooploong]
coach (bus) autóbusz [owtawboos]

(on train) kocsi [kochi]
coach station autóbusz állomás [owtawboos allomash]
coach trip autóbuszkirándulás [–kirandoolash]
coat kabát [kobat]
coathanger ruha akasztó [roo-ho okostaw]
cockroach svábbogár [shvabbogar]
cocoa kakaó [koko-aw]
coconut kókuszdió [kawkoosdi-aw]
code (for phoning) körzethívószám [kurzet-heevawsam]
what's the (dialling) code for Miskolc? mi a miskolci körzethívószám? [o mishkoltsi]
coffee kávé [kavay]
two coffees, please kérek két kávét [kayrek kayt kavayt]

You'll find plenty of coffee houses (**kávéház** [kavayhaz]) – an old and much-liked institution. Coffee is generally served super-strong, black and sweetened to taste, but drunk by the connoisseur unsweetened. Called **fekete** [feketeh] (black), this coffee may be ordered as **szimpla** [simplo] (small), **dupla** [dooplo] (large), or **rövid fekete** [ruhvid feketeh] (literally: 'short espresso'), where the same amount of coffee is made with less water. →

You can also get coffee with milk (**tejeskávé** [tayesh-kavay]) or whipped cream (**tejszínhabbal** [tayseen-hobbol]), although more and more eating places serve cappuccino rather than coffee with milk or cream. Most coffee houses have some pastries on offer, although you'll find much more choice in patisseries, which, of course, also sell coffee. It's also possible in most coffee houses to order a salad or an egg dish, but the choice of food is very limited.

coffee house kávéház [kavayhaz]
coin érme [ayrmeh]
Coke® kola [kolo]
cold hideg
I'm cold fázom
I have a cold meg vagyok fázva [vodjok fazvo]
collapse: he/she has collapsed összeesett [uhsseh-eshet]
collar gallér [gollayr]
collect (fetch) elvinni
I've come to collect ... azért jöttem, hogy elvigyem ... [ozayrt yuhttem hodj elvidjem]
collect call R-beszélgetés [ayr besaylgetaysh]
college kollégium [kollay-gi-oom]
colour szín [seen]
do you have this in other colours? ez más színben is kapható? [ez mash seenben ish kop-hotaw]

colour film színes 'film' [seenesh]
comb fésű [fayshew]
come jönni [yuhnni]

•••••• DIALOGUE ••••••

where do you come from? honnan jött? [honnon yuht]
I come from Edinburgh Edinburghból jöttem [–bawl yuhttem]

come back visszajönni [vissoy-uhnni]
I'll come back tomorrow holnap visszajövök [holnop vissoy-uhvuhk]
come in bejönni [beh-yuhnni]
come in! tessék! [tesh-shayk]
comfortable kényelmes [kay-nyelmesh]
compact disc kompakt lemez [kompokt]
company (business) társaság [tarshoshag], vállalat [vallolot]
compartment (on train) fülke [fewlkeh]
compass iránytű [ira^nyuh^tew]
complain panaszkodni [ponoskodni]
complaint panasz [ponos]
I have a complaint panaszt akarok emelni [okorok]
completely teljesen [tel-yeshen]
computer számítógép [sameetawgayp]
concert koncert [kontsert]
concussion agyrázkódás [odjrazkawdash]
conditioner (for hair) hajkondicionáló [hoykonditsi-onalaw], hajbalzsam [hoyboljom]
condom óvszer [awvser]
conference konferencia [konferentsi-o]
confirm megerősíteni [megerursheeteni]
congratulations! gratulálok! [grotoolalok]
connecting flight csatlakozó repülőjárat [chotlokozaw repewlur-yarot]
connection csatlakozás [chotlokozash]
constipation székrekedés [saykrekedaysh]
consulate konzulátus [konzoolatoosh]
contact (verb) érintkezésbe lépni ...-val/-vel [ayrint-kezayshbeh laypni ...-vol/-vel]
contact lenses kontaktlencse [kontoktlencheh]
contraceptive fogamzásgátló [fogomzashgatlaw]
convenient megfelelő [megfelelur]
that's not convenient az nem felel meg [oz]
cook (verb) főzni [furzni]
not cooked félig nyers [faylig nyersh]
cooker tűzhely [tewzheh^yuh^]
cookie keksz [keks]
cooking utensils edények [eday-nyek]
cool hűvös [hewvuhsh]
cork dugó [doogaw]
corkscrew dugóhúzó [doogaw-

hoozaw]
corner sarok [shorok]
on the corner a sarkon [o shorkon]
in the corner a sarokban [–bon]
cornflakes 'cornflakes'
correct (right) helyes [heh-yesh]
corridor folyosó [fo-yoshaw]
cosmetics kozmetikai szerek [kozmetiko-ee serek]
cost (verb) ...-ba/-be kerülni [-bo/-beh kerewlni]
how much does it cost? mennyibe kerül? [men-nyibeh kerewl]
cot kiságy [kishadj]
cotton gyapot [djopot]
cotton wool vatta [votto]
couch (sofa) díván [deevan], heverő [heverur]
couchette kusett [kooshet]
cough (noun) köhögés [kuh-huhgaysh]
cough medicine köhögés elleni gyógyszer [djawdjser]
could: could you ...? lenne szíves ...? [lenneh seevesh]
could I have ...? kaphatnék ...? [kop-hotnayk]
I couldn't ... nem tudtam ... [toodtom]
country (nation) ország [orsag]
(countryside) vidék [vidayk]
countryside vidék
couple (two people) pár
a couple of ... két ... [kayt]
courgette cukkini [tsookkini]
courier útikalauz [ootikolowz]
course (main course etc) fogás [fogash]
of course persze [perseh]
of course not persze, hogy nem [hodj]
cousin unokatestvér [oonokotesht-vayr]
cow tehén [tehayn]
cracker (biscuit) keksz [keks]
craft shop iparművészeti üzlet [ipormew-vayseti ewzlet]
crash (noun) karambol [korombol]
I've had a crash karamboloztam [koromboloztom]
crazy őrült [ur-rewlt]
cream (in cake, in coffee) tejszín [tayseen]
(lotion) kenőcs [kenurch]
whipped cream tejszínhab [tayseenhob]
creche bölcsőde [buhlchurdeh]
credit card kreditkártya [kreditkar-tyo]
do you take credit cards? fizethetek kreditkártyával? [kreditkar-tyavol]

Amex (the safest bet), Visa, Mastercard, Diners' Club, Carte Blanche and Eurocard credit and charge cards can be used to rent cars, buy airline tickets or pay your bills directly in hotels, restaurants and many upmarket shops. Outside the main tourist centres their usefulness is more restricted.

••••• DIALOGUE •••••

can I pay by credit card?
kreditkártyával fizethetek?
which card do you want to use?
melyik kártyával akar fizetni?
[meh-yik kar-tyavol okor]
Access/Visa Accesszel/Visával
yes, sir igenis [igenish]
what's the number? mi a száma?
[o samo]
and the expiry date? és mikor jár le? [aysh mikor yar leh]

crisps 'chips'
Croatia Horvátország [horvatorsag]
Croatian horvát
crockery asztali edények [ostoli eday-nyek]
crossroads útkereszteződés [ootkeres-tezurdaysh]
crowd tömeg [tuh-meg]
crowded zsúfolt [Joofolt]
crown (on tooth) korona [korono]
crutches mankó [monkaw]
cry (verb) sírni [sheerni]
cucumber uborka [ooborko]
cup csésze [chayseh]
a cup of ..., please egy csésze ... kérek [edj chayseh ... kayrek]
cupboard szekrény [sekray^nyuh]
cure (verb) kigyógyítani [kidjawdjeetoni]
curly göndör [guhndur]
current (electrical, in water) áram [arom]
curtains függöny [fewgguh^nyuh]
cushion párna [parno]
custom szokás [sokash]
Customs (vám)kezelés [(vam)kezelaysh]
cut (noun) vágás [vagash]
(verb) vágni
I've cut myself megvágtam magam [megvagtom mogom]
cutlery evőeszközök [evur-eskuhzuhk]
cycling kerékpározás [keraykparozash]

Given the general flat terrain, and the light winds and low rainfall from July until the end of September, cycling should be a good way to see Hungary. Cyclists are not allowed on main roads (with single-digit numbers), however, nor on some secondary roads between peak hours (7–9.30am and 4–6pm); bikes can be carried on most passenger trains, except for Intercity, Express and international trains. There are restrictions on the number of bicycles allowed on trains during rush hour (before 8am and from 2–3.30pm on weekdays), and if you're departing from mainline stations in Budapest it's tricky getting hold of the right paperwork, so allow plenty of time.
It's possible to rent bikes (by the day or week) in most large towns and the Balaton resorts, from MÁV, private operators or certain campsites. Unfortunately, most →

machines are low-slung and heavy, with limited gears, although superior models are increasingly available. There are repair shops in most larger towns, including several in Budapest.

cycling tour kerékpártúra [keraykpartooro]
cyclist kerékpáros [keraykparosh]
Czech cseh [cheH]
Czech Republic Cseh Köztársaság [cheH kuhztarshoshag]

D

dad apu [opoo]
daily naponta [noponto]
(adj) napi [nopi]
damage (verb) kárt tenni ...-ban/ben [...-bon/ben]
damaged megrongálódott [megrongalawdot]
I'm sorry, I've damaged this elnézét kérek, de kárt tettem benne [elnayzayt kayrek deh kart tettem benneh]
damn! a fene egye meg! [o feneh edjeh]
damp (adj) nedves [nedvesh]
dance (noun) tánc [tants]
(verb) táncolni [tantsolni]
would you like to dance? táncoljunk? [tantsol-yoonk]
dangerous veszélyes [vesay-yesh]
Danish dán
Danube Duna [doono]
Danube Bend Dunakanyar [doonoko-nyor]
dark (adj) sötét [shuhtayt]
it's getting dark sötétedik [shuhtaytedik]
date* dátum [datoom]
what's the date today? hányadika van? [ha-nyodiko von]
let's make a date for next Monday egyezzünk meg, hogy jövő hétfőn találkozunk [edjezzewnk meg hodj yuhvur haytfurn tolalkozoonk]
daughter lány [la^{nyuh}]
daughter-in-law meny [meh^{nyuh}]
dawn hajnal [hoynol]
at dawn hajnalban [–bon]
day nap [nop]
the day after másnap [mashnop]
the day after tomorrow holnapután [holnopootan]
the day before előző nap [elurzur]
the day before yesterday tegnapelőtt [tegnopelurt]
every day minden nap
all day egész nap [egays]
in two days' time két nap múlva [kayt nop moolvo]
day trip egész napos kirándulás [egays noposh kirandoolash]
dead halott [holot]
deaf süket [shewket]
deal (business) üzlet [ewzlet]
it's a deal! megegyeztünk! [megedjeztewnk], áll az alku! [al oz olkoo]

decaffeinated coffee koffeinmentes kávé [koffehinmentesh kavay]
December december [detsember]
decide eldönteni [elduhnteni]
we haven't decided yet még nem döntöttük el [mayg nem duhntuhttewk]
deckchair nyugágy [nyoogadj]
deep mély [may^{yuh}]
definitely határozottan [hotarozotton]
definitely not semmiesetre sem [shemmi-eshetreh shem]
degree (qualification) diploma [diplomo]
delay (noun) késés [kayshaysh]
deliberately szándékosan [sandaykoshon]
delicatessen csemege [chemegeh]
delicious finom
deliver leszállítani [lesalleetoni]
delivery (of mail) kézbesítés [kayzbesheetaysh]
Denmark Dánia [dani-o]
dental floss fogtisztító szál [fogtisteetaw sal]
dentist (man/woman) fogorvos/fogorvosnő [fogorvosh/fogorvoshnur]

•••••• DIALOGUE ••••••

it's this one here ez az [oz]
this one? ez?
no, that one nem, az
here itt
yes igen

see **doctor**

dentures hamis fogsor [homish fogshor]
deodorant szagtalanító [sogtoloneetaw]
department osztály [osta^{yuh}]
department store áruház [aroohaz]
departure indulás [indoolash]
departure bay (for buses) kocsiállás [koch-shi-allash]
departure lounge indulóváró [indoolaw-varaw]
depend: it depends attól függ [ottawl fewg]
it depends on ... ...-tól/-től függ [-tawl/-turl]
deposit (as security) letét [letayt]
(as part payment) előleg [elurleg]
dessert édesség [aydesh-shayg]
destination rendeltetési hely [rendeltetayshi heh^{yuh}]
develop (film) előhívni [elurheevni]

•••••• DIALOGUE ••••••

could you develop these films? lenne szíves előhívni ezt a filmet? [lenneh seevesh]
yes, certainly igen, hogyne [hodjneh]
when will they be ready? mikor lesz kész? [les kays]
tomorrow afternoon holnap délután [holnop daylootan]
how much is the four-hour service? mennyibe kerül a négyórás szolgálat? [men-nyibeh kerewl o naydjawrash solgalot]

diabetic (noun) cukorbeteg

[tsookorbeteg]
diabetic foods diétás ételek [di-aytash aytelek]
dial (verb) tárcsázni [tarchazni]
dialling code telefon kódszám [kawdsam]

To ring abroad from Hungary, dial the following numbers followed by the area code and subscriber number:

Australia	00 61
Ireland	00 353
New Zealand	00 64
UK	00 44
USA and Canada	00 1

diamond gyémánt [djaymond]
diaper pelenka [pelenko]
diarrhoea hasmenés [hoshmenaysh]
do you have something for diarrhoea? tud adni valamit hasmenés ellen? [tood odni volomit hoshmenaysh]
diary (business) naptár [noptar] (for personal experiences) napló [noplaw]
dictionary szótár [sawtar]
didn't* see **not**
die meghalni [megholni]
diesel dízel (olaj) [deezel (oloy)]
diet étrend [aytrend]
I'm on a diet fogyókúrázom [fodjawkoorazom]
I have to follow a special diet különleges diétát kell tartanom [kewluhnlegesh di-aytat kel tortonom]
difference különbség [kewluhnbshayg]
what's the difference? mi a különbség?
different különböző [kewluhnbuhzur]
this one is different ez másmilyen [mashmi-yen]
a different table másik asztal [mashik ostol]
difficult nehéz [nehayz]
difficulty nehézség [nehayshayg]
dinghy csónak [chawnok]
dining room ebédlő [ebaydlur], étterem [aytterem]
dinner (evening meal) vacsora [vochoro]
to have dinner vacsorázni [vochorazni]
direct (adj) közvetlen [kuhzvetlen]
is there a direct train? van közvetlen járat? [von kuhzvetlen yarot]
direction irány [ira[nyuh]]
which direction is it? merre van? [merreh von]
is it in this direction? erre van? [erreh]
directory enquiries tudakozó [toodokozaw]

For national directory enquiries dial 198 and for international enquiries dial 199.

dirt piszok [pisok]
dirty piszkos [piskosh]
disabled rokkant [rokkont],

mozgássérült [mozgash-shayrewlt]
is there access for the disabled? mozgássérültek is be tudnak menni? [mozgash-shayrewltek ish beh toodnok]
disappear eltűnni [eltewnni]
it's disappeared elveszett [elveset]
disappointed csalódott [cholawdot]
disappointing kiábrándító [ki-abrandeetaw]
disaster szerencsétlenség [serenchaytlen-shayg]
disco diszko [disko]
discount árengedmény [arengedmay^{nyuh}]
is there a discount? van árengedmény? [von]
disease betegség [betegshayg]
disgusting undorító [oondoreetaw]
dish (meal) fogás [fogash]
(bowl) tál
dishcloth konyharuha [ko^{nyuh}horoo-ho]
disinfectant fertőtlenítő [ferturt-leneetur]
disk (for computer) lemez
disposable diapers/nappies eldobható pelenka [eldob-hotaw pelenko]
distance távolság [tavolshag]
in the distance a messzeségben [o messeh-shaygben]
district (region) körzet [kurzet]
(in town) kerület [kerewlet]
disturb zavarni [zovorni]
diversion (detour) kerülő [kerewlur]
diving board ugródeszka [oograwdesko]
divorced elvált
dizzy: I feel dizzy szédülök [saydewluhk]
do (verb) tenni, csinálni [chinalni]
what shall we do? mit csináljunk? [chinal-yoonk]
how do you do it? hogy csinálja? [hodj chinal-yo]
will you do it for me? megtenné nekem? [megtennay]

•••••• DIALOGUES ••••••

how do you do? örvendek [urvendek]
nice to meet you én is [ayn ish]
what do you do? (work) mivel foglalkozik? [foglolkozik]
I'm a teacher, and you? (said by man/woman) tanár/tanárnő vagyok, és Ön? [tonar/tonarnur vodjok aysh uhn]
I'm a student diák vagyok [di-ak]
what are you doing this evening? mit csinál ma este? [chinal mo eshteh]
we're going out for a drink, do you want to join us? kimegyünk egy italra, nem jön velünk? [kimedjewnk edj itolro nem yuhn velewnk]

do you want cream? tejszínt parancsol? [tayseent poronchol]

I do, but she doesn't én igen, de ő nem [ayn igen deh ur]

doctor (man) orvos [orvosh], doktor
(woman) orvosnő [orvoshnur], doktornő [doktornur]
we need a doctor orvosra van szükségünk [orvoshro von sewkshaygewnk]
please call a doctor legyen szíves orvost hívni [ledjen seevesh orvosht heevni]

•••••• DIALOGUE ••••••

where does it hurt? hol érez fájdalmat? [ayrez fīdolmot]
right here itt
does that hurt now? ez fáj? [fī]
yes igen
take this to the chemist's menjen el ezzel a patikába [men-yen el ezzel o potikabo]

Provincial tourist offices can direct you to local medical centres or **orvosi rendelő** [orvoshi rendelur] (doctors' surgeries), while your embassy in Budapest will have the addresses of English-speaking doctors and dentists, who will probably be in private (**magán**) practice. Private medicine is much cheaper than in the West. For muscular, skin or gynaecological complaints, doctors often prescribe a soak at one of Hungary's numerous **gyógyfürdő** [djawdj-fewrdur] (medicinal baths). →

The national health service (**OTBF**) will provide free emergency treatment in any hospital or doctor's surgery for citizens of Britain, Finland, Norway, Sweden, the countries of the former Soviet Union, and former Eastern Bloc countries, but there is a charge for drugs and non-emergency care.
The standard of hospitals varies enormously; both nursing and medical staff are used to tips, called **hálapénz** (gratitude money).
It's advisable to have some sort of travel insurance, since with this you're covered for loss of possessions and money, as well as the cost of all medical and dental treatment.

document irat [irot]
dog kutya [koo-tyo]
doll baba [bo-bo]
don't!* ne! [neh]
don't do that! ne csinálja ezt! [chinal-yo]
see **not**
door ajtó [oytaw]
doorman portás [portash]
double kettős [kettursh]
double bed kettős ágy [adj]
double room kétágyas szoba [kaytadjosh sobo]
doughnut fánk
down lenn
(direction) le [leh]

down here idelenn
put it down over there ott tegye le [tedjeh leh]
it's down there on the right ott van, lenn a jobb oldalon [von lenn o yob oldolon]
it's further down the road még messzebb van ezen az úton [mayg messeb von ezen oz ooton]
downmarket (restaurant etc) egyszerűbb [edjsérewb]
downstairs lenn
dozen tucat [tootsot]
half a dozen féltucat [fayltootsot]
drain (noun: in sink) lefolyó [lefo-yaw]
(in road) csatorna [chatorno]
draught beer csapolt sör [chopolt shur]
draughty: it's draughty huzat van [hoozot von]
drawer fiók [fi-awk]
drawing rajz [royz]
dreadful szörnyű [sur-nyew]
dream (noun) álom [alom]
dress (noun) ruha [roo-ho]

When visiting churches, you should not wear shorts and should make sure your arms are covered. Hungarians usually dress up for theatres, the opera, concerts (even for open-air performances), for going out to restaurants or to visit friends in the evening. Unless clearly told otherwise, it's impolite to be dressed casually when invited to somebody's home.

dressed: to get dressed felöltözni [feluhltuhzni]
dressing (for cut) kötés [kuhtaysh]
salad dressing saláta öntet [sholato uhntet]
dressing gown hálókabát [halawkobat]
drink (noun: non-alcoholic) üdítő [ewdeetur]
(alcoholic) szeszesital [seseshitol]
(verb) inni
a cold drink egy hideg ital [edj hideg itol]
can I get you a drink? rendelhetek Önnek valamit inni? [rendelhetek uhnnek volomit]
what would you like (to drink)? mit szeretne inni? [seretneh]
no thanks, I don't drink köszönöm, nem, semmit sem akarok inni [kuhsuhnuhm nem shemmit shem okorok]
I'll just have a drink of water, please csak egy pohár vizet kérek [chok edj po-har vizet kayrek]
see **bar**
drinking water ivóvíz [ivaw-veez]
is this drinking water? ez ivóvíz?
drive (verb) vezetni
we drove here kocsin jöttünk [kochin yuhttewnk]
I'll drive you home hazaviszem kocsin [hozovisem]

driving

To drive in Hungary you'll need an international driving permit (issued by national motoring organizations for a small fee), and third-party insurance. If you're taking your own car, check with your insurance company to see if you're covered; you'll probably need a green card.

Speed limits for vehicles are 120kph on motorways, 100kph on highways, 80kph on other roads and 50kph in built-up areas. Offenders can expect to be heavily fined on the spot. Besides driving on the right, the most important rules are the prohibitions against repeatedly switching from lane to lane on highways, overtaking near pedestrian crossings, and sounding the horn in built-up areas unless to avert accidents. At crossroads, vehicles coming from the right have right of way, unless otherwise indicated by signs, and pedestrians have priority over cars turning onto the road. Trams always have right of way.

Drinking and driving is totally prohibited, and offenders with an excess of eight milligrams of alcohol are liable to felony charges.

The state requires cars to carry a triangular breakdown sign, spare bulbs, a first-aid kit, and a supplementary mudguard made →of a non-rigid material, attached to rear bumpers. Passengers must wear three-point safety belts in the front seats (and in back seats outside built-up areas). Children under the age of 14 or less than 150cm in height are not allowed to travel in the front seat and child seats are compulsory for children travelling in the back.

driver vezető [vezetur]

driving licence jogosítvány [yogosheetva^{nyuh}]

drop: just a drop, please (of drink) csak egész picit kérek [chok egays pitsit kayrek]

drug (medicine) orvosság [orvoshshag]

drugs (narcotics) kábítószer [kabeetawser]

drunk (adj) részeg [rayseg]

dry (adj) száraz [saroz]

dry-cleaner's vegytisztító [vedjtisteetaw]

duck kacsa [kocho]

due: he was due to arrive yesterday tegnap kellett volna érkeznie [tegnop kellet volno ayrkezni-eh]

when is the train due? mikor érkezik a vonat? [ayrkezik o vonot]

dull (weather) borús [boroosh]

(pain) tompa [tompo]

(uninteresting) unalmas [oonolmosh]

dummy (baby's) cucli [tsootsli]
during alatt [olot]
dust por
dustbin szemétláda [semaytlado]
dusty poros [porosh]
Dutch holland [hollond]
duty-free (goods) vámmentes (áru) [vammentesh (aroo)]
duty-free shop vámmentes üzlet [ewzlet], vámmentes áruk [arook]
duvet dunyha [doo^{nyuh}ho]

E

each (every) mindegyik [mindedjik]
how much are they each? mibe kerül darabja? [mibeh kerewl dorob-yo]
ear fül [fewl]
earache: I have earache fáj a fülem [fī o fewlem]
early korai [koro-ee]
too early túl korán [tool]
early in the morning korán reggel
I called by earlier korábban kerestem [korabbon kereshtem]
earrings fülbevaló [fewlbevolaw]
east Kelet
in the east keleten
Easter húsvét [hooshvayt]
eastern keleti
easy könnyű [kuhn-nyew]
eat enni
we've already eaten, thanks köszönöm, már ettünk [kuhsuhnuhm mar ettewnk]

eating habits

A Hungarian breakfast usually includes cheese, eggs or salami, together with bread and jam, and in rural areas is often accompanied by a shot of **pálinka** (brandy). By 8am cafés and snack bars are already functioning, and the rush hour is prime time for **tej-bár** [tay-bar] or **tejivó** [tayivaw]. These stand-up milk bars serve mugs of hot milk (**meleg tej** [tay]) and sugary cocoa (**kakaó** [koko-aw]), cheese-filled pastry cones (**sajtos pogácsa** [soytosh pogacho]) and cheese rolls (**sajtkrémes tekercs** [soytkraymesh tekerch]), envelopes of dough filled with curds (**túrós táska** [toorawsh tashko]), spongy milk-bread with raisins (**mazsolás kalács** [maJ-olash kolach]), and other dunkable pastries.

Lunch is normally eaten at about noon, but restaurants serve hot food all day, and set-lunch menus may be had in some places as late as 3pm. The time for the evening meal at home is 7–8pm.

Although cold starters are gaining in popularity, for most Hungarians a full meal begins with soup. The typical full meal ends with a sweet dish, cheese being →

considered as part of a cold meal or sandwich.

It's the custom to say '**jó étvágyat kívánok!**' [yaw aytvadjot keevanok] or at least the shorter version '**jó étvágyat!**', before starting a meal. It means 'enjoy your meal!'/'bon appetit!' In reply, you say the same to fellow diners or '**köszönöm**' [kuhsuhnuhm] (thank you) to the waiter. It's polite to say '**egészségünkre!**' [egays-shaygewnkreh] (to our good health!) to one's fellow diners after the meal.

eau de toilette kölni víz [kuhlni veez]
economy class tûrista osztály [toorishto ostayuh]
egg tojás [to-yash]
eggplant padlizsán [podliJan]
either: either ... or ... vagy ... vagy ... [vodj]
either of them akármelyikük [okarmeh-yikewk]
elastic band gumiszalag [goomisolog]
elbow könyök [kuh-nyuhk]
electric elektromos [elektromosh]
electrical appliances villamos eszköz [villomosh eskuhz]
electric fire villany hősugárzó [villanyuh hur-shoogarzaw]
electrician villanyszerelő [villonyuhserelur]
electricity villamosság [villomosh-shag]
elevator felvonó [felvonaw], 'lift'
else: something else valami más [volomi mash]
somewhere else valahol máshol [volohol mash-hol]

• • • • • • DIALOGUE • • • • • •

would you like anything else?
szeretne valami mást? [seretneh]
no, nothing else, thanks
köszönöm, semmi mást nem kérek [kuhsuhnuhm shemmi masht nem kayrek]

email 'email'
embassy nagykövetség [nodj-kuhvetshayg]
embroidery kézimunka [kayzimoonko]
emergency vészhelyzet [vays-hehyuhzet]
this is an emergency! vészhelyzet van! [von]
emergency exit vészkijárat [vayski-yarot]
empty üres [ewresh]
end (noun) vég [vayg]
at the end of the street az utca végén [oz oottso vaygayn]
when does it end? mikor lesz vége? [les vaygeh]
engaged (toilet) foglalt [foglolt]
(phone) mással beszél [mash-shol besayl]
(to be married) el van jegyezve [von yedj-ezveh]
engine (car) motor [mo-tor]
England Anglia [ongli-o]
English angol [ongol]

I'm English angol vagyok [vodjok]
do you speak English? tud angolul? [tood ongolool]
enjoy: to enjoy oneself jól érezni magát [yawl ayrezni mogat]

•••••• DIALOGUE ••••••

how did you like the film? hogy tetszett a film? [hodj tetset o]
I enjoyed it very much, did you enjoy it? nagyon tetszett, Önnek is? [nodjon tetset uhnnek ish]

enjoyable élvezetes [aylvezetesh]
enormous hatalmas [hotolmosh]
enough elég [elayg]
there's not enough nincs elég [ninch]
it's not big enough nem elég nagy [nodj]
that's enough ez elég
entrance bejárat [bay-arot]
envelope boríték [boreetayk]
epileptic (noun) epilepsziás [epilepsi-ash]
equipment felszerelés [felserelaysh]
error tévedés [tayvedaysh]
especially kivált
essential fontos [fontosh]
it is essential that ... fontos, hogy ... [hodj]
Eurocheque eurocsekk [eh-oorochek]
Eurocheque card eurocsekk kártya [kar-tyo]
Europe Európa [eh-oorawpo]
European európai [eh-oo-rawpo-ee]
even ... még ... is [mayg ... ish]
even if ... még akkor is, ha ... [okkor ish ho]
evening este [eshteh]
this evening ma este [mo]
in the evening este
evening meal vacsora [vochoro]
eventually végül [vaygewl]
ever valaha [voloho]

•••••• DIALOGUE ••••••

have you ever been to Szeged? volt valaha Szegeden? [segeden]
yes, I was there two years ago igen, két évvel ezelőtt voltam ott [ayvvel ezelurt voltom]

every minden
every day minden nap [nop]
everyone mindenki
everything minden
everywhere mindenütt [mindenewt]
exactly! úgy van! [oodj von]
exam vizsga [viJgo]
example példa [payldo]
for example például [paylda-ool]
excellent kitűnő [kitewnur]
excellent! nagyszerű! [nodj-serew]
except kivéve [kivayveh]
excess baggage poggyász túlsúly [pogdjas toolshoo[yuh]]
exchange rate valutaárfolyam [volooto-arfo-yom]
exciting (day, film) izgalmas [izgolmosh]
(holiday) érdekes [ayrdekesh]

excuse me (to get past) szabad? [sobod]
(to get attention) bocsánat, uram [bochanot oorom], hölgyem [huhldjem]
(to say sorry) bocsánatot kérek [kayrek]
exhaust (pipe) kipufogó [kipoofogaw]
exhausted (tired) kimerült [kimerewlt]
exhibition kiállítás [ki-alleetash]
exit kijárat [ki-yarot]
where's the nearest exit? hol a legközelebbi kijárat? [o legkuhzelebbi]
expect elvárni
expensive drága [drago]
experienced tapasztalt [topostolt]
explain megmagyarázni [megmodjorazni]
can you explain that? meg tudja ezt magyarázni? [tood-yo ezt modjorazni]
express (mail) expressz ['express']
(train) gyorsvonat [djorshvonot]
extension (telephone) mellék(állomás) [mellayk(allomash)]
extension 221, please a kétszázhuszonegyes melléket kérem [o – kayrem]
extension lead hosszabbító huzal [hossobbeetaw hoozol]
extra: can we have an extra one? kaphatnék külön még egyet? [kop-hotnayk kewluhn mayg edjet]
do you charge extra for that? felszámítanak ezért külön még valamit? [felsameetonok ezayrt kewluhn mayg volomit]
extremely rendkívül [rendkeevewl]
eye szem [sem]
will you keep an eye on my suitcase for me? lenne szíves vigyázni a bőröndömre egy kicsit? [lenneh seevesh vidjazni o bur-ruhnduhm-reh edj kichit]
eyeglasses (US) szemüveg [semew-veg]
eyeliner kihúzó ceruza [kihoozaw tseroozo]
eye make-up remover szemfesték lemosó [semfeshtayk lemoshaw]
eye shadow szemhéjfesték

F

face arc [orts]
factory gyár [djar]
faint (verb) elájulni [elī-oolni]
she's fainted elájult [elī-oolt]
I feel faint ájulás kerülget [ī-oolash kerewlget]
fair (noun) vásár [vashar]
(adj) igazságos [igoJagosh]
fairly eléggé [elayggay]
fake (noun) hamisítvány [homisheetva^nyuh]
fall (US) ősz [urs]
in the fall ősszel [urssel]
fall (verb) esni [eshni]
she's had a fall elesett [eleshet]

false hamis [homish]
family család [cholad]
famous híres [heeresh]
fan (electrical) ventillátor [ventilla-tor]
(handheld) legyező [ledjezur]
(sports) szurkoló [soorkolaw]
fantastic fantasztikus [fontostikoosh]
far messze [messeh]

••••• DIALOGUE •••••

is it far from here? messze van innen? [von]
no, not very far nem, nincs nagyon messze [ninch nodjon]
well, how far? mégis, milyen messze? [maygish mi-yen]
it's about 20 kilometres körülbelül húsz kilométerre van [kurewlbelewl – kilomayterreh]

fare (bus, rail etc) menetdíj [menetdee^{yuh}]
farm gazdaság [gozdoshag]
fashionable divatos [divotosh]
fast gyors [djorsh]
fat (person) kövér [kurvayr]
(on meat) zsír [Jeer]
father apa [opo]
father-in-law após [opawsh]
faucet csap [chop]
fault hiba [hibo]
sorry, it was my fault bocsánat, az én hibám [bochanot oz ayn]
it's not my fault nem az én hibám
faulty hibás [hibash]
favourite kedvenc [kedvents]
fax (noun) (tele)fax [(teleh-)foks]
(verb: person) faxolni [foksolni]
(document) elfaxolni [elfoksolni]
February február [febroo-ar]
feel érezni [ayrezni]
I feel hot melegem van [von]
I feel unwell rosszul érzem magam [rossool ayrzem mogom]
I feel like going for a walk sétálni lenne kedvem [shaytalni lenneh kedvem]
how are you feeling? hogy érzi magát? [hodj ayrzi mogat]
I'm feeling better jobban vagyok [yobbon vodjok]
fence kerítés [kereetaysh]
ferry (boat) komp [komp]
(service) rév [rayv]
festival fesztivál [festivahl]
fetch hozni
I'll fetch him majd elhozom [moyd]
will you come and fetch me later? lesz szíves értem jönni később? [les seevesh ayrtem yuhnni kayshurb]
feverish lázas [lazosh]
few: a few néhányan [nayha-nyon]
a few days néhány nap [nayha^{nyuh} nop]
fiancé vőlegény [vurlegay^{nyuh}]
fiancée menyasszony [meh-nyosso^{nyuh}]
field mező [mezur]
fight (noun) verekedés [verekedaysh]
fill in kitölteni [kituhlteni]
do I have to fill this in? ezt ki

kell töltenem? [tuhltenem]
fill up teletölteni [teleh-tuhlteni]
fill it up, please legyen szíves teletölteni [ledjen seevesh]
filling (in cake, sandwich) töltelék [tuhltelayk]
(in tooth) tömés [tuhmaysh]
film 'film'

•••••• DIALOGUE ••••••

do you have this kind of film? van ilyen filmje? [von i-yen film-yeh]
yes, how many exposures? igen, hány felvételre? [ha^{nyuh} felvay-telreh]
36 harminchatra [hormintshotro]

film processing 'film' előhívás [elurheevash]
filter coffee filteres kávé [filteresh kavay]
filthy mocskos [mochkosh]
find (verb) találni [tolalni]
I can't find it nem találom [tolalom]
I've found it megvan [megvon]
find out megtudni [megtoodni]
could you find out for me? lenne szíves megtudni nekem? [lenneh seevesh]
fine (weather) jó [yaw]
(punishment) bírság [beershag]

•••••• DIALOGUES ••••••

how are you? hogy van? [hodj von]
I'm fine, thanks köszönöm, jól [kuhsuhnuhm yawl]

is that OK? ez jó lesz? [yaw les]
that's fine, thanks köszönöm, remek

finger ujj [oo^{yuh}]
finish (verb) befejezni [befayezni]
I haven't finished yet még nem fejeztem be [mayg nem fayeztem beh]
when does it finish? mikor lesz vége? [les vaygeh]
fire tűz [tewz]
(campfire) tábortűz
fire! tűz van! [von]
can we light a fire here? tüzet gyújthatunk itt? [tewzet djoo-yuht-hotoonk]
it's on fire ég [ayg]
fire alarm tűzriadó [tewzri-odaw]
fire brigade tűzoltóság [tewzoltawshag], tűzoltók [tewzoltawk]

> Dial 105 to report a fire. In the event of injury, an ambulance should also be called on 104, as well as the police on 107.

fire escape vészkijárat [vayski-yarot]
fire extinguisher tűzoltó szerkezet [tewzoltaw serkezet]
first első [elshur]
I was first én voltam az első [ayn voltom oz]
at first először [elursur]
the first time első alkalommal [elshur olkolommol]
first on the left balra az első [bolro]
the first of June június elseje [elshayeh]
first aid elsősegély [elshur-

shegay^{yuh}]
first-aid kit elsősegély doboz [elshur-shegay^{yuh}]
first class (travel etc) első osztály [elshur osta^{yuh}]
first floor első emelet (US) földszint [fuhldsint]
first name keresztnév [kerestnayv]
fish (noun) hal [hol]
fishmonger's halas [holosh]
fit: it doesn't fit me nem illik rám
fitting room próbafülke [prawbofewlkeh]
fix (verb: arrange) elintézni [elintayzni]
can you fix this? (repair) meg tudja ezt javítani? [tood-yo ezt yoveetoni]
fizzy pezsgő [peJgur]
flag zászló [zaslaw]
flannel mosdókesztyű [moshdawkest-yew]
flash (for camera) vaku [vokoo]
flat (noun: apartment) lakás [lokash] (adj) lapos [loposh]
I've got a flat tyre gumidefektet kaptam [goomidefektet koptom]
flavour íz [eez]
flea bolha [bolho]
flight repülés [repewlaysh], járat [yarot]
flight number járatszám [yarotsam]
flood árvíz [arveez]
floor (of room) padló [podlaw] (storey) emelet
on the floor a földön [o fuhlduhn]
florist virágüzlet [viragewzlet]
flour liszt [list]
flower virág
flu 'influenza'
fluent: he speaks fluent Hungarian folyékonyan beszél magyarul [fo-yayko-nyon besayl modjorool]
fly (noun) légy [laydj] (verb) repülni [repewlni]
fog köd [kuhd]
foggy: it's foggy köd van [von]
folk dancing népi tánc [naypi tants]
folk music népzene [naypzeneh]
follow követni [kuhvetni]
follow me kövessen [kuhvesh-shen]
food étel [aytel]
food poisoning ételmérgezés [aytelmayr-gezaysh]
food shop/store élelmiszerüzlet [aylel-miserewzlet]
foot (of person) láb
on foot gyalog [djolog]
football (game) labdarúgás [lobdoroogash]
football match labdarúgó mérkőzés [lobdoroogaw mayrkurzaysh]
for: do you have something for ...? (headache/diarrhoea etc) tud adni valamit ... ellen? [tood odni volomit]

who's the goulash for? kié a gulyás? [ki-ay o goo-yash]
that's for me ezt én kértem [ayn kayrtem]
and this one? és ez? [aysh]
that's for her ez az övé [oz uhvay]

where do I get the bus for Esztergom? honnan indul az autóbusz Esztergomba? [honnon indool oz owtawboos estergombo]
the bus for Esztergom leaves from the Pest end of Árpád híd az esztergomi autóbusz az Árpád-híd pesti hídfőjétől indul [oz estergomi owtawboos oz arpad-heed peshti heedfur-yayturl]

how long have you been here? mióta van itt? [mi-awto von]
I've been here for two days, how about you? két napja vagyok itt, és Ön? [kayt nop-yo vodjok it aysh uhn]
I've been here for a week egy hete vagyok itt [edj heteh]

forehead homlok
foreign külföldi [kewlfuhldi]
foreigner külföldi
forest erdő [erdur]
forget elfelejteni [elfelayteni]
I forget, I've forgotten elfelejtettem [elfelaytettem]
fork villa [villo]
(in road) elágazás [elagozash]
form (document) űrlap [ewrlop]
formal formális [formalish]
fortnight két hét [kayt hayt]
fortunately szerencsére [serenchay-reh]
forward: could you forward my mail? lenne szíves továbbítani a leveleimet? [lenneh seevesh tovabbeetoni o leveleh-imet]
foundation (make-up) alapozó krém [olopozaw kraym]
fountain (ornamental) szökőkút [suhkurkoot]
(for drinking) forrás [forrash]
foyer (of hotel) hall [hol], előcsarnok [elurchornok]
(theatre) 'foyer'
fracture (noun) törés [turaysh]
France Franciaország [frontsio-orsag]
free szabad [sobod]
(no charge) ingyenes [indjenesh]
is it free (of charge)? ez ingyenes?
freeway autópálya [owtawpa-yo]
freezer mélyhűtő [mayhewtur]
French francia [frontsi-o]
French fries hasábburgonya [hoshabboorgo-nyo]
frequent gyakori [djokori]
how frequent is the bus to Vác? milyen gyakran járnak a buszok Vácra? [mi-yen djokron yarnok o boosok vatsro]
fresh (fruit etc) friss [frish-sh]
fresh orange juice friss narancslé [noronchlay]
Friday péntek [payntek]
fridge hűtőszekrény [hewtur-sekray^nyuh]
fried hirtelensült [hirtelenshewlt]
fried egg tükörtojás [tewkurto-yash]

friend (male/female) barát/ barátnő [borat/boratnur]
friendly barátságos [boratshagosh]
from*: **from Budapest** Budapestről [boodopeshtrurl]
from London Londonból [–bawl]
when does the next train from Vienna arrive? mikor érkezik a legközelebbi vonat Bécsből? [ayrkezik o legkuhzelebbi vonot baychburl]
from Monday to Friday hétfőtől péntekig [–turl]
from next Thursday jövő csütörtöktől [yuhvur –turl]
it's from me ez tőlem van [turlem von]
it's from him ez tőle van [turleh]

•••••• DIALOGUE ••••••

where are you from? Ön honnan jött? [uhn honnon yuht]
I'm from Slough Sloughból jöttem [–bawl]

front (part) eleje ...-nak/-nek [elayeh ...-nok/-nek]
in front elöl [eluhl]
in front of the hotel a szálloda előtt [o sallodo elurt]
frost fagy [fodj]
frozen fagyott [fodjot]
(food) mélyhűtött [may^yuh hewtuht]
frozen food mélyhűtött étel [aytel]
fruit gyümölcs [djewmuhlch]
fruit juice gyümölcslé [djewmuhlchlay]
frying pan serpenyő [sherpeh-nyur]
full tele [teleh]
it's full of ... tele van ...-val/vel [von ...-vol/vel]
I'm full jól vagyok lakva [yawl vodjok lokvo]
full board teljes ellátás [tel-yesh ellatash]
fun: it was fun jó mulatság volt [yaw moolotshag volt]
funeral temetés [temetaysh]
funny (strange) különös [kewluhnuhsh]
(amusing) mulatságos [moolotshagosh]
furniture bútor [bootor]
further távolabb [tavolob]
it's further down the road messzebb van ezen az úton [messebb von ezen oz ooton]

•••••• DIALOGUE ••••••

how much further is it to Kecskemét? milyen messze van még Kecskemét? [mi-yen messeh von mayg kechkemayt]
about 5 kilometres körülbelül öt kilométerre [kurewlbelewl uht kilomayterreh]

fuse biztosíték [bizto-sheetayk]
the lights have fused a lámpa kicsapta a biztosítékot [o lampo kichopto o bizto-sheetaykot]
fuse box biztosíték tábla [bizto-sheetayk tablo]

future jövő [yuhvur]
in future ezután [ezootan]

G

game (played by one or more) játék [yatayk]
(played by two or more) társasjáték [tarshosh-yatayk]
(of cards) kártyajáték [kar-tyo-yatayk]
(match) mérkőzés [mayrkurzaysh]
(meat) vad [vod]
garage (for fuel) benzinkút [benzinkoot], töltőállomás [tuhltur-allomash]
(for repairs) autójavítóműhely [owtaw-yovitaw-mew-heh^yuh], szervíz [serveez]
(for parking) garázs [goraJ]
see **petrol**
garden kert [kert]
garlic fokhagyma [fokhodjmo]
gas gáz
(US: gasoline) benzin
see **petrol**
gas can (US) benzinkanna [benzinkonno]
gas cylinder gáz palack [gaz polotsk]
(camping gas) 'camping' gáz
gas fire gáz konvektor
gasoline benzin
gas permeable lenses gázáteresztő lencse [gazaterestur lencheh]
gas station benzinkút [benzinkoot], töltőállomás [tuhltur-allomash]
gate kijárat [ki-yarot]
(at airport) beszállóhely [besallaw-heh^yuh]
gay homoszexuális [homoseksoo-alish]
gearbox sebességváltóház [shebesh-shayg-valtaw-haz]
gears sebességek [shebesh-shaygek]
general (adj) általános [altolanosh]
gents (toilet) urak [oorok]
genuine (antique etc) eredeti
German német [naymet]
Germany Németország [naymetorsag]
get (fetch) hozni
could you get me another one? lenne szíves még egyet hozni? [lenneh seevesh mayg edjet]
how do I get to ...? hogyan jutok el ...-ba/-be? [hodjon yootok el ...-bo/-beh]
do you know where I can get them? tudja, hol kaphatnék ilyet? [tood-yo hol kop-hotnayk i-yet]

•••••• DIALOGUE ••••••

can I get you a drink? parancsol egy italt? [poronchol edj itolt]
no, I'll get this one, what would you like? nem, ezt én fizetem, mit szeretne? [ayn – seretneh]
a glass of red wine egy pohár vörös bort [edj po-har vuruhsh]

get back (return) visszatérni

[vissotayrni]
get in (arrive) megérkezni [megayrkezni]
get off kiszállni [kisalni]
where do I get off? hol kell leszállnom? [lesalnom]
get on (to train etc) felszállni [felsalni]
get out (of car etc) kiszállni [kisalni]
get up (in the morning) felkelni
gift ajándék [oy-andayk]

> When visiting people, Hungarians always take a gift, and will often take flowers for the hostess, especially when invited to a main meal. It's also customary to take sweets for any children. If going to a party, it's usual to take a bottle of wine or champagne.

gift shop ajándéktárgy üzlet [oy-andayk-tardj ewzlet]
gin gin [jin]
a gin and tonic, please gint és tonicot kérek [jint aysh tonikot kayrek]
girl lány [la[nyuh]]
girlfriend barátnő [boratnur]
give adni [odni]
can you give me some change? tudna aprópénzt adni nekem? [toodno oprawpaynzt odni]
I gave it to him odaadtam neki [odo-odtom]
will you give this to ...? lenne szíves átadni ezt ...-nak/-nek? [lenneh seevesh atodni ezt ...-nok/-nek]
give back visszaadni [visso-odni]
glad boldog
glass (material) üveg [ewveg]
(for drinking) pohár [po-har]
a glass of red/white wine egy pohár vörös/fehér bor [edj pohar vuruhsh/fehayr]
glasses szemüveg [semew-veg]
gloves kesztyű [kest-yew]
glue (noun) ragasztó [rogostaw]
go menni
we'd like to go to the Royal Castle a Várba szeretnénk menni [seretnaynk]
where are you going? hova megy/mennek? [hovo medj]
where does this bus go? hova megy ez az autóbusz? [oz owtawboos]
let's go! gyerünk! [djerewnk]
hamburger to go hamburger utcán át [oot-tsan at]
she's gone (left) elment
where has he gone? hova ment? [hovo]
I went there last week a múlt héten mentem oda [o moolt hayten mentem odo]
go away elmenni
go away! hagyj békén! [hodj[yuh] baykayn]
go back (return) visszamenni [vissomenni]
go down (the stairs etc) lemenni
go in bemenni
go out: do you want to go out tonight? menjünk valahova

ma este? [menyewnk volo-hovo mo eshteh]

go through átmenni

go up (the stairs etc) felmenni

God Isten [ishten]

gold arany [oro^nyuh]

golf 'golf'

golf course golfpálya [golfpa-yo]

good jó [yaw]

good! jó!

it's no good nem jó

goodbye viszontlátásra [visontlatashro]

good evening jó estét kívánok [yaw eshtayt keevanok]

Good Friday nagypéntek [nodjpayntek]

good morning jó reggelt [yaw]

good night jó éjszakát [yaw aysokat]

goose liba [libo]

got: we've got to leave mennünk kell [mennewnk]

have you got any fresh bread? van friss kenyere? [von frish-sh keh-nyereh]

government kormány [korma^nyuh]

gradually fokozatosan [fokozo-toshon]

gram(me) gram [grom]

grammar nyelvtan [nyelvton]

grandchild unoka [oonoko]

grandfather nagyapa [nodjopo]

grandmother nagyanya [nodjo-nyo]

grapefruit 'grapefruit'

grapefruit juice 'grapefruit' lé [lay]

grapes szőlő [surlur]

grass fű [few]

grateful hálás [halash]

gravy lé [lay]

great (excellent) nagyszerű [nodjserew]

that's great! ez nagyszerű!

a great success nagy siker [nodj shiker]

Great Britain Nagy-Britannia [nodj-britonni-o]

Great Plain az Alföld [oz olfuhld]

greedy mohó [mo-haw]

(for food) falánk [folank]

green zöld [zuhld]

green card (car insurance) zöld kártya [kar-tyo]

greengrocer's zöldséges [zuhldshaygesh]

greeting people

There are different ways of greeting people in Hungarian, depending on their age and how well you know them. If you are under 20 and are speaking to someone of a similar age, '**szervusz**' [servoos] or even the slangy but very common '**szia**' [si-a] will do. Both of these mean 'hello' and 'goodbye', like 'ciao' in italian. The plural forms '**szervusztok**' [servoostok] and '**sziasztok**' [si-astok] are used when speaking to more than one person. Plurals of this kind must not be used if the company includes older people.

Formal greetings are obligatory →

in Hungarian when you are clearly not on familiar terms with the person(s) addressed, and when they are obviously over 14 years of age. The best, and most general, formal greeting is '**jó napot kívánok**' [yaw nopot keevanok] (literally: 'I wish you good day'). This may be used to greet any person, at any time of the day until it gets dark. '**Jó reggelt kívánok**' [yaw reggelt keevanok] ('I wish you good morning') can be used until about 9am. In the evening, after nightfall, use '**jó estét kívánok**' [yaw eshtayt keevanok] ('I wish you good evening').

When being introduced, it's quite acceptable to say simply '**örvendek**' [urvendek] ('pleased to meet you') in lieu of any other greeting.

The oddest, but a very common, form of greeting is '**kezét csókolom**' [kezayt chawkolom] (which means literally: 'I kiss your hand'), which is almost invariably abbreviated to '**kezicsókolom**' [kezichawkolom] or simply '**csókolom**' [chawkolom]. It can be used both to greet someone and to take one's leave. '**Csókolom**' is used by children and teenagers greeting anyone of their parents' generation or older, and by most people greeting grandparents or other elderly relatives.

The most general way of saying 'goodbye' to any age group at any time of day, is '**viszontlátásra**' [visontlatashro] ('so long', 'see you'). A formal, polite way of saying 'goodbye' or 'good night' after about 10pm is '**jó éjszakát**' [yaw aysokat]. '**Üdvözlöm**' [ewdvuhzluhm] (which means literally: 'I greet you', said to one person) or '**üdvözlöm Önöket**' [ewdvuhzluhm uhnuhket] (said to more than one person) may be used to greet people you do not know.

see **name**

grey szürke [sewrkeh]

grill (noun) rost [rosht]

grilled rostonsült [roshtonshewlt]

grocer's fűszerüzlet [fewserewzlet], fűszeres [fewseresh]

ground föld [fuhld]

  on the ground a földön [o fuhlduhn]

ground floor földszint [fuhldsint]

group csoport [choport]

guarantee (noun) garancia [gorontsi-o]

  is it guaranteed? garantált? [gorontalt]

guest vendég [vendayg]

guesthouse penzió [penzi-aw]

  see **accommodation**

guide (person) idegenvezető [idegenvezetur]

guidebook útikönyv [ootikuh[nyuh]v]

guided tour csoportos látogatás [choportosh latogotash]
guitar gitár
gum (in mouth) íny [ee^{nyuh}]
gun (pistol) pisztoly [pisto^{yuh}]
(rifle) puska [pooshko]
gym tornaterem [tornoterem]
gypsy cigány [tsiga^{nyuh}]
gypsy band cigányzenekar [–zenekor]
gypsy music cigányzene [–zeneh]

H

hair haj [hoy]
hairbrush hajkefe [hoy-kefeh]
haircut hajvágás [hoyvagash]
hairdresser's (men's) borbély [borbay^{yuh}]
(women's) fodrász [fodras]
hairdryer hajszárító [hoysareetaw]
hairgrips hajcsat [hoychot]
hair spray hajlakk [hoylok]
half* fél [fayl]
half an hour félóra [faylawro]
half a litre fél liter
about half that ennek körülbelül a fele [kurewlbelewl o feleh]
half board fél penzió [fayl penzi-aw]
half-bottle fél üveg [ewveg]
half fare félárú menetdíj [faylaroo menetdee^{yuh}]
half-price félár [faylar]
ham sonka [shonko]
hamburger hamburger [homboorger]
hammer (noun) kalapács [kolopach]
hand kéz [kayz]
handbag kézitáska [kayzitashko]
handbrake kézifék [kayzifayk]
handkerchief zsebkendő [Jebkendur]
handle (on door) kilincs [kilinch]
(on suitcase etc) fogantyú [fogon-tyoo]
(of tool, appliance) nyél [nyayl]
hand luggage kézipoggyász [kayzipodjas]
hang-gliding sárkányrepülés [sharka^{nyuh}repewlaysh]
hangover macskajaj [mochko-yoy]
I've got a hangover másnapos vagyok [mashnoposh vodjok]
happen történni [turtaynni]
what's happening? mi van? [von]
(what's going on?, what's on?) mi a program? [o progrom]
what has happened? mi történt? [turtaynt]
happy boldog
(pleased) elégedett [elaygedet]
I'm not happy about this ez nem tetszik nekem [tetsik]
I am not happy with the service elégedetlen vagyok a kiszolgálással [elaygedetlen vodjok o kisolgalash-shol]
hard kemény [kemay^{nyuh}]
(difficult) nehéz [nehayz]
hard-boiled egg keménytojás [kemay^{nyuh}to-yash]
hard lenses merev lencse

[lencheh]
hardly: hardly ever szinte soha [sinteh sho-ho]
hardware shop vasáru [vosharoo]
hat kalap [kolop]
hate (verb) útálni [ootalni]
have* van (nekem/neked) [von]
can I have a ...? kaphatnék egy ...? [kop-hotnayk edj]
do you have ...? van önöknek ...? [von uhnuhk-nek]
what'll you have (to drink)? mit iszik? [isik]
I have to leave now most el kell mennem [mosht]
do I have to ...? muszáj ...? [moosī]
can we have some ...? kaphatnánk ...? [kop-hotnank]
hayfever szénanátha [saynonat-ho]
hazelnuts mogyoró [modjoraw]
he* ő [ur]
head fej [fay]
headache fejfájás [fayfī-ash]
headlights országúti lámpa [orsagooti lampo]
health food shop natura termék bolt [notooro termayk]
healthy egészséges [egayshaygesh]
hear hallani [holloni]

•••••• DIALOGUE ••••••

can you hear me? hall engem? [holl]
I can't hear you, could you repeat that? nem hallom, lenne szíves megismételni? [lenneh seevesh megishmaytelni]

hearing aid hallókészülék [hollawkaysewlayk]
heart szív [seev]
heart attack szívroham [seevro-hom]
heat hő [hur]
heater (in room) radiátor [rodi-ator]
(in car) fűtőkészülék [fewtur-kaysewlayk]
heating fűtés [fewtaysh]
heavy nehéz [nehayz]
heel (of foot, of shoe) sarok [shorok]
could you heel these? lenne szíves megsarkalni? [lenneh seevesh megshorkolni]
height magasság [mogosh-shag]
helicopter helikopter
hello (to one person) szervusz [servoos]
(to more than one person) szervusztok [servoostok]
(answer on phone) halló [hollaw]
helmet (for motorbike) bukósisak [bookaw-shishok]
help (noun) segítség [shegeet-shayg]
(verb) segíteni [shegeeteni]
help! segítség!
can you help me? tudna segíteni rajtam? [toodno – roytom]
thank you very much for your help nagyon köszönöm a segítségét [nodjon kuhsuhnuhm o shegeet-shaygayt]
helpful (person) segítőkész [shegeet-urkays]
(advice) hasznos [hosnosh]

hepatitis májgyulladás [mīdjoollodash]
her*: **I haven't seen her** nem láttam [lattom]
to her neki
with her vele [veleh]
for her érte [ayrteh]
that's her ő az [ur oz]
that's her towel ez az ő törülközője
herbal tea herbatea [herboteh-o]
herbs gyógyfű [djawdj-few]
here itt
here is/are ... itt van/vannak ... [von/vonnok]
here you are tessék [tesh-shayk]
hers* az övé [oz uhvay]
that's hers ez az övé
hi! (to one person) szia! [si-o]
(to more than one person) sziasztok! [si-ostok]
hide (verb) elrejteni [elrayteni]
high magas [mogosh]
highchair etetőszék [etetursayk]
highway (US) autópálya [owtawpa-yo]
hiking gyalogtúra [djologtooro]
hill domb
him*: **I haven't seen him** nem láttam [lattom]
to him neki
with him vele [veleh]
for him érte [ayrteh]
that's him ő az [ur oz]
hip csípő [cheepur]
hire bérelni [bayrelni]
for hire bérelhető [bayrelhetur]
where can I hire a bike? hol tudok biciklit bérelni? [toodok bitsiklit bayrelni]
see **rent**
his*: **it's his car** ez az ő kocsija [oz ur]
that's his az az övé [uhvay]
hit (verb) ütni [ewtni]
hitch-hike autóstoppolni [owtawshtoppolni]

Hitch-hiking is widely practised by young Hungarians, and only forbidden on motorways. Although a fair number of drivers seem willing to give lifts, hitch-hiking is not recommended as a means of getting around the country, especially for women travelling alone.

hobby 'hobby'
hold (verb) tartani [tortoni]
hole lyuk [yook]
holiday szabadság [sobodshag], ünnep [ewnnep]
on holiday szabadságon [sobodshagon]
Holland Hollandia [hollondi-o]
home otthon [ot-hon]
at home (in my house/country) otthon
we go home tomorrow holnap hazautazunk [holnop hozowtozoonk]
honest becsületes [bechewletesh]
honey méz [mayz]
honeymoon nászút [nasoot]
hood (US: of car) motorház fedő [mo-torhaz fedur]

hope remélni [remaylni]
I hope so remélem [remaylem]
I hope not remélem, nem
hopefully remélhetőleg [remaylheturleg]
horn (of car) duda [doodo]
horrible borzalmas [borzolmosh]
horse ló [law]
horse riding lovaglás [lovoglash]
horse-riding tour lovastúra [lovoshtooro]
hospital kórház [kawrhaz]
hospitality vendégszeretet [vendayg-seretet]
thank you for your hospitality köszönöm a szíves vendéglátást [kuhsuhnuhm o seevesh vendayglatasht]

Refusing hospitality can be tricky, especially with older people or people in rural areas. If you drink the contents of your glass it will almost certainly be refilled, and if you finish what's on a plate in the centre of the table, the hostess will almost certainly bring more, as it's a sign of poor hospitality to leave a guest with nothing to eat or drink. The best policy, if you've had enough, is to leave your glass full until the last possible moment.

hostel (in towns) Túristaszálló [tooristo-sallaw]
(in country) Túristaház [tooristo-haz]

Although many are due to close or become private guesthouses in the future, hostels are currently the cheapest available lodgings in Hungary. There are two kinds of official tourist hostels: **Túristaszálló**, generally found in provincial towns, and **Túristaház**, located in highland areas favoured by hikers. Both are graded 'A' or 'B' depending on the availablility of hot water and the number of beds per room. It's generally advisable to make bookings through the regional tourist office. Some hostels are official hostels, for which you'll need a membership card though, in practice, many hostels in Hungary don't insist you have the card.
In many towns, you can also stay in vacant college dormitories. Generally, these accept tourists at weekends throughout the year, and over the whole of the summer vacation (roughly July to mid-August). It's usually possible to make bookings through the local Express agency or the regional tourist office, but otherwise you can just turn up.

hot forró [forraw]
(spicy) csípős [cheepursh]
I'm hot melegem van [von]
it's hot today meleg van ma [von mo]

hotel szálló [sallaw], szálloda [sallodo]

> Although Hungarians call hotels **szálló** or **szálloda**, everyone understands the English word. For the moment, most hotels have an official three- or four-star rating (five-star establishments are restricted to Budapest and the Balaton region), although this gives only a vague idea of prices, which vary according to the locality and the time of year; high season is June to September. Four- and five-star establishments are reliably comfortable, with private bathrooms, a TV and central heating, but three-star places can be not so pleasant. One- and two-star hotels probably won't have private bathrooms, but might have a sink in the room. Single rooms are rare.
> Many places post current room rates in Deutschmarks (although you pay in forints). Prices in Budapest and the Balaton region are 15–35 per cent higher than in other areas, though rates can drop by as much as 30 per cent over winter. Breakfast is invariably included in the price.
> see **accommodation**, **hostel** and **private room**

hotel room szállodaszoba [sallodosobo]
hour óra [awro]
house ház
house wine házi bor
how hogy [hodj]
how many? hány? [ha^nyuh]
how much is it? mennyibe kerül? [men-nyibeh kerewl]
how do you do? örvendek [urvendek]
how are you? (fam) hogy vagy? [hodj vodj]
(pol) hogy van? [von]

•••••• DIALOGUES ••••••

how are you? hogy van?
fine, thanks, and you? köszönöm, jól, és Ön? [kuhsuhnuhm yawl aysh uhn]

how much is it? mennyibe kerül? [men-nyibeh kerewl]
1,500 forints ezerötszáz forint
I'll take it megveszem [megvesem]

humid párás [parash]
Hungarian magyar [modjor]
Hungary Magyarország [modjororsag]
hungry éhes [ay-hesh]
are you hungry? (pol) éhes?
(fam) éhes vagy? [vodj]
hurry (verb) sietni [shi-etni]
I'm in a hurry sietek [shi-etek]
there's no hurry nem kell sietni
hurry up! siessen! [shi-esh-shen]
hurt (verb) fájni [fī-ni]
it really hurts nagyon fáj [nodjon fī]
husband férj [fayr^yuh]
hydrofoil szárnyashajó [sar-nyosh-ho-yaw]

I

I én [ayn]
ice jég [yayg]
with ice jéggel [yayggel]
no ice, thanks köszönöm, jeget nem kérek [kuhsuhnuhm yeget nem kayrek]
ice cream fagylalt [fodjlolt]
ice-cream cone fagylalt tölcsér [tuhlchayr]
ice lolly nyalóka [nyolawko]
ice rink jégpálya [yaygpa-yo]
ice skates korcsolya [korcho-yo]
idea ötlet [uhtlet]
idiot bolond
if ha [ho]
ignition gyújtás [djoo^{yuh}tash]
ill beteg
I feel ill rosszul érzem magam [rossool ayrzem mogom]
illness betegség [betegshayg]
imitation (leather etc) utánzat [ootanzot]
immediately azonnal [ozonnol]
important fontos [fontosh]
it's very important nagyon fontos a dolog [nodjon – o]
it's not important nem fontos a dolog
impossible lehetetlen
impressive elismerésre méltó [elish-merayshreh mayltaw]
improve javítani [yoveetoni]
(get better) javulni [yovoolni]
I want to improve my Hungarian szeretném jobban megtanulni a magyar nyelvet [seretnaym yobbon megtonoolni o modjor nyelvet]
in*: in my car a kocsimban [o kochimbon]
in Budapest Budapesten [boodopeshten]
in London Londonban [–bon]
it's in the centre a város központjában van [o varosh kuhzpont-yabon von]
in two days from now két nap múlva [nop moolvo]
in five minutes öt perc múlva [perts moolvo]
in May májusban [mī-ooshbon]
in English angolul [ongolool]
in Hungarian magyarul [modjorool]
is he in? otthon van? [ot-hon von]
include: does that include meals? ebben a koszt is benne van? [o kost ish benneh von]
is that included? ez is benne van?
inconvenient (time) alkalmatlan [olkolmotlon]
incredible hihetetlen [hi-hetetlen]
Indian indiai [indi-o-ee]
indicator index [indeks]
indigestion emésztési zavar [emaystayshi zovor]
indoor pool uszoda [oosodo]
indoors fedett
inexpensive olcsó [olchaw]
infection fertőzés [ferturzaysh]
infectious fertőző [ferturzur]
inflammation gyulladás [djoollodash]
informal informális [informalish]

information felvilágosítás [felvilagosheetash]
do you have any information about ...? tud felvilágosítást adni ...-ról/ről? [tood felvilagosheetasht odni ...-rawl/rurl]
information desk információ [informatsi-aw]
injection injekció [in-yektsi-aw]
injured sérült [shayrewlt]
she's been injured megsérült [megshayrewlt]
inn csárda [chardo]
inner tube belső [belshur]
innocent ártatlan [artotlon]
insect rovar [rovor]
insect bite rovarcsípés [rovorcheepaysh]
do you have anything for insect bites? tud valamit adni rovarcsípésre? [tood volomit odni rovorcheepayshreh]
insect repellent rovarirtó [rovorirtaw]
inside: inside the hotel benn a szállodában [o sallodabon]
let's sit inside menjünk be [men-yewnk beh]
he's inside benn van
insist ragaszkodni [rogoskodni]
I insist ragaszkodom hozzá [rogoskodom]
insomnia álmatlanság [almotlonshag]
instant coffee azonnal oldódó kávépor [ozonnol oldawdaw kavaypor]
instead helyett [heh-yet]
instead of ... ... helyett
give me that one instead adja helyette azt [od-yo heh-yetteh ozt]
insulin inzulin [inzoolin]
insurance biztosítás [biztosheetash]
intelligent értelmes [ayrtelmesh]
interested: I'm interested in ... érdekelne ... [ayrdekelneh]
interesting érdekes [ayrdekesh]
that's very interesting ez nagyon érdekes [nodjon]
international nemzetközi [nemzetkuhzi]
interpret tolmácsolni [tolmacholni]
interpreter tolmács [tolmach]
intersection útkereszteződés [ootkeres-tezurdaysh]
interval (at theatre) szünet [sewnet]
into ...-ba/-be [-bo/-beh]
I'm not into ... nem vagyok otthonos a ...-ban/-ben [vodjok ot-honosh o ...-bon/-ben]
introduce bemutatni [bemoototni]
may I introduce ...? hadd mutassam be ... [hod mootosh-shom beh]
invitation meghívás [megheevash]
invite meghívni [megheevni]
Ireland Írország [eerorsag]
Irish ír(országi) [eer(orsagi)]
I'm Irish ír vagyok [vodjok]
iron (for ironing) vasaló [vosholaw]
can you iron these for me? kivasalná ezt nekem? [kivosholna]

is* van
island sziget [siget]
it (that) az [oz]
(this) ez
it is ... az/ez ...
is it ...? az/ez ...?
where is it? hol van? [von]
it's him ő az [ur]
it was ... ... volt
Italian olasz [olos]
Italy Olaszország [olosorsag]
itch: it itches viszket [visket]

J

jack (for car) emelő [emelur]
jacket zakó [zokaw]
jam lekvár
jammed: it's jammed beszorult [besoroolt]
January január [yonoo-ar]
jar (noun) tégely [taygeh^yuh]
jaw állkapocs [alkopoch]
jazz dzsezz [dJezz]
jealous féltékeny [fayltay-keh^nyuh]
jeans farmernadrág [formernodrag]
jetty móló [mawlaw]
jeweller's ékszerüzlet [aykserewzlet], ékszerész [aykserays]
jewellery ékszer [aykser]
Jewish zsidó [Jidaw]
job (employment) állás [allash]
(task) munka [moonko]
jogging kocogás [kotsogash]
to go jogging kocogni [kotsogni]
joke vicc [vits]
journey utazás [ootozash]
have a good journey! jó utat! [yaw ootot]
jug korsó [korshaw], kancsó [konchaw]
a jug of water egy kancsó víz [edj – veez]
juice lé [lay]
July július [yooli-oosh]
jump (verb) ugrani [oogroni]
jumper pulóver [poolawver]
junction csatlakozás [chotlokozash]
June június [yooni-oosh]
just (only) csak [chok]
just two csak kettő
just for me csak nekem
just here pontosan itt [pontoshon]
not just now nem ebben a pillanatban [o pillonotbon]
we've just arrived épp megérkeztünk [ayp megayrkeztewnk]

K

keep (verb) megtartani [megtortoni]
keep the change a többi a magáé [o tuhbbi o moga-ay]
can I keep it? megtarthatom? [megtort-hotom]
please keep it kérem, tartsa meg [kayrem tortsho]
ketchup kecsup [kechoop]
kettle teáskanna [teh-ashkonno]
key kulcs [koolch]
the key for room ..., please

kérem a ... szoba kulcsát [kayrem o ... sobo koolchat]
keyring kulcskarika [koolchkoriko]
kidneys vesék [veshayk]
kilo kiló [kilaw]
kilometre kilométer [kilomayter]
how many kilometres is it to ...? hány kilométer innen ...? [ha^{nyuh}]
kind (generous) kedves [kedvesh]
that's very kind nagyon kedves [nodjon]

•••••• DIALOGUE ••••••

which kind do you want? melyik fajtát akarja? [meh-yik foytat okor-yo]
I want this/that kind ezt/azt a fajtát kérem [ezt/ozt o foytat kayrem]

king király [kira^{yuh}]
kiosk bódé [bawday], fülke [fewlkeh]
kiss (noun) csók [chawk]
(verb) csókolni [chawkolni]
kitchen konyha [ko^{nyuh}ho]
Kleenex® papírzsebkendő [popeerJebkendur]
knee térd [tayrd]
knickers bugyi [boodji]
knife kés [kaysh]
knock (verb) kopogni
knock over (object) felborítani [felboreetoni]
(pedestrian) elgázolni [elgazolni]
he's been knocked over elgázolták [elgazoltak]
know (somebody) ismerni [ishmerni]
(something, a place) tudni [toodni]
I don't know nem tudom [toodom]
I didn't know that azt nem tudtam [ozt nem toodtom]
do you know where I can find ...? tudja, hol tudnám megtalálni ...? [tood-yo hol toodnam megtolalni]

L

label címke [tseemkeh]
ladies' room, ladies' toilets női W.C. [nuh-i vay tsay]
ladies' wear női ruha [nuh-i roo-ho]
lady hölgy [huhldj]
lager világos sör [vilagosh shur]
see **beer**
lake tó [taw]
Lake Balaton a Balaton [o boloton]
Lake Neusiedlersee Fertő tó [fertur taw]
lamb (meat) bárány [bara^{nyuh}]
lamp lámpa [lampo]
lane (on motorway) sáv [shav]
(small road) dűlő [dewlur]
language nyelv
language course nyelvtanfolyam [nyelvtonfo-yom]
language school nyelviskola [nyelvi-shkolo]
large nagy [nodj]
last utolsó [ootolshaw]
last week múlt héten [moolt

hayten]
last Friday múlt pénteken
last night múlt éjjel [ay-yel]
what time is the last train to Pécs? mikor indul az utolsó vonat Pécsre? [oz ootolshaw vonot paychreh]

late késő [kayshur]
sorry I'm late bocsánat a késésért [bochanot o kayshay-shayrt]
the train was late késett a vonat [kayshet o vonot]
we must go – we'll be late mennünk kell – nem szabad elkésnünk [mennewnk – sobod elkayshnewnk]
it's getting late későre jár [kayshur-reh yar]

later később [kayshurb]
I'll come back later később visszajövök [visso-yuhvuhk]
later on később
see you later viszontlátásra [visontlatashro]

latest legkésőbb [legkayshurb]
by Wednesday at the latest legkésőbb szerdára [serdaro]
the latest fashion/news a legújabb divat/hír [o legoo-yob]

laugh (verb) nevetni

launderette, laundromat önkiszolgáló mosoda [uhnkisolgalaw moshodo]

laundry (clothing) szennyes [sen-nyesh]
(place) mosoda [moshodo]

Self-service launderettes (**mosoda** [moshodo]) are rare, and **Patyolat** [pa-tyolot] (local cleaning services) are unlikely to have your washing or dry-cleaning back in less than 48 hours. More upmarket hotels have a laundering service. If you are staying in private lodgings, you are usually allowed to use your host's washing machine.

lavatory mosdó [moshdaw]

law törvény [turvay^{nyuh}]

lawn gyep [djep]

lawyer (man/woman) ügyvéd/ügyvédnő [ewdjvayd/ewdjvaydnur]

laxative hashajtó [hosh-hoytaw]

lazy lusta [looshto]

lead (electrical) vezeték [vezetayk]
(verb) vezetni
where does this lead to? hova fog ez vezetni? [hovo]

leaf levél [levayl]

leaflet röpirat [ruh-pirot]

leak (noun) lék [layk]
(verb) kiszivárogni [kisivarogni]
the roof leaks beszivárog a víz a tetőn [besivarog o veez o teturn]

learn tanulni [tonoolni]

least: not in the least a legkevésbé sem [o legkevayshbay shem]
at least legalább [legolab]

leather bőr [bur]

leave (go away) elmenni

(set off, go on ahead) indulni [indoolni]
(behind, with someone) hagyni [hodjni]
I am leaving tomorrow holnap elmegyek [holnop elmedjek]
he left yesterday tegnap elment [tegnop]
may I leave this here? itt hagyhatom ezt? [hodjhotom]
I left my coat in the bar a kabátomat a bárban hagytam [hodjtom]
when does the bus for Pécs leave? mikor indul a busz Pécsre? [mikor indool o boos paychreh]

left bal [bol]
on the left baloldalt [bololdolt]
to the left balra [bolro]
turn left forduljon balra [fordool-yon]
there's none left egy sem maradt [edj shem morot]

left-handed balkezes [bolkezesh]

left luggage (office) csomagmegőrző [chomogmegurzur]

Most train stations have a left luggage office or automatic left luggage lockers (**csomagmegőrző szekrény** [chomogmegurzur sekray[nyuh]), where you can store your baggage for up to 24 hours.

leg láb

lemon citrom [tsitrom]

lemonade lemonádé [lemonaday]

lemon tea citromos tea [tsitromosh teh-o]

lend kölcsönadni [kuhlchuhnodni]
will you lend me your ...? kölcsönadnád a ...-edet/odat? [kuhlchuhnodnad o]

lens (of camera) lencse [lencheh]

lesbian leszbikus [lesbikoosh]

less kevesebb [kevesheb]
less than ... kevesebb mint ...
less expensive olcsóbb [olchawb]

lesson lecke [letskeh]

let (allow) hagyni [hodjni]
will you let me know? értesít majd? [ayrtesheet moyd]
I'll let you know értesíteni fogom [ayrtesheeteni]
let's go for something to eat menjünk és együnk valamit [men-yewnk aysh edjewnk volomit]

let off letenni
will you let me off at ...? letennél ...? [letennayl]

letter levél [levayl]
do you have any letters for me? van postám? [von poshtam]

letterbox levélszekrény [levaylsekray[nyuh]], postaláda [poshtolado]

Nearly all letterboxes in Hungary are red and are fixed on the outside of buildings. There are still →

a few light blue boxes for airmail letters only, mostly outside main post offices.

lettuce saláta [sholato]
lever (noun) fogantyú [fogon-tyoo]
library könyvtár [kuh^{nyuh}vtar]
licence engedély [engeh-day^{yuh}]
(driver's) jogosítvány [yogosheetva^{nyuh}]
lid fedő [fedur]
lie (verb: tell untruth) hazudni [hozoodni]
lie down lefeküdni [lefekewdni]
life élet [aylet]
lifebelt mentőöv [mentur-uhv]
lifeguard életmentő [ayletmentur]
life jacket mentőkabát [menturkobat]
lift (in building) felvonó [felvonaw], 'lift'
could you give me a lift? elvinne a kocsiján? [elvinneh o kochi-yan]
would you like a lift? elvigyem a kocsimon? [elvidjem o kochimon]
light (noun) lámpa [lampo]
(not heavy) könnyű [kurn-nyew]
do you have a light? (for cigarette) tudna tüzet adni? [toodno tewzet odni]
light green világoszöld [vilagosh-zuhld]
light blue világoskék [vilagoshkayk]
light bulb körte [kurteh]
I need a new light bulb új körtére van szükségem [oo^{yuh} kurtayreh von sewkshaygem]
lighter (cigarette) öngyújtó [uhndjoo^{yuh}taw]
lightning villám
like: I like it tetszik nekem [tetsik]
I like going for walks szeretek sétálni [seretek shaytalni]
I like you maga tetszik nekem [mogo tetsik]
I don't like it nem tetszik nekem
do you like ...? szeretsz ...? [serets]
I'd like ... szeretnék ... [seretnayk]
would you like a drink? kér valamit inni? [kayr volomit]
would you like to go for a walk? szeretne sétálni? [seretneh shaytalni]
what's it like? milyen az? [mi-yen oz]
I want one like this olyat szeretnék, mint ez [o-yot]
lime zöld citrom [zuhld tsitrom]
line (on paper) sor [shor]
(phone) vonal [vonol]
could you give me an outside line? kaphatnék egy városi vonalat? [kop-hotnayk edj varoshi vonolot]
lips ajkak [oykok]
lip salve szőlőzsír [surlurJeer]
lipstick ajakrúzs [oyokrooJ]
liqueur likőr [likur]
litre liter
a litre of white wine egy liter

fehér bor [edj liter fehayr]
little kicsi [kichi]
just a little, thanks köszönöm, egész keveset kérek [kuhsuhnuhm egays keveshet kayrek]
a little milk egy kis tej [edj kish tay]
a little bit more egy kicsit több [kichit tuhb]
live (verb: in town etc) lakni [lokni]
we live together együtt élünk [edjewt aylewnk]

•••••• DIALOGUE ••••••

where do you live? hol lakik? [lokik]
I live in London Londonban lakom [–bon lokom]

lively eleven [eh-lehven]
liver máj [mī]
loaf cipó [tsipaw]
lobby (in hotel) 'lobby'
local helyi [heh-yi]
can you recommend a local wine/restaurant? tudna ajánlani egy helyi bort/vendéglőt? [toodno o-yanloni edj heh-yi bort/vendayglurt]
lock (noun) zár
(verb) kulcsra zárni [koolchro]
it's locked kulcsra van zárva [von zarvo]
lock in bezárni
lock out kizárni
I've locked myself out kizártam magam a szobámból [kizartom mogom o sobambawl]
locker (for luggage etc) szekrény [sekray[nyuh]]
lollipop nyalóka [nyolawko]
long hosszú [hossoo]
how long will it take to fix it? meddig tart, míg megjavítják? [tort meeg meg-yoveet-yak]
how long does it take? meddig tart?
a long time soká [shoka]
one day/two days longer egy nappal/két nappal tovább
long-distance call távolsági beszélgetés [tavolshagi besaylgetaysh]
look: I'm just looking, thanks köszönöm, csak körülnézek [kuhsuhnuhm chok kurewlnayzek]
you don't look well rosszul néz ki [rossool nayz]
look out! vigyázat! [vidjazot]
can I have a look? megnézhetem? [megnayz-hetem]
look after gondozni
look at nézni [nayzni]
look for keresni [kereshni]
I'm looking for ... ...-t keresem [kereshem]
look forward to örömmel várom [uruhmmel]
I'm looking forward to it már alig várom [olig]
loose (handle etc) laza [lozo]
lorry teherautó [teher-owtaw]
lose elveszteni [elvesteni]
I've lost my way eltévedtem [eltayvedtem]

I'm lost, I want to get to ... eltévedtem, ...-ba akarok menni [-bo okorok]
I've lost my bag elvesztettem a táskámat [elvestettem]

lost property (office) talált tárgyak (osztálya) [tolalt tardjok (osta-yo)]

lot: a lot, lots sok [shok]
not a lot nem nagyon sok [nodjon]
I like it a lot nagyon tetszik nekem [tetsik]
a lot of people sok ember
a lot bigger sokkal nagyobb [shokkol nodjob]

lotion krém [kraym]

loud hangos [hongosh]

lounge (in house, hotel) szalon [solon]
(in airport) indulóváró [indoolaw-varaw]

love (verb) szeretni [seretni]
I love Hungary szeretem Magyarországot [seretem modjororsagot]

lovely szép [sayp]
(meal) finom

low alacsony [olocho^{nyuh}]

luck szerencse [serencheh]
good luck! sok szerencsét! [shok serenchayt]

luggage poggyász [pogdjas]

luggage trolley kuli [kooli]

lump (on body) daganat [dogonot]

lunch ebéd [ebayd]

lungs tüdő [tewdur]

luxurious luxus [looksoosh]

luxury fényűzés [fay-nyewzaysh]

M

machine gép [gayp]

mad (insane) őrült [urewlt]
(angry) dühös [dewhuhsh]

magazine folyóirat [foy-aw-irot]

maid (in hotel) szobalány [sobola^{nyuh}]

maiden name lánynév [la^{nyuh}nayv]

mail (noun) posta [poshto]
(verb) feladni [felodni]
is there any mail for me? nem jött levelem? [yuht]
see **post office**

mailbox levélszekrény [levaylsekray^{nyuh}], postaláda [poshtolado]

main fő [fur]

main course főétel [furaytel]

main post office főposta [furposhto]

main road (in town) út [oot]
(in country) országút [orsagoot]

mains switch hálózati kapcsoló [halawzoti kopcholaw]

make (brand name) márka [marko]
(verb) csinálni [chinalni]
I make it 500 forints nekem ötszáz forintra jön ki [forintro yuhn]
what is it made of? miből van? [miburl von]

make-up arcszínező [orts-zeenezur]

man ember, férfi [fayrfi]

manager igazgató [igozgotaw], ügyvezető [ewdj-vezetur]

can I see the manager? beszélhetnék az igazgatóval? [besaylhetnayk oz igozgotawvol]
manageress igazgatónő [igozgotawnur]

manners
Hungarians believe in old-fashioned manners: men letting women through doors first, for example. If a woman tries to go against this on the Metro, insisting the man goes first, this can cause confusion and even anger if the doors shut with no-one getting off! However, there is an exception to this: men go into restaurants first, supposedly to protect the woman in case there's a fight or something else unpleasant inside.

manual (car with manual gears) kézi sebességváltós kocsi [kayzi shebeshayg-valtawsh kochi]
many sok [shok]
not many nem sok
map térkép [tayrkayp]
(city plan) város-térkép [varosh-tayrkayp]
(road map) autós térkép [owtawsh]
(hiking map) turistatérkép [toorristo-tayrkayp]
network map tömegközlekedési térkép [tuhmeg-kuhzlekedayshi]

Hungarian city plans (**város-térkép**) also show tram and bus routes. They are available from local tourist offices or, failing that, from bookshops (**könyvesbolt**). Better value is the **Magyar Auto Atlasz** [modjor owto atlas], which contains plans of most towns (some of the street names may be out of date) plus road maps, and can also be bought from bookshops. Bookshops also stock **turistatérkép** (hiking maps) covering the Mátra, Bükk and the other highland regions, which should be purchased in advance wherever possible. The tourist information organization, Tourinform, issues a variety of useful free road maps, including one showing Budapest's one-way streets and bypasses.

March március [martsi-oosh]
margarine margarin [morgorin]
market piac [pi-ots]
(indoor) vásárcsarnok [vasharchornok]

Piac (outdoor markets) are colourful affairs, sometimes with the bizarre sight of rows of poultry sheltered beneath sunshades; in **vásárcsarnok** (market halls) people select their fish fresh from glass tanks, and their mushrooms from a staggering array of →

gomba, which are displayed alongside toxic fungi in a 'mushroom parade' to enable shoppers to recognize the difference. Both outdoor markets and market halls have stalls selling household objects, kitchenware and folk craft objects which tend to be a great deal cheaper than in folk art shops. In addition, there are many street vendors of such handmade folk-artsy objects as table linen, embroidery etc. Prices are better than in shops, but factory-made fakes abound.

marmalade marmaládé [mormoladay], narancslekvár [noronchlekvar]
married: I'm married (said by man/woman) nős/asszony vagyok [nursh/osso[nyuh] vodjok]
are you married? (to man/woman) van Önnek felesége/férje? [von uhnnek feleshaygeh/fayr-yeh]
mascara arcfesték [ortsfeshtayk]
match (football etc) mérkőzés [mayrkurzaysh]
matches gyufa [djoofo]
material (fabric) anyag [o-nyog]
matter: it doesn't matter nem baj [boy]
what's the matter? mi a baj? [o]
mattress matrac [motrots]
May május [mī-oosh]
may: may I have another one? kaphatok még egyet? [kophotok mayg edjet]
may I come in? bejöhetek? [bayuh-hetek]
may I see it? megnézhetném? [megnayz-hetnaym]
may I sit here? leülhetek ide? [leh-ewl-hetek ideh]
maybe talán [tolan]
mayonnaise majonéz [moyonayz]
me* engem
that's for me ez az enyém [oz eh-nyaym]
send it to me küldje el nekem [kewld-yeh]
me too én is [ayn ish]
meal étkezés [aytkezaysh]
mean (verb) jelenteni [yelenteni]
what do you mean? hogy érti ezt? [hodj ayrti]

•••••• DIALOGUE ••••••

what does this word mean? mit jelent ez a szó? [yelent ez o saw]
it means ... in English ez angolul ...-t jelent [ongolool]

measles kanyaró [ko-nyoraw]
German measles rubeóla [roobeh-awlo]
meat hús [hoosh]
mechanic szerelő [serelur]
medicinal baths gyógyfürdő [djawdj-fewrdur]
medicine orvosság [orvosh-shag]
medium (adj: size) középméret [kuhzayp-mayret]
medium-dry középszáraz [kuhzayp-saroz]
medium-rare kissé angolosan

sütve [kish-shay ongoloshon shewtveh]

medium-sized közepes nagyságú [kuhzepesh nodjshagoo]

meet találkozni [tolal-kozni]

nice to meet you örülök a találkozásnak [urewluhk o tolal-kozashnok]

where shall I meet you? hol találkozunk? [tolal-kozoonk]

meeting (with several people) értekezlet [ayrtekezlet]

(with one person) találkozó [tolalkozaw]

meeting place találkozó hely [heh^{yuh}]

melon dinnye [din-nyeh]

men férfiak [fayrfi-ok]

mend megjavítani [megyoveetoni]

could you mend this for me? meg tudná ezt javítani? [toodna ezt yoveetoni]

men's room urak [oorok]

menswear férfiviselet [fayrfivishelet]

mention (verb) említeni [emleeteni]

don't mention it szívesen [seeveshen]

menu étlap [aytlop]

may I see the menu, please? kérem az étlapot [kayrem oz aytlopot]

see **menu reader** page 231

message üzenet [ewzenet]

are there any messages for me? nincs üzenet a számomra? [ninch ewzenet o samomro]

I want to leave a message for ... szeretnék üzenetet hagyni ...-nak/-nek [seretnayk ewzenetet hodjni ...-nok/-nek]

metal (noun) fém [faym]

metre méter [mayter]

microwave (oven) mikrohullámú sütő [mikro-hoollamoo shewtur]

midday dél [dayl]

at midday délben [daylben]

middle: in the middle a középen [o kuhzaypen]

in the middle of the night az éjszaka közepén [oz ay^{yuh}soko]

the middle one a középső [kuhzaypshur]

midnight éjfél [ay^{yuh}fayl]

at midnight éjfélkor [ay^{yuh}faylkor]

might: I might go lehet, hogy megyek [hodj medjek]

I might not go lehet, hogy nem megyek

I might want to stay another day lehet, hogy még egy napig szeretnék itt maradni [mayg edj nopig seretnayk it morodni]

migraine migrén [migrayn]

mild enyhe [eh^{nyuh}heh]

milk tej [tay]

millimetre milliméter [milimayter]

minced meat darált hús [doralt hoosh]

mind: never mind nem baj [boy]

I've changed my mind meggondoltam magam

[meggondoltom mogom]

•••••• DIALOGUE ••••••

do you mind if I open the window? megengedi, hogy kinyissam az ablakot? [hodj kinyish-shom oz oblokot]

no, I don't mind hogyne, nyugodtan [hodjneh nyoogodton]

mine*: **it's mine** ez az enyém [oz en-yaym]

mineral water ásványvíz [ashva[nyuh]veez]

mints mentolos bonbon [mentolosh]

minute perc [perts]

in a minute mindjárt [mind-yart]

just a minute egy pillanat [edj pillonot]

mirror tükör [tewkur]

(car) visszapillantótükör [vissopillontaw-tewkur]

Miss kisasszony [kishosso[nyuh]]

miss: **I missed the bus** lekéstem az autóbuszt [lekayshtem oz owtawboost]

missing eltűnt [eltewnt]

one of my ... is missing eltűnt az egyik ...-m [oz edjik]

there's a suitcase missing az egyik bőrönd eltűnt

mist köd [kuhd]

mistake (noun) tévedés [tayvedaysh]

I think there's a mistake azt hiszem, ez tévedés [ozt hisem ez tayvedaysh]

sorry, I've made a mistake bocsánat, tévedtem [bochanot tayvedtem]

mix-up: **sorry, there's been a mix-up** bocsánat, valami félreértés történt [bochanot volomi faylreh-ayrtaysh turtaynt]

mobile phone rádiótelefon [radi-aw–]

modern korszerű [korserew]

moisturizer hidratáló [hidrotalaw]

moment: **I won't be a moment** rögtön jövök [ruhgtuhn yuhvuhk]

Monday hétfő [haytfur]

money pénz [paynz]

The Hungarian unit of currency is the forint (Ft or HUF). The forint comes in notes of 100, 500, 1,000 and 5,000Ft, with 1, 2, 10, 20, 50 and 100Ft coins; the 100Ft note is valid, but is gradually being withdrawn. The little **fillér** [fillayr] (0.01Ft) coins, in denominations of 1, 2, 10 and 50, are practically worthless. It is necessary to order your Hungarian currency well in advance from your bank, but Hungarian currency can quickly and easily be bought at Ferihegy (Budapest) Airport, and all major railway stations.

Providing you produce your passport, changing money or travellers' cheques is a painless operation at any Ibusz or regional tourist office, or at the majority of large hotels and campsites. →

Valuta desks in banks take longer over transactions, and work shorter hours (Mon–Fri 8.30am–3.30pm) than tourist offices. Keep the receipts, as these may be required to change forints back into foreign currency when you leave Hungary.

month hónap [hawnop]
monument emlékmű [emlaykmew]
moon hold
moped 'moped'
more* több [tuhb]
can I have some more water? kaphatnánk még vizet? [kop-hotnank mayg]
more expensive/interesting drágább/érdekesebb
more than ... több mint ...
more than that ennél több [ennayl]
a lot more sokkal több [shokkol]

•••••• DIALOGUE ••••••

would you like some more? kér még? [kayr mayg]
no, no more for me, thanks köszönöm, nem kérek többet [kuhsuhnuhm nem kayrek tuhbbet]
how about you? és Ön? [aysh uhn]
I don't want any more, thanks köszönöm, nem kell több

morning reggel
this morning (9am–noon) ma délelőtt [mo daylelurt]
(4–9am) ma reggel
(midnight–4am) ma éjjel [ay-yel]
in the morning reggel
mosque mecset [mechet], dzsámi [dJami]
mosquito szúnyog [soo-nyog]
mosquito net szúnyogháló [soo-nyog-halaw]
mosquito repellent szúnyogirtó [soo-nyogirtaw]
most: I like this one most of all ezt szeretném a legjobban [seretnaym o leg-yobbon]
most of the time legtöbbször [legtuhbsur]
most tourists a legtöbb látogató [o legtuhb]
mostly többnyire [tuhb-nyireh]
motel 'motel'
mother anya [o-nyo]
mother-in-law anyós [o-nyawsh]
motorbike motorbicikli [motorbitsikli], motorkerékpár [motorkeraykpar]
motorboat motorcsónak [motorchawnok]
motorway autópálya [owtawpa-yo]
mountain hegy [hedj]
in the mountains a hegyek közt [o hedjek kuhzt]
mountaineering alpinizmus [olpinizmoos]
mouse egér [egayr]
moustache bajusz [bo-yoos]
mouth száj [sī]
move (verb: change position) mozogni

(something) mozgatni
(elsewhere) költözni [kuhltuhzni]
he's moved to another room átköltözött egy másik szobába [atkuhltuhzuht edj mashik sobabo]
could you move your car? lenne szíves elvinni a kocsiját? [lenneh seevesh elvinni o kochi-yat]
could you move up a little? lenne szíves egy kicsit arrább menni? [lenneh seevesh edj kichit orrab]
where has it moved to? (shop etc) hova költözött? [hovo kuhltuhzuht]

movie 'film'
movie theater mozi
Mr ... úr [oor]
Mrs ...-né [-nay]
much sok [shok]
much better/worse sokkal jobb/rosszabb [shokkol yobb/rossob]
much hotter sokkal melegebb
not much nem sok
not very much nem nagyon sok [nodjon]
I don't want very much nem akarok nagyon sokat? [okorok nodjon shokot]

mud sár [shar]
mug (for drinking) bögre [buh-greh]
I've been mugged kiraboltak [kiroboltok]

mum anyu [o-nyoo]
mumps mumpsz [mooms]
museum múzeum [moozeh-oom]

Museums are generally open Tuesday to Sunday 10am–6pm; in winter, hours are generally 9am–5pm, but the closing time can be earlier. Museum admission charges vary; student cards secure reductions, or free entry in many cases. Some places have free admission on Saturdays or Wednesdays.
Few of Hungary's museums have captions in any language but Hungarian, although the main museums in provincial centres and the capital might sell catalogues in German, French or English.

mushrooms gomba [gombo]
music zene [zeneh]
musician zenész [zenays]
Muslim mohamedán [mohomedan]
must*: **I must** ... ...-om/-em kell
I must go mennem kell
I mustn't drink alcohol nem szabad szeszesitalt innom [sobod seseshitolt]

mustard mustár [mooshtar]
my* az én ...-m/-im [oz ayn]
myself: **I'll do it myself** megcsinálom én magam [megchinalom ayn mogom]
by myself egyedül [edjedewl]

N

nail (finger) **köröm** [kuhruhm]
(metal) **szög** [suhg]
nailbrush körömkefe [kuhruhmkefeh]
nail varnish körömlakk [kuhruhmlok]
name név [nayv]
my name's John a nevem John [o]
what's your name? hogy hívják? [hodj heev-yak]
what's the name of this street? hogy hívják ezt az utcát? [oz ootsat]

Surnames precede Christian names in Hungary. When addressing someone, the use of the Christian name is inappropriate until you are fairly well-acquainted or unless both speakers are under 20. If a new acquaintance introduces themselves, however, '**Ilona vagyok**' ('I am Ilona'), without the surname, this is an invitation to use the Christian name. Without this encouragement, using a person's Christian name is patronizing if the other person is younger, and disrespectful if he/she is older than yourself.
In addressing someone, the use of '**úr**' [oor] ('Mr') is more frequent than the use of 'Mrs' or 'Miss', simply because the female versions are so cumbersome. 'Mrs', in Hungarian, is simply **-né** [-nay] (for example, 'Mrs Nagy' is '**Nagyné**') the use of which is downright rude without any qualification (such as '**kedves Nagyné**' meaning 'dear Mrs Nagy'), while the equivalent of 'Miss', '**kisasszony**' [kishosso[nyuh]], is quite a mouthful. Hence, you can say '**mondja, Nagy úr**' ('tell me, Mr Nagy', but speaking to his wife or daughter it's easier to say '**mondja, asszonyom**' [asson[nyuh]] ('tell me, Madam') or '**mondja, kisasszony**' ('tell me, Miss').
Finally, when the name is unknown and the person is a stranger, the proper way to address him or her is '**Uram**' [oorom] 'Sir' or '**Hölgyem**' [huhldjem] ('Madam'). When the person addressed has a professional or academic title, it's usual to use the title without the name: '**Doktor úr**' ('Doctor') is the proper form of address for a medical doctor or any man with a doctorate. Men are frequently addressed according to their profession: '**mérnök úr**' ('Mr Engineer'), '**tanár úr**' ('Mr Teacher'), '**Professzor úr**' ('Mr Professor').
see **greeting people**

name day névnap [nayvnop]

> In Hungary, especially for Catholics, name days are at least as important as birthdays. Each name has one or more designated days in the calendar, the majority of them being Catholic feast days of saints (for example, 20th August, St Stephen's day). It's not customary to give presents on name days, except for giving flowers to women, but the day is often celebrated with a party.

napkin asztalkendő [ostolkendur]
nappy pelenka [pelenko]
narrow (street) keskeny [keshkeh^{nyuh}]
nasty rossz [ross]
national nemzeti
natural természetes [termaysetesh]
nausea hányinger [ha^{nyuh}inger]
navy (blue) sötétkék [shuhtayt-kayk]
near közel [kuhzel]
is it near the city centre? közel van a belvároshoz? [von o belvarosh-hoz]
do you go near the National Museum? elmegy a Nemzeti Múzeum közelében? [elmedj o – kuhzelayben]
where is the nearest ...? hol van a legközelebbi ...? [von o legkuhzelebbi]
nearby közel(i) [kuhzel(i)]
nearly majdnem [moydnem]
necessary szükséges [sewkshaygesh]
neck nyak [nyok]
necklace nyaklánc [nyoklants]
necktie nyakkendő [nyokkendur]
need: I need ... (could do with) ...-ra/-re van szükségem [-ro/-reh von sewkshaygem]
(have to) ...-nem/-nom kell
I need to go to the bank el kell mennem a bankba
do I need to pay? kell fizetnem?
needle tű [tew]
negative (film) negatív [negoteev]
neither: neither (one) of them egyikük sem [edjikewk shem]
neither ... nor ... sem ... sem ...
nephew unokaöccs [oonoko-uhch]
net (in sport) háló [halaw]
Netherlands Hollandia [hollondi-o]
never soha [sho-ho]

•••••• DIALOGUE ••••••

have you ever been to Vienna? volt már Bécsben? [volt mar baychben]
no, never, I've never been there nem, ott még sosem voltam [mayg shoshem voltom]

new új [oo^{yuh}]
news újság [oo^{yuh}shag]
(radio, TV etc) hírek [heerek]
newsagent's újságárus [oo^{yuh}shagaroosh], újságos [oo^{yuh}shagosh]
newspaper újság [oo^{yuh}shag]

newspaper kiosk újságos bódé [oo^{yuh}shagosh bawday]

New Year Újév [oo-yayv]

Happy New Year! Boldog Újévet! [oo-yayvet]

New Year's Eve is elaborately, noisily, often rowdily celebrated all over the country, but nowhere quite so enthusiastically as in Budapest. All public performances, especially the obligatory late-night performance of Johann Strauss's Fledermaus (**Denevér**) as well as tables in practically any restaurant, bar or nightclub are sold out or reserved many weeks in advance. House-parties and balls also abound and younger people tend to 'make the rounds' (**pendlizni**), going to three, four or more parties or balls in a row. If invited to a house-party, the thing to bring is a bottle of champagne and, maybe, a chocolate piglet for the children. Pigs are considered lucky at New Year's Eve and the traditional dish for the occasion is a whole roast sucking pig. The traditional midnight dish is **korhelyleves** [korheh^{yuh}levesh] (sour cabbage soup with sausages in it), sometimes followed by doughnuts filled with ham and sprinkled with grated cheese.

New Year's Eve Szilveszter este [silvester eshteh]

New Zealand Új-Zéland [oo^{yuh}zaylond]

New Zealander: I'm a New Zealander új-zélandi vagyok [vodjok]

next következő [kuhvetkezur]

the next turning on the left a következő saroknál balra [o kuhvetkezur shoroknal bolro]

at the next stop a következő megállónál [megallawnal]

next week jövő héten [yuhvur hayten]

next to mellett

nice (food) finom

(looks, view etc) szép [sayp]

(place) kellemes [kellemesh]

(person) rokonszenves [rokonsenvesh]

niece unokahúg [oonoko-hoog]

night éjszaka [ay^{yuh}soko]

at night éjjel [ay-yel]

good night jó éjszakát [yaw ay^{yuh}sokat]

•••••• DIALOGUE ••••••

do you have a single room for one night? van egy egyágyas szobája egy éjszakára? [von edj edjadjosh sobī-o edj ay^{yuh}sokaro]

yes, madam van, kérem [von kayrem]

how much is it per night? mennyi egy éjszakára? [men-nyi edj ay^{yuh}sokaro]

it's 10,000 forints for one night tízezer forint egy éjszakára

thank you, I'll take it köszönöm, kiveszem [kuhsuhnuhm kivesem]

nightclub éjjeli mulató [ay-yeli moolotaw]
nightdress hálóing [halawing]
night porter éjszakai recepciós [ay^{yuh}soko-ee retseptsi-awsh]
no* nem
  I've no change nincs aprópénzem [ninch oprawpaynzem]
  there's no ... left nincs több ... [ninch tuhb]
  no way! szó sem lehet róla! [saw shem lehet rawlo]
  oh no! (upset) jaj, Istenem! [yoy ishtenem]
nobody* senki [shenki]
  there's nobody there senki sincs itt [shinch]
noise zaj [zoy]
noisy: it's too noisy túl zajos [tool zo-yosh]
non-alcoholic alkoholmentes [olkoholmentesh]
none* semmi [shemmi]
nonsmoking compartment nem-dohányzó szakasz [nem-doha^{nyuh}zaw sokos]
noon dél [dayl]
  at noon délben [daylben]
no-one* senki [shenki]
nor: nor do I én sem [ayn shem]
normal normális [normalish]
north Észak [aysok]
  in the north északon [aysokon]
  to the north északra [aysokro]
  north of Szeged Szegedtől északra [segedturl aysokro]
northeast észak-kelet [aysok-kelet]
northern északi [aysoki]
Northern Ireland Észak-Írország [aysok-eerorsag]
northwest északnyugat [aysok-nyoogot]
Norway Norvégia [norvaygi-o]
Norwegian norvég [norvayg]
nose orr
nosebleed orrvérzés [orvayrzaysh]
not* nem
  no, I'm not hungry nem, nem vagyok éhes [vodjok]
  I don't want any, thank you köszönöm, nem kell [kuhsuhnuhm]
  it's not necessary nem szükséges [sewkshaygesh]
  I didn't know that azt nem tudtam [ozt nem toodtom]
  not that one – this one nem az – ez [oz – ez]
note (banknote) bankjegy [bonkyedj]
notebook notesz [notes]
notepaper (for letters) levélpapír [levaylpopeer]
nothing semmi [shemmi]
  nothing for me, thanks köszönöm, nem kérek semmit [kuhsuhnuhm nem kayrek shemmit]
  nothing else semmi más [shemmi mash]
novel regény [regayny]
November 'november'
now most [mosht]
number szám [sam]
  (figure) számjegy [sam-yedj]

I've got the wrong number téves számot hívtam [tayvesh samot heevtom]
what is your phone number? mi az Ön telefonszáma? [oz uhn telefonsamo]
number plate (rend)számtábla [(rend)samtablo]
nurse (man/woman) ápoló/ápolónő [apolaw/apolawnur]
nut (for bolt) anyacsavar [o-nyochovor]
nuts dió [di-aw]

O

occupied (toilet) foglalt [foglolt]
(phone) mással beszél [mash-shol besayl]
o'clock* óra [awro]
October október [oktawber]
odd (strange) különös [kewluhnuhsh]
off (lights) kikapcsolva [kikopcholvo]
it's just off the Boulevard a Körútról nyílik [o kuhrootrawl nyeelik]
we're off tomorrow holnap elutazunk [holnop elootozoonk]
offensive (language, behaviour) sértő [shayrtur]
office (place of work) iroda [irodo]
officer (said to policeman) biztos úr [biztosh oor]
often gyakran [djokron]
not often nem gyakran
how often are the buses? milyen gyakran jár az autóbusz? [mi-yen djokron yar oz owtawboos]
oil olaj [oloy]
ointment kenőcs [kenurch]
OK jó [yaw]
are you OK? nincs semmi baja? [ninch shemmi bo-yo]
is that OK with you? ez megfelel Önnek? [uhnnek]
is it OK to smoke? szabad dohányozni? [sobod doha-nyozni]
that's OK, thanks köszönöm, ez jó lesz [kuhsuhnuhm ez yaw les]
I'm OK (nothing for me) köszönöm, nem kérek [kayrek]
(I feel OK) jól vagyok [yawl vodjok]
is this train OK for Szeged? ez a vonat megy Szegedre? [o vonot medj segedreh]
I said I'm sorry, OK? már mondtam egyszer, hogy bocsánatot kérek! [mondtom edjser hodj bochanotot kayrek]
old (person) idős [idursh]
(thing) régi [raygi]

•••••• DIALOGUE ••••••

how old are you? Ön hány éves? [uhn ha^nyuh ayvesh]
I'm 25 huszonöt éves vagyok [ayvesh vodjok]
and you? és Ön? [aysh uhn]

old-fashioned divatjamúlt [divo-tyomoolt]

old town (old part of town) óváros [awvarosh]
in the old town az óvárosban [oz awvaroshbon]
olives olajbogyó [oloybodjaw]
omelette omlet
on* ...-n/-on/-en/-ön
(date) ...-án/-én
on the street/tram az utcán/villamoson [oz oot-tsan/villomoshon]
on the plane a repülőgépen [o repewlurgaypen]
is it on this road? ebben az utcában van? [oz oot-tsabon von]
on Saturday szombaton [somboton]
on television a tévén [o tayvayn]
I haven't got it on me nincs nálam [ninch nalom]
this one's on me (drink) ezt én fizetem [ayn]
the light wasn't on nem égett a lámpa [ayget o lampo]
what's on tonight? mit adnak ma este? [odnok mo eshteh]
once (one time) egyszer [edjser]
at once (immediately) azonnal [ozonnol]
one egy [edj]
the white one a fehér [o fehayr]
one-way ticket egyszeri utazásra szóló jegy [edj-seri ootozashro sawlaw yedj]
a one-way ticket to ... egyszeri utazásra szóló jegyet ...-ra/-re [-ro/-reh]
onion hagyma [hodjmo]
only csak [chok]
only one csak egy [edj]
it's only 6 o'clock még csak hat óra van [mayg – awro von]
I've only just got here csak most érkeztem [mosht ayrkeztem]
on/off switch be/kikapcsoló [beh/kikopcholaw]
open (adj) nyitott
(shop) nyitva [nyitvo]
(verb: door) kinyitni
(of shop) nyitni
when do you open? mikor nyit?
I can't get it open nem tudom kinyitni [toodom]
in the open air a szabadban [o sobodbon]
opening times nyitvatartási idők [nyitvotortashi idurk]
open ticket dátum nélküli jegy [datoom naylkewli yedj]
opera opera [opero]
operation (medical) műtét [mewtayt]
operator (telephone) (telefon)központ [–kuhzpont]
opposite ... szemben [semben]
opposite my hotel a szállodámmal szemben [sallodammol]
the opposite direction ellenkező irányban [ellenkezur ira[nyuh]bon]
the bar opposite a szemközti bár [o semkuhzti]
optician optikus [optikoosh],

látszerész [latserays]
or vagy [vodj]
orange (fruit) narancs [noronch] (colour) narancssárga [noronch-shargo]
fizzy orange szénsavas narancslé [saynshovosh noronchlay]
orange juice friss narancslé [frish-sh noronchlay]
orchestra zenekar [zenekor]
order: we'd like to order (in restaurant) szeretnénk rendelni [seretnaynk]
I've already ordered, thanks köszönöm, már rendeltem [kuhsuhnuhm]
I didn't order this én nem ezt rendeltem [ayn]
out of order nem működik [mewkuhdik]
ordinary közönséges [kuhzuhnshaygesh]
other másik [mashik]
the other one a másik [o]
the other day a minap [minop]
I'm waiting for the others a többiekre várok [tuhbbi-ekreh varok]
do you have any others? van más is? [von mash ish]
otherwise különben [kewluhnben]
our* a mi ...-unk/-ünk/-aink/-eink [o mi ...-oonk/-ewnk/-o-eenk/-aynk]
ours* a miénk [o mi-aynk]
out: he's out nincs otthon [ninch ot-hon]
three kilometres out of town három kilométerrel a városon kívül [kilomayterrel o varoshon keevewl]
outdoors a szabadban [o sobodbon]
outside* ...-n kívül [keevewl]
can we sit outside? ülhetünk kinn? [ewlhetewnk]
oven sütő [shewtur]
over: over here emitt
over there amott [omot]
over 500 több mint ötszáz [tuhb mint]
over 60 years hatvan év fölött [ayv fuhluht]
it's over kész [kays]
overcharge: you've overcharged me túl sokat számított fel [tool shokot sameetott]
overcoat felsőkabát [felshurkobat]
overlooking: I'd like a room overlooking the courtyard udvarra néző szobát szeretnék [oodvorro nayzur sobat seretnayk]
overnight (travel) éjszakai [ay^{yuh}soko-ee]
overtake megelőzni [megelurzni]
owe: how much do I owe you? mivel tartozom? [tortozom]
own: my own car a saját autóm [o sho-yat owtawm]
are you on your own? egyedül van? [edjedewl von]
I'm on my own egyedül vagyok [vodjok]
owner tulajdonos [tooloy-donosh]

P

pack (verb) csomagolni [chomogolni]
a pack of ... egy csomag ... [edj chomog]
package (parcel) csomag
package holiday társasutazás [tarsho-shootozash]
packed lunch becsomagolt ebéd [bechomogolt ebayd]
packet: a packet of cigarettes csomag (cigaretta) [chomog (tsigoretto)]
padlock (noun) lakat [lokot]
page (of book) lap [lop]
could you page Mr ...? legyen szíves kerestesse ... urat [ledjen seevesh kereshtesh-sheh ... oorot]
pain fájdalom [fīdolom]
I have a pain here itt fáj [it fī]
painful fájdalmas [fīdolmosh]
painkillers fájdalomcsillapító [fīdolomchillopeetaw]
paint (noun) festék [feshtayk]
painting festmény [feshtmay^{nyuh}]
pair: a pair of ... egy pár ... [edj]
Pakistani pakisztáni [pokistani]
palace palota [poloto]
pale (face) sápadt [shapodt]
(colour) halvány [holva^{nyuh}]
pale blue halvány kék
pan lábas [labosh]
panties bugyi [boodji]
pants (underwear: men's) alsónadrág [olshawnodrag]
(women's) bugyi [boodji]
(US: trousers) nadrág [nodrag]
pantyhose harisnyanadrág [horish-nyonodrag]
paper papír [popeer]
(newspaper) újság [oo^{yuh}shag]
a piece of paper egy darab papír [edj dorob]
paper handkerchiefs papírzsebkendő [popeerJeb-kendur]
parcel csomag [chomog]
pardon (me)? (didn't understand/hear) tessék? [tesh-shayk]
parents szülők [sewlurk]
park (noun) park [pork]
(verb) parkolni [porkolni]
can I park here? parkolhatok itt? [porkolhotok]
parking lot autópark [owtawpork]
part (noun) rész [rays]
partner (boyfriend, girlfriend etc) élettárs [aylettarsh]
party (group) csoport [choport]
(celebration) vendégség [vendaygshayg]
passenger utas [ootosh]
passport útlevél [ootlevayl]

> If you lose your passport, the first place to go is the police. If your embassy provides you with a new passport, you have to go to the Aliens' Registration Division of the police, in Andrássy út in Budapest, to get the replacement passport endorsed.

past*: in the past a múltban [o mooltbon]
just past the information office

mindjárt az információs iroda után [mindyart oz informatsi-awsh irodo ootan]
pastry (cake etc) sütemény [shewtemay[nyuh]]
path ösvény [uhshvay[nyuh]]
pattern minta [minto]
pavement járda [yardo]
on the pavement a járdán [o yardan]
pay (verb) fizetni
can I pay, please? szeretnék fizetni [seretnayk]
it's already paid for már ki van fizetve [von fizetveh]
where do I pay? hol lehet fizetni?

•••••• DIALOGUE ••••••

who's paying? ki fizet?
I'll pay én fizetek [ayn]
no, you paid last time, I'll pay nem, utoljára is Ön fizetett, most én fizetek [ootol-yaro ish uhn fizetet mosht ayn]

payphone perselyes telefon [pershayesh]
peaceful békés [baykaysh]
peach őszibarack [ursiborotsk]
peanuts amerikai mogyoró [omeriko-ee modjoraw]
pear körte [kurteh]
peas borsó [borshaw]
peculiar (strange) furcsa [foorcho]
pedestrian crossing gyalogos átkelőhely [djologosh atkelurheh[yuh]]

> Never assume that a car will stop for you on a pedestrian crossing. Drivers in Hungary will often do anything to avoid having to slow down and make way for pedestrians.

peg (for washing) ruhacsipesz [roohochipes]
(for tent) sátorcövek [shatortsuhvek]
pen toll [tol]
pencil ceruza [tseroozo]
penfriend levelező partner [levelezur portner]
penicillin penicillin [penitsillin]
penknife zsebkés [Jebkaysh]
pensioner nyugdíjas [nyoogdeeyosh]
people emberek
the other people in the hotel a többi vendég a szállodában [o tuhbbi vendayg o sallodabon]
too many people túl sok ember [tool shok]
pepper (spice) bors [borsh]
(large, green, red etc) zöldpaprika [zuhldpopriko]
chilli pepper csilipaprika [chilipopriko]
peppermint (sweet) erős cukor [erursh tsookor]
per: per night éjszakánként [ay[yuh]sokankaynt]
how much per day? mennyibe kerül naponként? [men-nyibeh kerewl noponkaynt]

per cent százalék [sazolayk]
perfect tökéletes [tuhkayletesh]
perfume parfüm [porfewm]
perhaps talán [tolan]
perhaps not talán nem
period (of time) időszak [idursok]
(menstruation) menstruáció [menshtroo-atsi-aw]
perm tartóshullám [tortawsh-hoollam]
permit (noun) engedély [engeday^{yuh}]
person személy [semay^{yuh}]
personal stereo 'Walkman'
petrol benzin

> Most service stations (**benzinkút, töltőállomás**) stock 98 octane **extra**, 92 octane **szuper** (closest to four-star), 86 octane **normál**, and diesel. Lead-free fuel (**ólommentes benzin** [awlommentesh]) is available at stations in big cities and along major routes. If you are travelling in the country, you're best advised to get an AFOR (the state petrol company) map of country service stations from the Hungarian Automobile Association, or buy a map of Shell outlets at one of their stations. Service stations usually function daily from 6am–10pm, except on highways and in the capital, where many operate around the clock.

petrol can benzinkanna [benzinkonno]
petrol station benzinkút [benzinkoot], töltőállomás [tuhltur-allomash]
pharmacy patika [potiko], gyógyszertár [djawdj-sertar]

> All towns and most villages have a pharmacy, with staff (most likely to understand German rather than English) authorized to issue a wide range of drugs, including painkillers. Pharmacies are not allowed to issue listed drugs upon foreign prescriptions. Opening hours are normally Mon–Fri 9am–6pm, Sat 9am–noon or 1pm; signs in the window give the location or telephone number of the nearest all-night (**éjjeli** [ay-yeli] or **ügyeleti szolgálat** ewdjeleti solgalot]) pharmacy.

phone (noun) telefon
(verb) telefonálni

> In towns and cities, local calls can be made from public phones with 5, 10 or 20 forint coins. Long-distance calls are more problematic and communications between smaller localities are poor because all calls must be placed through the post office or the operator (01). Elsewhere, it should be possible to make direct calls by dialling 06, followed by the area code and the sub- →

scriber's number. Even so, you might still achieve better results by getting the post office operator to place the call.
In downtown Budapest and the Balaton resorts there are now booths taking phonecards, which can be bought from main post offices. You can use the cards in the special red or grey booths (also taking 10Ft and 20Ft coins) that allow you to make international calls. As an alternative, you can place calls through the international operator (09), the Central Telephone Bureau in Budapest, or fancy hotels in the provinces (which levy a hefty surcharge).

phone book telefonkönyv [–kuhnyuhv]
phone box telefonfülke [–fewlkeh]
phone call hívás [heevash]
phonecard telefonkártya [–kartyo]
phone number telefonszám [–sam]
photo fénykép [faynyuhkayp]
excuse me, could you take a photo of us? bocsánat, lenne szíves lefényképezni minket? [bochanot lenneh seevesh lefaynyuhkaypezni]
phrasebook nyelvkönyv [nyelvkuhnyuhv]
piano zongora [zongoro]
pickpocket zsebtolvaj [Jebtolvoy]
pick up: will you be there to pick me up? ott leszel, hogy felvegyél? [lesel hodj felvedjayl]
picnic piknik
picture (painting) kép [kayp]
(photo) fénykép [faynyuhkayp]
pie (meat) pástétom [pashtaytom]
(fruit) pite [piteh]
piece darab [dorob]
a piece of ... egy darab ... [edj]
pig disznó [disnaw]
(in restaurants) sertés [shertaysh]

pig-killing
Pig-killing time is in January or February, a tradition of pre-refrigerator times. The killing itself is serious business, done usually by a professional butcher in the small hours of the morning. Even townspeople with no facility to breed pigs sometimes arrange for their own pig-killing somewhere in the country, by buying the animal and paying for the services of the butcher and other helpers. In the countryside, the evening of the pig-killing is called **disznótor** ('the wake for the pig'), and is an enormous feast.
In the pig-killing season most restaurants have **disznótoros vacsora** [disnawtorosh vochoro] (pig-killing dinner) on their menus. This usually consists of two or three kinds of grilled or →

roast meats, with a variety of grilled or cooked sausages, as well as potatoes, sauerkraut and pickles.

pill fogamzásgátló [fogomzashgatlaw]
I'm on the pill fogamzásgátlót szedek [sedek]
pillow párna [parno]
pillow case párnahuzat [parnohoozot]
pin (noun) gombostű [gomboshtew]
pineapple ananász [ononas]
pineapple juice ananász lé [lay]
pink rózsaszín [rawJoseen]
pipe (for smoking) pipa [pipo]
(for water) cső [chur]
pity: it's a pity milyen kár [mi-yen]
pizza 'pizza'
place (noun) hely [heh^{yuh}]
at your place Önnél [uhnnayl]
at his place nála [nalo]
plain (not patterned) egyszínű [edjseenew]
plane repülőgép [repewlurgayp]
by plane repülőgépen
plant növény [nuhvay^{nyuh}]
plasters ragtapasz [rogtopos], leukoplaszt [leh-ookoplast]
plastic műanyag [mew-o-nyog]
(credit cards) hitelkártyák [hitelkar-tyak]
plastic bag műanyag zacskó [mew-o-nyog zochkaw]
plate tányér [ta-nyayr]
platform (where passengers wait) peron
(track) vágány [vaga^{nyuh}]
which platform is it for Miskolc? melyik vágányról indul a miskolci vonat? [may-yik vaga^{nyuh}rawl indool o mishkoltsi vonot]
play (verb) játszani [yatsoni]
(noun: in theatre) (szín)darab [(seen)dorob]
playground játszótér [yatsawtayr]
pleasant kellemes [kellemesh]
please kérem [kayrem]
(offering something) tessék [tesh-shayk]
yes, please igen, kérek [kayrek]
could you please ...? lenne szíves ...? [lenneh seevesh]
please don't ... kérem, ne ... [neh]
pleased: pleased to meet you van szerencsém [von serenchaym], örvendek [urvendek]
pleasure: my pleasure nagyon szívesen [nodjon seeveshen]
plenty: plenty of ... elég ... [elayg], sok ... [shok]
there's plenty of time még sok időnk van [mayg shok idurnk von]
that's plenty, thanks ez nagyonis elegendő, köszönöm [nodjonish elegendur kuhsuhnuhm]
plug (electrical, in sink) dugó [doogaw]

plumber vízvezetékszerelő [veezvezetayk-serelur]
pm* délután [daylootan]
poached egg buggyantott tojás [boog-djontot toyash]
pocket zseb [Jeb]
point: two point five két egész öt tized [egays]
there's no point nincs értelme [ninch ayrtelmeh]
poisonous mérges [mayrgesh]
Poland Lengyelország [lendjelorsag]
police rendőrség [rendurshayg]
call the police! hívják a rendőrséget! [heev-yak o rendurshayget]

> The emergency telephone number is 107 for the police. The **Magyar Államrendőrség** (Hungarian State Police Force) has special divisions for airports, railway stations, the Budapest Metro, for traffic control and there is also a river police division on the Danube. Policemen and women wear blue uniforms with peaked caps (police officers on traffic control duty may wear white uniforms in the summer) and they are usually armed.
> The police are entitled to impose on-the-spot fines on pedestrians and motorists for traffic offences, for which they should supply a receipt.

policeman rendőr [rendur]
police station rendőr őrszoba [ursobo]
policewoman rendőrnő [rendurnur]
polish (noun) fényezés [fay-nyezaysh]
Polish lengyel [lendjel]
polite udvarias [oodvori-osh]
polluted szennyezett [sen-nyezet]
pony póni [pawni]
pool (for swimming) uszoda [oosodo]
poor (not rich) szegény [segayny]
(quality) silány [shila^{nyuh}]
pop music popzene [popzeneh]
pop singer (man/woman) 'pop' énekes/énekesnő [aynekesh/aynekeshnur]
popular népszerű [naypserew]
population lakosság [lokosh-shag]
pork sertéshús [shertaysh-hoosh]
port (drink) portói [portaw-i]
porter (in hotel) portás [portash]
portrait arckép [ortskayp]
posh (restaurant, people) elegáns [elegansh]
possible lehetséges [lehet-shaygesh]
is it possible to ...? lehetne ...? [lehetneh]
as ... as possible amilyen ... csak lehet [omi-yen ... chok]
post (noun: mail) posta [poshto]
(verb) feladni [felodni]
could you post this for me? lenne szíves ezt feladni? [lenneh seevesh]
postbox postaláda [poshtolado]

postcard levelezőlap [levelezurlop]
picture postcard képeslap [kaypeshlop]
postcode irányítószám [ira-nyeetawsam]
poster poszter [poster]
(in street) falragasz [folrogos]
poste restante poste restante [posteh reshtonteh]
post office posta(hivatal) [poshto(hivotol)]

Post offices are usually open Mon–Fri 8am–6pm, and until noon on Saturday, although in Budapest you'll find several offices that are open 24 hours. Mail from abroad should be addressed '**poste restante, posta**' followed by the name of the town; tell your friends to write your surname first, Hungarian-style, and underline it; even this may not prevent your mail being misfiled, so ask them to check under all your names. To collect mail, show your passport and ask '**van posta a részemre?**' [von poshto o raysemreh]. It's probably safer to send mail to the American Express office in Budapest – where letters marked 'c/o American Express' are kept safely until collection, and the staff speak English.
It's quicker to buy **bélyeg** [bayyeg] (stamps) at tobacconists; → post offices are often full of people making complicated transactions or sending telegrams.

potato burgonya [boorgo-nyo]
potato chips (US) 'chips'
pots and pans edények [edaynyek]
pottery (objects) cserépedények [cheraypedaynyek]
pound (money) font(sterling) [–shterling]
power cut áramszünet [aromsewnet]
power point konnektor
practise: I want to practise my Hungarian gyakorolni akarom a magyar nyelvet [djokorolni okorom o modjor]
prefer: which do you prefer? melyiket szereted jobban? [may^yuh^ket sereted yobbon]
I prefer this one ezt szeretem jobban [seretem yobbon]
pregnant terhes [terhesh]
prescription (for medicine) recept [retsept]
see **pharmacy**
present (gift) ajándék [o-yandayk]
president (of country: man/woman) elnök/elnökasszony [elnuhk/elnuhkosso^nyuh^]
pretty (attractive) csinos [chinosh]
(quite) elég(gé) [elayg(gay)]
it's pretty expensive elég drága
price ár
priest pap [pop]

prime minister (man/woman) miniszterelnök/ miniszterelnök asszony [ministerelnuhk/ministerelnuhk osso^{nyuh}]

printed matter nyomtatvány [nyomtotva^{nyuh}]

prison börtön [burtuhn]

private magán [mogan]

private bathroom külön fürdőszoba [kewluhn fewrdursobo]

private room fizetővendégszolgálat [fizet-urvendayg-solgalot]

private rooms (suite) lakosztály [lokosta^{yuh}]

> In Budapest and many towns, renting a private room in someone's house is often cheaper than staying in a guesthouse or hotel, especially in the centre of town. This type of private accommodation (known as **fizetővendégszolgálat**) can be arranged by local tourist offices for a fee, or by knocking on the door of places with **szoba kiadó** or **Zimmer frei** signs. Unfortunately, many landladies also charge thirty per cent extra if you stay fewer than three nights, and a general lack of single rooms means that solo travellers have to pay for a double.
>
> As a rule of thumb, a town's **Belváros** (inner section) is likely → to consist of spacious apartments with parquet floors, high ceilings and a balcony overlooking a courtyard, whereas the outlying zones are probably charmless, high-rise modern developments. Some landladies will provide breakfast for a fee, although most leave early for work. For this reason, it's usually impossible to take possession of the room before 5pm; after that you can come and go with a key.

probably valószínűleg [volawseenewleg]

problem probléma [problaymo]

no problem! semmi gond! [shemmi]

program(me) (noun) program [progrom]

promise: I promise ígérem [eegayrem]

pronounce: how is this pronounced? hogy kell ezt kiejteni? [hodj –ki-ayteni]

properly (repaired, locked etc) rendesen [rendeshen]

protection factor (of suntan lotion) védelmi tényező [vaydelmi taynyezur]

Protestant protestáns [proteshtansh]

public holiday ünnepnap [ewnnepnop]

> On the following days most things in Hungary shut down and, should any of the public holidays fall on a Tuesday or Thursday, the day between the holiday and the weekend also becomes a holiday:
>
> 1 January
> 15 March
> Easter Monday
> 1 May
> 20 August
> 23 October
> 25 December
> 26 December

public toilet nyilvános illemhely [nyilvanosh illemheh[yuh]]
pudding (dessert) édesség [aydesh-shayg]
pull húzni [hoozni]
pullover pulóver [poolawver]
puncture gumidefekt [goomidefekt]
purple lila [lilo]
purse (for money) pénztárca [paynztartso]
(US: handbag) kézitáska [kayzitashko]
push tolni
pushchair tolókocsi [tolaw-kochi]
put tenni
where can I put ...? hova tehetem ...? [hovo]
could you put us up for the night? el tudna szállásolni minket ma éjszakára? [toodno sallasholni minket mo ay[yuh]sokaro]
pyjamas pizsama [piJomo]

Q

quality minőség [minurshayg]
quarantine egészségügyi zárlat [egayshaygewdji zarlot]
quarter negyed [nedjed]
quay rakpart [rokport]
question kérdés [kayrdaysh]
queue (noun) sor [shor]
quick gyors [djorsh]
that was quick ez hamar ment [homor]
what's the quickest way there? hogyan lehet a leggyorsabban odajutni? [hodjon lehet o legdjor-shobbon odo-yootni]
fancy a quick drink? van kedve egy gyors italra? [von kedveh edj djorsh itolro]
quickly gyorsan [djorshon]
quiet (place, hotel) csendes [chendesh]
quiet! csend legyen! [chend ledjen]
quite (fairly) egészen [egaysen]
(very) meglehetősen [meglehetursheh]
that's quite right tökéletesen igaz [tuhkayleteshen igoz]
quite a lot egész sok [egays shok]

R

rabbit nyúl [nyool]
race (for runners, cars) verseny [versheh^nyuh]
racket (tennis, squash) ütő [ewtur]
radiator (of car) radiátor [rodiator]
(in room) fűtőtest [fewturtesht]
radio rádió [radi-aw]
on the radio a rádióban [o radiawbon]
rail: by rail vonaton [vonoton]
railway vasút [voshoot]
rain (noun) eső [eshur]
in the rain az esőben [oz]
it's raining esik [eshik]
raincoat esőkabát [eshurkobat]
rape (verb) megerőszakolni [megerursokolni]
rare (uncommon) ritka [ritko]
(steak) véres [vayresh]
rash (on skin) kiütés [ki-ewtaysh]
raspberry málna [malno]
rat patkány [potka^nyuh]
rate (for changing money) átváltási arány [atvaltashi ora^nyuh]
rather: it's rather good nagyon jó [nodjon yaw]
I'd rather walk inkább gyalog mennék [djolog mennayk]
razor borotva [borotvo]
razor blades borotvapengék [borotvo-pengayk]
read olvasni [olvoshni]
ready kész [kays]
are you ready? kész van? [von]
I'm not ready yet még nem vagyok kész [mayg nem vodjok]

•••••• DIALOGUE ••••••
when will it be ready? mikorra lesz kész? [mikorro les]
it should be ready in a couple of days két napon belül kész lesz [nopon belewl kays les]

real igazi [igozi]
really igazán [igozan]
I'm really sorry igazán sajnálom [shoynalom]
that's really great ez igazán nagyszerű [nodjserew]
really? (doubt) tényleg? [tay^nyuh leg]
(polite interest) igazán?
rear lights hátsólámpa [hatshawlampo]
rearview mirror visszapillantó tükör [vissopillontaw tewkur]
reasonable (prices etc) ésszerű [aysserew]
receipt nyugta [nyoogto]
(for collecting purchases) blokk
see shop
recently nemrég [nemrayg]
reception (in hotel) recepció [retseptsi-aw], porta [porto]
(for guests) fogadás [fogodash]
at reception a recepciónál [o retsepti-awnal]
reception desk recepció [retseptsi-aw]
receptionist recepciós [retseptsi-awsh], portás [portash]
recognize felismerni [felishmerni]
recommend: could you recommend ...? tudna

ajánlani ...? [toodno o-yanloni]
record (music) hanglemez [honglemez]
red vörös [vuruhsh]
red wine vörösbor [vuruhshbor]
refund (noun) visszatérítés [vissotayreetaysh]
can I have a refund? kérem vissza a pénzemet [kayrem visso o paynzemet]
region régió [raygi-aw]
registered: by registered mail ajánlott levélben [o-yanlot levaylben]
registration number rendszám [rendsam]
religion vallás [vollash]
remember: I don't remember nem emlékszem [emlayksem]
I remember emlékszem
do you remember? emlékszik? [emlayksik]
rent (noun) bér [bayr]
(verb) bérelni [bayrelni]
to rent bérelhető [bayrelhetur]

••••• DIALOGUE •••••

I'd like to rent a car kocsit szeretnék bérelni [kochit seretnayk]
for how long? mennyi időre? [mennyi idur-reh]
two days két napra [nopro]
this is our range ez a választék [o valostayk]
I'll take the ... a ...-t választom [valostom]
is that with unlimited mileage? távolságkorlátozás nélkül? [tavolshag-korlatozash naylkewl]
it is igen
can I see your licence please? szabad megnéznem a jogosítványát? [sobod megnayznem o yogosheetva-nyat]
and your passport és az útlevelét [aysh oz ootlevelayt]
is insurance included? a biztosítás benne van? [o bizto-sheetash benneh von]
yes, but you pay the first 50,000 forints igen, de az első ötvenezer forintot Önnek kell kifizetni [deh oz elshur – uhnnek]
can you leave a deposit of 50,000 forints? lesz szíves ötvenezer forint biztosítékot letenni? [les seevesh – bizto-sheetaykot]

rented car bérelt autó [bayrelt owtaw]
repair (verb) megjavítani [meg-yoveetoni]
can you repair it? meg tudja javítani? [tood-yo yoveetoni]
repeat ismételni [ish-maytelni]
could you repeat that? lesz szíves megismételni? [les seevesh megish-maytelni]
reservation foglalás [foglolash]
I'd like to make a reservation szeretnék foglalni egy ...-t [seretnayk foglolni edj]

••••• DIALOGUE •••••

I have a reservation foglaltam egy szobát [fogloltom edj sobat]
yes sir, what name please? igen, kérem, milyen névre? [kayrem mi-yen nayvreh]

reserve (verb) foglalni [foglolni]

•••••• DIALOGUE ••••••

can I reserve a table for tonight? foglalhatnék egy asztalt ma estére? [foglol-hotnayk edj ostolt mo eshtayreh]
yes madam, for how many people? igen, asszonyom, hány személynek? [osso-nyom ha^{nyuh} semay^{nyuh}nek]
for two kettőnek [ketturnek]
and for what time? és hány órára? [aysh ha^{nyuh} awraro]
for 8 o'clock nyolc órára [nyolts]
and could I have your name please? szabad kérnem a nevét? [sobod kaymem o nevayt]
see **alphabet** for spelling

rest: I need a rest pihennem kell
the rest of the group a csoport többi tagja [o choport tuhbbi togyo]

restaurant vendéglő [vendayglur], étterem [aytterem]

Hungarians have a variety of words implying fine distinctions between restaurants. In theory, an **étterem** is a proper restaurant, while a **vendéglő** is supposed to be like a French-style bistro, but in practice the terms are often used interchangeably. The term **söröző** [shuruhzur], although it indicates a beer hall, is also more often than not a reasonably good but not upmarket restaurant. The old word for an inn, **csárda** [chardo], applies to posh places specializing in certain dishes (for example, **halászcsárda** [holas-chardo] – a 'Fisherman's Inn'), restaurants alongside roads or with rustic pretensions, as well as to the humbler rural establishments that the name originally signified. In the provinces, the word **kocsma** [kochmo] or, sometimes, **korcsma** [korchmo] indicates a drinking place where, in most cases, a rudimentary meal or snack may also be obtained.
You'll usually be asked if you want an **előétel** [eluraytel] (starter), which is generally soup or salad. Nobody will mind, however, if you just have one of the **főételek** [furaytelek] (main courses) or, alternatively, order just a soup and a starter without a main course.
Places used to tourists often have menus in German (and sometimes English), a language of which most waiters and waitresses have a smattering. Particularly in Budapest, tourist-oriented establishments may give you a menu without prices – a sure sign that they're expensive, or plan to rip you off. You should demand a menu with prices clearly indicated (**árazott menü** [arozot menew]). While some →

restaurants offer a bargain set menu (**napi menü**) of basic dishes, the majority of places are strictly à la carte.
Many places still close early, around 10pm, although this is changing, particularly in Budapest. Many restaurants employ musicians at lunchtime and in the evening. It isn't necessary to put money in the collection plate of the musicians, but if the violinist stops at your table and you unwisely encourage him, then a hefty and immediate tip is expected. It's not the custom, nor is it very wise, to treat the musicians to drinks as this usually results in a rip-off of gargantuan proportions.
see **bill** and **eating habits**

restaurant car étkezőkocsi [aytkezur-kochi]
rest room W.C. [vay tsay], mosdó [moshdaw]
retired: I'm retired nyugdíjas vagyok [nyoogdee-yosh vodjok]
return: a return to ... visszatérés ...-ba/-be [vissotayraysh ...-bo/-beh]
return ticket menettérti jegy [menettayrti yedj], retúrjegy [retoor-yedj]
see **ticket**
reverse charge call R-beszélgetés [ayr besaylgetaysh]
reverse gear hátráló sebesség [hatralaw shebesh-shayg]
revolting felháborító [felhaboreetaw]
rib borda [bordo]
rice rizs [riJ]
rich (person) gazdag [gozdog]
(food) nehéz [nehayz]
ridiculous nevetséges [nevetshaygesh]
riding school lovaglóiskola [lovoglawishkolo], lovarda [lovordo]
right (correct) helyes [hay-yesh]
(not left) jobb [yob]
you were right Önnek volt igaza [uhnnek volt igozo]
that's right úgy van [oodj von]
this can't be right ez nem lehet igaz [igoz]
right! rendben!
is this the right road for ...? ez az út vezet ...-ba? [oz oot vezet ...-bo]
on the right jobboldalt [yobboldolt]
to the right jobbra [yobbro]
turn right forduljon jobbra [fordool-yon]
right-hand drive jobbkormányos autó [yobkorma-nyosh owtaw]
ring (on finger) gyűrű [djewrew]
I'll ring you majd felhívom [moyd felheevom]
ring back visszahívni [visso-heevni]
ripe (fruit) érett [ayret]
rip-off: it's a rip-off ez rablás [roblash]
rip-off prices rabló árak [roblaw

arok]
risky kockázatos [kotskazotosh]
river folyó [fo-yaw]
road (main) út [oot]
(smaller) utca [oot-tso]
is this the road for ...? ezen az utcán kell ... menni? [oz oot-tsan]
down the road az úton [ooton]
road accident közlekedési baleset [kuhzleh-kedayshi boleshet]
road map autóstérkép [owtawsh-tayrkayp]
roadsign útjelző tábla [ootyelzur tablo]
rob: I've been robbed kiraboltak [kiroboltok]
rock szikla [siklo]
(music) 'rock' zene [zeneh]
on the rocks (with ice) jéggel [yayggel]
roll (bread) zsemle [Jemleh]
Romania Románia
Romanian román [roman]
roof tető [tetur]
room szoba [sobo]
in my room a szobámban [o sobambon]

•••••• DIALOGUE ••••••

do you have any rooms? van kiadó szobája? [von ki-odaw sobī-o]
for how many people? hány személynek? [ha[nyuh] semay[yuh]nek]
for one/for two egynek/kettőnek [edjnek/ketturnek]
yes, we have rooms free igen, van üres szobánk [von ewresh sobank]
for how many nights will it be? hány éjszakára lesz? [ha[nyuh] ay[yuh]sokaro les]
just for one night csak egy éjszakára [chok edj]
how much is it? mennyibe kerül? [men-nyibeh kerewl]
... with bathroom fürdőszobával ... [fewrdursobavol]
... without bathroom fürdőszoba nélkül ... [fewrdursobo naylkewl]
can I see a room with bathroom? megnézhetnék egy fürdőszobás szobát? [megnayz-hetnayk edj fewrdursobash sobat]
OK, I'll take it rendben van, kiveszem [von kivesem]

room service szobaszervíz [soboserveez]
rope kötél [kuhtayl]
rosé (wine) rózsaszínű bor [rawJoseenew]
roughly (approximately) körülbelül [kuhrewl-belewl]
round: it's my round ezt a rundot én fizetem [o roondot ayn]
round-trip ticket menettérti jegy [menettayrti yedj], retúrjegy [retoor-yedj]
a round-trip ticket to ... visszatérés ...-ba/-be [vissotayraysh ...-bo/-beh]
route útvonal [ootvonol]
what's the best route? merre a legjobb menni? [merreh o leg-yob]
rowing evezés [evezaysh]

rowing boat evezős csónak [chawnok]
rubber (material) gumi [goomi]
(eraser) radir [rodir]
rubber band gumiszalag [goomisolog]
rubbish (waste) szemét [semayt]
(poor-quality goods) hitvány áru [hitva^nyuh aroo]
rubbish! (nonsense) szamárság! [somarshag]
rucksack hátizsák [hatiJak]
rude goromba [gorombo]
ruins romok
rum rum [room]
rum and Coke® cola rummal [kolo roommol]
run (verb: person) futni [footni]
how often do the buses run? milyen gyakran járnak a buszok? [mi-yen djokron yarnok o boosok]
I've run out of money kifogyott a pénzem [kifodjott o paynzem]
rush hour csúcsforgalom [choochforgolom]
Russia Oroszország [orosorsag]
Russian orosz [oros]

S

sad szomorú [somoroo]
saddle nyereg
safe (not in danger) biztonságban [bizton-shagbon]
(not dangerous) biztonságos [bizton-shagosh]
safety pin biztosítótű [biztoshee-tawtew]
sailboard (noun) surfdeszka [surfdesko]
sailboarding szélvitorlázás [saylvitor-lazash]
sailing vitorlázás [vitorlazash]
salad saláta [sholato]
salad dressing saláta öntet [uhntet]
salami szalámi [solami]
sale: for sale eladó [elodaw]
salmon łazac [lozots]
salt só [shaw]
same: the same ugyanaz [oodjonoz]
the same as this ugyanaz mint ez
the same again, please megint ugyanazt kérem [kayrem]
it's all the same to me nekem mindegy [mindedj]
sandals szandál [sondal]
sandwich szendvics [sendvich]
sanitary napkin/towel egészségügyi tampon [egayshay-gewdji tompon]
Saturday szombat [sombot]
sauce mártás [martash]
saucepan fazék [fozayk]
saucer kistányér [kishta-nyayr]
sauna szauna [sowno]
sausage kolbász [kolbas]
say (verb) mondani [mondoni]
how do you say ... in Hungarian? hogy mondják magyarul, hogy ...? [hodj mond-yak modjorool]
what did he say? mit mondott?

she said ... azt mondta, hogy ... [ozt mondto]
could you say that again? lesz szíves megismételni? [les seevesh megish-maytelni]
scarf (for neck) sál [shal]
(for head) fejkendő [faykendur]
scenery táj [tī]
schedule (US: timetable) menetrend
scheduled flight menetrendszerű járat [menetrend-serew yarot]
school iskola [ishkolo]
scissors: a pair of scissors olló [ollaw]
scooter robogó [robogaw]
scotch viski
Scotch tape® ragasztószalag [rogostaw-solog]
Scotland Skócia [shkawtsi-o]
Scottish skót [shkawt]
I'm Scottish skót vagyok [vodjok]
scrambled eggs rántotta [rantotto]
screw (noun) csavar [chovor]
screwdriver csavarhúzó [chovorhoozaw]
search (verb) keresni [kereshni]
seat ülés [ewlaysh]
(place) hely [heh^{yuh}]
is this seat taken? foglalt ez a hely? [foglolt ez o]
seat belt biztonsági öv [biztonshagi uhv]
secluded magányos [mogan-yosh]
second (adj) második [mashodik]
(of time) másodperc [mashodperts]
just a second! egy pillanat! [edj pillonot]
second class (travel etc) második osztály [mashodik ostay]
second floor második emelet
(US) első emelet [elshur]
second-hand használt [hosnalt]
see látni
can I see? láthatnám? [lat-hotnam]
have you seen ...? látta már ...-t? [latto]
I saw him this morning ma reggel láttam [mo – lattom]
see you! viszlát! [vislat]
I see (I understand) értem [ayrtem]
self-catering apartment bérlakás [bayrlokash]
self-service önkiszolgálás [uhnkisolgalash]
sell eladni [elodni]
do you sell ...? eladja ...-t? [elod-yo]
Sellotape® ragasztószalag [rogostawsolog]
send küldeni [kewldeni]
I want to send this to England ezt Angliába akarom küldeni [ongli-abo okorom kewldeni]
senior citizen (man/woman) idősebb férfi/asszony [idurshebb fayrfi/osso^{nyuh}]
separate külön [kewluhn]
separated: I'm separated különváltan élek [kewluhnvalton aylek]
separately (pay, travel) külön

September szeptember [september]
Serbia Szerbia [serbi-o]
Serbian szerb [serb]
serious (problem, illness) súlyos [shoo-yosh]
(person, offer) komoly [komo^{yuh}]
service charge (in restaurant) kiszolgálási díj [kisolgalashi dee^{yuh}]
service station benzinkút [benzinkoot], töltőállomás [tuhltur-allomash]
serviette szalvéta [solvayto]
set menu napi menü [nopi menew]
several több [tuhb]
sew varrni [vorni]
could you sew this back on? vissza tudná ezt varrni? [visso toodna]
sex nem
sexy nemileg vonzó [vonzaw]
shade: in the shade az árnyékban [oz arn-yaykbon]
shake: let's shake hands rázzunk kezet [razzoonk]
shallow (water) sekély [shekay^{yuh}]
shame: what a shame! milyen kár! [mi-yen kar]
shampoo (noun) sampon [shompon]
shampoo and set mosás és berakás [moshash aysh berokash]
share (verb: room, table etc) megosztani [megostoni]
sharp éles [aylesh]
shaver villanyborotva [villo^{nyuh}borotvo]
shaving foam borotvahab [borotvo-hob]
shaving point konnektor villanyborotva számára [villo^{nyuh}borotvo samaro]
she* ő [ur]
is she here? itt van? [von]
sheet (for bed) lepedő [lepedur]
shelf polc [polts]
sherry 'sherry'
ship hajó [ho-yaw]
by ship hajón [ho-yawn]
shirt ing
shit! a frász törje ki! [o fras tuhr-yeh]
shock (noun) sokk [shok]
I got an electric shock from the ... megrázott a ... [megrazott o]
shock-absorber lökésgátló [luhkayshgatlaw]
shocking botrányos [botran-yosh]
shoe cipő [tsipur]
a pair of shoes egy pár cipő [edj par tsipur]
shoelaces cipőfűző [tsipurfewzur]
shoe polish cipőkrém [tsipurkraym]
shoe repairer cipész [tsipays]
shoe shop cipőbolt [tsipurbolt]
shop üzlet [ewzlet], bolt

Shops are open Mon–Fri 10am–6pm, with supermarkets and grocery stores open 8am–6pm or until 7pm in larger towns. On Saturday most places close at →

1pm. There are exceptions: one or two shops have extended their Saturday opening hours, and in Budapest and other larger centres there are numerous 24-hour shops: the signs to look for are **Non-Stop**, **0-24** or **Éjjel-Nappali**. In areas frequented by tourists, Sunday opening is becoming fairly general.

Department stores are called **Áruház**, while shops are usually named after their wares, for example **húsbolt** (butcher's), **italbolt** (drink), **papír és írószerbolt** (stationery shop) and **cipőbolt** (shoe shop).

In most shops (except supermarkets, some smaller food shops, pharmacies and small boutiques) you first select the goods, the assistant issues you a bill, you pay at the cash desk and then collect your goods against the receipt (**blokk**).

In the old-fashioned ex-state-run shops, there are usually separate exit and entrance doors. **Bejárat** is the entrance and **kijárat** is the exit. In supermarkets, you are expected to take a trolley or a basket, even if you're just looking, and assistants can get very shirty if you don't use the right door and/or take a basket.

shopping: I'm going shopping megyek vásárolni [medjek vasharolni]

shopping centre bevásárló központ [bevasharlaw kuhzpont]

shop window kirakat [kirokot]

shore part [port]

short (person) alacsony [olocho^nyuh]
  (time, journey) rövid [ruhvid]

shortcut rövidre vágot haj [ruhvidreh vagot hoy]

shorts térdnadrág [tayrdnodrag]

should: what should I do? mit csináljak? [chinal-yok]
  you should go to the police menjen a rendőrségre [men-yen o rendur-shaygreh]
  you shouldn't go to the police ne menjen a rendőrségre [neh men-yen o rendur-shaygreh]
  he should be back soon hamarosan vissza kell érnie [homoroshon visso kel ayrni-eh]

shoulder váll

shout (verb) kiabálni [ki-obalni]

show (in theatre) előadás [elurodash]
  could you show me? legyen szíves megmutatni [ledjen seevesh megmoototni]

shower (in bathroom) zuhany [zoo-ho^nyuh]
  (of rain) zápor
  with shower zuhanyozó fülkével [zoo-ho-nyozaw fewlkayvel]

shower gel tusfürdő [toosh-fewrdur]

shut (verb) zárni
  when do you shut? mikor zár be? [beh]

when does it shut? mikor zárják be? [zar-yak beh]
they're shut be vannak zárva [beh vonnok zarvo]
I've shut myself out kizártam magam [kizartom mogom]
shut up! kuss! [koosh-sh]

shutter (on camera) zár
(on window) redőny [redur^{nyuh}]

shy félénk [faylaynk]

sick (ill) beteg
I feel sick hányingerem van [ha-nyingerem von]
I'm going to be sick (vomit) hánynom kell [ha^{nyuh}nom]

side oldal [oldol]
the other side of the street az utca másik oldala [oz oot-tso mashik oldolo]

side lights városi lámpa [varoshi lampo]

side salad saláta [sholato]

side street mellékutca [mellaykoot-tso]

sidewalk járda [yardo]
on the sidewalk a járdán [o yardan]

sight: the sights of ... ... látnivalói [latnivolaw-i]

sightseeing: we're going sightseeing megyünk városnézőbe [medjewnk varoshnay-zurbeh]

sightseeing tour városnéző kirándulás [varoshnay-zur kirandoolash]

sign (roadsign etc) jel [yel]

signal: he didn't give a signal (driver, cyclist) nem jelzett [yelzet]

signature aláírás [ola-eerash]

signpost útjelző tábla [oot-yelzur tablo]

silence csend [chend]

silk selyem [sheh-yem]

silly buta [booto]

silver (noun) ezüst [ezewsht]

similar hasonló [hoshonlaw]

simple (easy) könnyű [kuhn-nyew]

since: since last week múlt hét óta [moolt hayt awto]
since I got here mióta idejöttem [mi-awto iday-yuhttem]

sing énekelni [aynekelni]

singer (man/woman) énekes/énekesnő [aynekesh/aynekeshnur]

single: a single to ... egyszeri utazásra szóló jegyet ...-ra/-re [edj-seri ootozashro sawlaw ...-ro/-reh]
I'm single (said by man/woman) nőtlen/lány vagyok [nurtlen/la^{nyuh} vodjok]

single bed egyszemélyes ágy [edj-semay-yesh adj]

single room egyágyas szoba [edj-adjosh sobo]

single ticket egyszeri utazásra szóló jegy [edj-seri ootozashro sawlaw yedj]

sink (in kitchen) mosogató [moshogotaw]

sister nővér [nurvayr]

sister-in-law sógornő [shawgornur]

sit: can I sit here? leülhetek ide? [leh-ewl-hetek ideh]
is anyone sitting here? ül itt valaki? [ewl it voloki]
sit down leülni [leh-ewlni]
sit down! foglaljon helyet! [foglol-yon heh-yet]
size méret [mayret]
ski (noun) sí [shee]
(verb) síelni [shee-elni]
a pair of skis egy pár sítalp [edj par sheetolp]
skiing sízés [sheezaysh]
ski-lift sílift [sheelift]
skin bőr [bur]
skin-diving buvárúszás [boovaroosash]
skinny vézna [vayzno]
skirt szoknya [sok-nyo]
sky ég [ayg]
sleep (verb) aludni [oloodni]
did you sleep well? jól aludt? [yawl oloodt]
sleeper (on train) hálókocsi [halawkochi]
sleeping bag hálózsák [halawJak]
sleeping car hálókocsi [halawkochi]
sleeping pill altató [oltotaw]
sleeve ujj [oo^{yuh}]
slide (photographic) diapozitív [di-opoziteev]
slip (garment) kombiné [kombinay]
slippery csúszós [choosawsh]
Slovakia Szlovákia [slovaki-o]
Slovenia Szlovén Köztársaság [slovayn kuhztarshoshag]
slow lassú [losh-shoo]
slow down! (driving) lassabban hajtson! [losh-shobbon hoytshon]
slowly lassan [losh-shon]
very slowly nagyon lassan [nodjon]
small kicsi [kichi]
smell: it smells (smells bad) **rossz** szaga van [ross sogo von]
smile (verb) mosolyogni [mosho-yogni]
smoke (noun) füst [fewsht]
do you mind if I smoke? megengedi, hogy dohányozzam? [megengedi hodj do-ha^{nyuh}ozzom]
I don't smoke nem dohányzom [do-ha^{nyuh}zom]
do you smoke? Ön dohányzik? [uhn do-ha^{nyuh}zik]
smoking (compartment) dohányzó szakasz [do-ha^{nyuh}zaw sokos]
snack: just a snack csak egy keveset akarok enni [chok edj keveshet okorok]

A whole range of places purvey snacks, notably **csemege** [chemegeh] (delicatessens), a few of which let you eat on the premises. Many delis (like the **tej-bár** [tay-bar]) use the system whereby customers order and pay at the cash desk (**kassza** [kassa]) in return for a receipt to be exchanged at the food counter.
For sit-down nibbles, people patronize either a **bisztró** [bistraw], which tends to offer a couple of →

hot dishes besides the inevitable salami rolls, a **snackbár**, which is a superior version of the same, or a **büfé** [bewfay]. Many small eateries are called **eszpresszó** [espressaw]. Büfés are found in department stores and stations, and are sometimes open around the clock. The food on offer, though, is often limited to sandwiches and sausages (**hurka** [hoorko] and **kolbász** [kolbas]). On the streets, according to season, vendors preside over vats of **kukorica** [kookoritso] (corn on the cob) or trays of **gesztenye** [gesteh-nyeh] (roast chestnuts), while fried fish (**sült hal** [sewlt hol]) shops are common in towns near rivers or lakes. **Szendvics** [sendvich], **hamburger** [homboorger] and **gofri** (waffle) stands are mushrooming in the larger towns, while McDonald's and Burger King are spreading across the country. Around resorts, another popular munch is **lángos** [langosh]: the Hungarian, mega-size equivalent of doughnuts, often sold with a sprinkling of cheese or a dash of syrup.

sneeze (noun) **tüsszenteni** [tewssenteni]
snorkel légzőcső [laygzurchur]
snow (noun) **hó** [haw]
  it's snowing havazik [hovozik]
so: it's so good olyan jó [o-yon yaw]
  it's so expensive olyan drága
  not so much nem olyan sok [shok]
  not so bad nem olyan rossz [ross]
  so am I, so do I én is [ayn ish]
  so-so úgy-ahogy [oodj-o-hodj]
soaking solution (for contact lenses) **áztató oldat** [aztotaw oldot]
soap szappan [soppon]
soap powder mosópor [moshawpor]
sober józan [yawzon]
socket (electrical) **konnektor**
socks zokni
soda (water) szódavíz [sawdoveez]
sofa díván [deevan]
soft (material etc) **puha** [poo-ho]
soft-boiled egg lágytojás [ladjto-yash]
soft drink üdítő [ewdeetur]

Pepsi® and Coke® and various sugary, fruit-flavoured soft drinks are sold everywhere. A few (mostly German) brands of unsweetened fruit juices can be found in supermarkets and Vitamin Porta shops. Most supermarkets also stock bottled **limonádé** [limonaday], mineral water (**ásványvíz** ashva[nyuh]veez), soda water (**szódavíz** [sawdoveez]) and a range of fruit juices.

soft lenses lágy lencse [ladj

lencheh]

sole (of shoe, of foot) talp [tolp]

could you put new soles on these? lenne szíves ezeket megtalpalni? [lenneh seevesh ezeket megtolpolni]

some: can I have some water? kaphatnék egy kis vizet? [kop-hotnayk edj kish vizet]

can I have some rolls? kaphatnék néhány zsemlét? [nay-han^{yuh}]

can I have some? kaphatnék abból? [obbawl]

somebody, someone valaki [voloki]

something valami [volomi]

something to eat valami ennivaló [ennivolaw]

sometimes néha [nayho]

somewhere valahol [volo-hol]

son fia [fi-o]

song dal [dol]

son-in-law vő [vur]

soon hamar [homor]

I'll be back soon nemsokára újra itt leszek [nemshokaro oo^{yuh}ro it lesek]

as soon as possible mihelyt lehet [mi-hayt]

sore: it's sore sajog [sho-yog]

sore throat torokfájás [torokfī-ash]

sorry: sorry! bocsánatot kérek! [bochanotot kayrek]

sorry? (didn't understand/hear) tessék? [tesh-shayk]

sort: what sort of ...? miféle ...? [mifayleh]

soup leves [levesh]

sour (taste) savanyú [shovo-nyoo]

sour cream tejfel [tayfel]

south Dél [dayl]

in the south délen [daylen]

South Africa Dél-Afrika [dayl-ofriko]

South African dél-afrikai [dayl-ofriko-ee]

I'm South African dél-afrikai vagyok [vodjok]

southeast dél-kelet [dayl-kelet]

southern déli [dayli]

southwest dél-nyugat [dayl-nyoogot]

souvenir emléktárgy [emlayktardj]

spa gyógyfürdőhely [djawdj-fewrdur-heh^{yuh}]

Spain Spanyolország [shpo^{nyuh}olorsag]

Spanish spanyol [shpo-nyol]

spanner franciakulcs [frontsi-okoolch]

spare parts pótalkatrész [pawtolkotrays]

spare tyre pótkerék [pawtkerayk]

spark plug gyújtógyertya [djoo^{yuh}tawdjer-tyo]

speak beszélni [besaylni]

do you speak English/German? tud Ön angolul/németül? [tood uhn ongolool/naymetewl]

I don't speak Hungarian nem tudok magyarul [toodok modjorool]

•••••• DIALOGUE ••••••

can I speak to Zoltán? szeretnék Zoltánnal beszélni? [seretnayk]
who's calling? ki beszél?
it's Patricia Patricia beszél
I'm sorry, he's not in, can I take a message? sajnálom, nincs itthon, akar üzenetet hagyni? [shoynalom ninch it-hon okor ewzenetet hodjni]
no thanks, I'll call back later köszönöm, nem, majd megint telefonálok később [kuhsuhnuhm nem moyd megint telefonalok kayshurb]
please tell him I called legyen szíves megmondani, hogy hívtam [ledjen seevesh megmondoni hodj heevtom]

spectacles szemüveg [semewveg]
spell: how do you spell it? hogy írják? [hodj eer-yak]
see **alphabet**
spend költeni [kuhlteni]
spider pók [pawk]
spin-dryer szárítógép [sareetawgayp]

> **spirits**
> As long as you stick to native brands, spirits are cheap. The best-known type of **pálinka** – brandy – is distilled from apricots (**barack**), and is a speciality of the Kecskemét region, but spirits are also produced from peaches (**őszibarack**), pears (**kőrte**), plums (**szilva**) and other fruit. Sometimes it's possible to get hold of the **kisüsti** [kisewshti] (small cauldron) variety of these brandies. Distilled on a smaller scale, these tend to be clearer, stronger and more genuine altogether.
> Hungarians with money to burn order whisky (**viszki** [viski]) to impress, but most people find its cost prohibitive. Vodka isn't popular, despite the availability of excellent Russian **Stolichnaya**.

spoon kanál [konal]
sport sport [shport]
sports centre sport telep [shport]
sprain: I've sprained my ... kificamítottam a ... [kifitsomee-tottom o]
spring (season) tavasz [tovos]
(of car, seat) rúgó [roogaw]
in the spring tavasszal [tovossol]
square (in town) tér [tayr]
stairs lépcső [laypchur]
stale állott
stall: the engine keeps stalling a motor mindig leáll [o mo-tor mindig leh-al]
stamp (noun) bélyeg [bay-yeg]

•••••• DIALOGUE ••••••

a stamp for England, please kérek egy bélyeget Angliába [kayrek edj bay-yeget ongli-abo]
what are you sending? milyen küldeményre? [mi-yen kewldeh-may[nyuh]reh]

ENGLISH ❖ HUNGARIAN | Sp

this postcard erre a lapra [erreh o lopro]
see post office

standby várólista [varawlishto]
star csillag [chillog]
(in film) filmsztár [filmstar]
start (noun) kezdet
(verb) kezdeni
when does it start? mikor kezdődik? [kezdurdik]
the car won't start az autó nem akar beindulni [oz owtaw nem okor beh-indoolni]
starter (of car) önindító [uhnindeetaw]
(food) előétel [eluraytel]
starving: I'm starving farkaséhes vagyok [forkoshayhesh vodjok]
state (country) állam [allom]
the States (USA) az Egyesült Államok [oz edjeshewlt allomok]
station állomás [allomash]
(main) pályaudvar [pa-yowdvor]
stationery írószer és papíráru [eerawser aysh popeeraroo]
statue szobor [sobor]
stay: where are you staying? hol szállt meg? [sallt]
I'm staying at ... a ...-ban/-ben lakom [...-bon/-ben lokom]
I'd like to stay another two nights szeretnék még két éjszakára itt maradni [seretnayk mayg kayt ay[yuh]sokaro it morodni]
steak szték [stayk]
steal lopni
my bag has been stolen ellopták a táskámat [o tashkamot]
steep (hill) meredek
steering kormánymű [korma[nyuh]mew]
step: on the steps a lépcsőn [o laypchurn]
stereo sztereó [stereh-aw]
sterling sterling [shterling]
steward (on plane) légiutaskisérő [laygi-ootosh-kishayrur], pincér (hajón) [pintsayr (ho-yawn)]
stewardess légikisasszony [laygi-kishosso[nyuh]], 'stewardess'
still: I'm still here még mindig itt vagyok [mayg – vodjok]
is he still there? itt van még? [von]
keep still! maradj nyugton! [morodj nyoogton]
sting: I've been stung by a wasp megcsípett egy darázs [megcheepett edj doraJ]
stockings harisnya [horish-nyo]
stomach gyomor [djomor]
stomachache gyomorfájás [djomorfī-ash]
stone (rock) kő [kur]
stop (verb) megállni
please, stop here (to taxi driver etc) itt álljon meg, kérem [al-yon meg kayrem]
do you stop near ...? megáll a ... közelében? [o ... kuhzelayben]
stop it! hagyd abba! [hodjd obbo]
stopover rövid tartózkodás [ruhvid tortawzkodash]

(for an hour or two) útmegszakítás [ootmegsokeetash]
storm vihar [vi-hor]
straight (whisky etc) tisztán [tistan]
it's straight ahead egyenesen előre kell menni [edjeneshen elurreh]
straightaway azonnal [ozonnol]
strange (odd) különös [kewluhnuhsh]
stranger idegen
I'm a stranger here idegen vagyok errefelé [vodjok errefelay]
strap szíj [see^yuh]
strawberry eper
stream patak [potok]
street utca [oot-tso]
on the street az utcán [oz oot-tsan]
streetmap várostérkép [varosh-tayrkayp]
string spárga [shpargo]
strong erős [erursh]
stuck megakadt [megokodt]
it's stuck megakadt
student (male/female) egyetemi hallgató/hallgatónő [edjetemi hollgotaw/hollgotawnur]
stupid buta [booto]
suburbs külvárosok [kewlvaroshok]
subway (US: railway) metró [metraw]
suddenly hirtelen
suede szarvasbőr [sorvoshbur]
sugar cukor [tsookor]
suit (noun: man's) öltöny [uhltuh^nyuh]
(woman's) kosztüm [kostewm]
it doesn't suit me (jacket etc) nem áll jól nekem [al yawl]
it suits you jól áll Önnek [uhnnek]
suitcase bőrönd [buruhnd]
summer nyár
in the summer nyáron
sun nap [nop]
in the sun a napon [o nopon]
out of the sun árnyékban [ar-nyaykbon]
sunbathe napozni [nopozni]
sunblock (cream) napolaj [nopoloy]
sunburn leégés [leh-aygaysh]
sunburnt lesült [leshewlt]
Sunday vasárnap [vosharnop]
sunglasses napszemüveg [nopsemewveg]
sun lounger nyugágy [nyoogadj]
sunny: it's sunny napos az idő [noposh oz idur]
sunroof (in car) ablaktető [obloktetur]
sunset naplemente [noplementeh]
sunshade napellenző [nopellenzur]
sunshine napsütés [nopshewtaysh]
sunstroke napszúrás [nopsoorash]
suntan lesülés [leshewlaysh]
suntan lotion napolaj [nopoloy]
suntanned lesült [leshewlt]
suntan oil napolaj [nopoloy]
super remek

supermarket szupermárket [soopermarket]
supper vacsora [vochoro]
supplement (extra charge) melléklet [mellayklet]
sure: are you sure? tényleg? [tay^{nyuh}leg]
sure! persze! [perseh]
surname vezetéknév [vezetayknayv]
swearword szitok [sitok]
sweater pulóver [poolawver]
sweatshirt alsóing [olshawing]
Sweden Svédország [shvaydorsag]
Swedish svéd [shvayd]
sweet (taste) édes [aydesh]
(noun: dessert) édesség [aydesh-shayg]
sweets cukorka [tsookorko]
swelling daganat [dogonot]
swim (verb) úszni [oosni]
I'm going for a swim megyek úszni [medjek]
let's go for a swim menjünk úszni [men-yewnk]
swimming costume fürdőruha [fewrdur-roo-ho]
swimming pool (indoor) uszoda [oosodo]
(outdoor) strand [shtrond]
swimming trunks úszónadrág [oosawnodrag]
switch (noun) kapcsoló [kopcholaw]
switch off (TV) kikapcsolni [kikopcholni]
(light) eloltani [eloltoni]
(engine) leállítani [leh-aleetoni]
switch on (TV) bekapcsolni [bekopcholni]
(light) meggyújtani [megdjoo^{yuh}toni]
(engine) beindítani [beh-indeetoni]
Switzerland Svájc [shvīts]
swollen dagadt [dogot]
synagogue zsinagóga [Jinogawgo]

T

table asztal [ostol]
a table for two egy asztalt szeretnék két személyre [edj ostolt seretnayk kayt semay^{yuh}reh]
tablecloth terítő [tereetur]
table tennis asztali tenisz [ostoli tenis]
table wine asztali bor
tailor szabó [sobaw]
take (verb: lead) elvinni
(accept) venni
can you take me to the ...? legyen szíves vigyen el a ... [ledjen seevesh vidjen el o]
do you take credit cards? fizethetek kreditkártyával? [kreditkar-tyavol]
fine, I'll take it jól van, megveszem [yawl von megvesem]
can I take this? (leaflet etc) elvehetem?
how long does it take? meddig tart? [tort]
it takes three hours három óráig tart [awra-ig]

is this seat taken? foglalt ez a hely? [foglolt ez o heh^yuh]
hamburger to take away hamburger utcán át [homboorger oot-tsan]
can you take a little off here? (to hairdresser) itt vegyen le belőle egy kicsit [vedjen leh belurleh edj kichit]
talcum powder púder [pooder]
talk (verb) beszélni [besaylni]
tall magas [mogosh]
tampon tampon [tompon]
tan (noun) lesülés [leshewlaysh]
to get a tan lesülni [leshewlni]
tank (of car) benzintartály [benzintortay]
tap csap [chop]
tape (for cassette) kazetta [kozetto]
tape measure mérőszalag [mayrursolog]
tape recorder magnó [mognaw]
taste (noun) ízlés [eezlaysh]
can I taste it? megkóstolhatom? [megkawshtol-hotom]
taxi taxi [toksi]
will you get me a taxi? legyen szíves, hívjon egy taxit nekem [ledjen seevesh heev-yon edj toksit]
where can I find a taxi? hol találhatok taxit? [tolal-hotok toksit]

••••• DIALOGUE •••••

to the airport/to the ... Hotel, please a repülőtérre/a ... szállóba megyek [o repewlurtayrreh/o ... sallawbo medjek]
how much will it be? mennyi lesz? [men-nyi les]
900 forints kilencszáz forint
that's fine right here, thanks itt jó lesz, köszönöm [yaw les kuhsuhnuhm]

The use of taxis is increasingly problematic as meters are habitually rigged, night-rates exaggerated out of all proportion, and many drivers will simply name a sum at the outset without reference to the meter altogether. This racket affects especially Ferihegy (Budapest) Airport and the taxi ranks outside some of the major international hotels.
Some taxi companies are better than others; the 'chequered taxis' (distinguished by a stripe of red and white squares) have a better reputation than the rest. That said, the foreign visitor with little or no Hungarian should ignore the taxi rank at Ferihegy, and go for the Airport Minibus Service (**repülőtéri minibusz** [repewlurtayri miniboos]), which is announced in several languages while passengers queue for passport control. These minibuses will take the passenger and his/her luggage anywhere in Budapest for a very reasonable fare.
see **tip**

taxi-driver taxisofőr [toksi-shoffur]
taxi rank taxiállomás [toksi-allomash]
tea (drink) tea [teh-o]
tea for one/two please teát kérek egy/két személyre [teh-at kayrek edj/kayt semay^{yuh}reh]
teabags teazacskók [teh-ozoch-kawk]
teach: could you teach me? megtanítana? [megtoneetono]
teacher (secondary school: man/woman) **tanár/tanárnő** [tonar/tonarnur]
(primary school: man/woman) tanító/tanítónő [toneetaw/toneetawnur]
team csapat [chopot]
teaspoon kávéskanál [kavaysh-konal]
tea towel konyharuha [ko^{nyuh}horoo-ho]
teenager (male/female) **kamasz/kamasz lány** [komos/komos la^{nyuh}]
telegram távirat [tavirot]
telephone telefon
see **phone**
television televízió [televeezi-aw], tévé [tayvay]
tell: could you tell him ...? megmondaná neki, hogy ...? [megmondona neki hodj]
temperature (weather) hőmérséklet [hurmayrshayklet]
tennis tenisz [tenis]
tennis court teniszpálya [tenispa-yo]
tennis racket teniszütő [tenis-ewtur]
tent sátor [shator]
terminus (rail) végállomás [vaygallomash]
terrible rettenetes [rettenetesh]
terrific nagyszerű [nodjserew]
than mint
smaller than kisebb mint
thank: thank you köszönöm [kuhsuhnuhm]
thank you very much köszönöm szépen [saypen]
thanks köszönet [kuhsuhnet]
no thanks köszönöm, nem
thanks for the lift köszönöm, hogy elhozott [hodj]

•••••• DIALOGUE ••••••

thanks köszönet
that's OK, don't mention it
szívesen, nincs mit [seeveshen ninch]

that* (adj) az a [oz o]
that one az
I hope that ... remélem, hogy ... [remaylem hodj]
that's nice nagyon kedves [nodjon kedvesh]
is that ...? ...-val/-vel beszélek? [-vol/-vel besaylek]
that's it (that's right) úgy van [oodj von]
the* a [o]
(plural) az [oz]
theatre színház [seenhaz]
their* az ő ...-juk/-jük [oz ur ...-yook/-yewk]
theirs* az övék [oz urvayk]

them* azokat [ozokot]
(people) őket [urket]
for them, to them nekik
with them velük [velewk]
who? – them ki? – ők [urk]
then (at that time) akkor [okkor]
(after that) aztán [oztan]
there ott
over there amott [omot]
up there odafönn [odofuhn]
is/are there ...? van/vannak ...? [von/vonnok]
there is/are ... van/vannak ...
there you are (giving something) tessék [tesh-shayk]
thermal baths gyógyfürdő [djawdj-fewrdur]
thermometer hőmérő [hurmayrur]
Thermos® flask termosz [termos]
these* ezek a [o]
I'd like these ezeket szeretném [seretnaym]
they* ők [urk]
thick vastag [voshtog]
(stupid) ostoba [oshtobo]
thief tolvaj [tolvoy]
thigh comb [tsomb]
thin vékony [vayko^{nyuh}]
thing dolog
my things a holmim [o]
think: I think so azt hiszem, igen [ozt hisem]
I don't think so nem hiszem
I'll think about it majd meggondolom [moyd meggondolom]
third party insurance kötelező biztosítás [kuhtelezur biztosheetash]
thirsty: I'm thirsty szomjas vagyok [som-yosh vodjok]
this* (adj) ez a [o]
this one ez
this is my wife ez a feleségem [feleshaygem]
is this ...? ez ...?
those* (adj) azok a [ozok o]
which ones? – those melyikek? – azok [meh-yikek – ozok]
thread (noun) cérna [tsayrno]
throat torok
throat pastilles torokfájás elleni cukorka [torokfī-ash – tsookorko]
through keresztül [kerestewl]
does it go through ...? (train, bus) átmegy ...-en/-on/-ön [atmedj ...-en/-on/-uhn]
throw (verb) dobni
throw away eldobni
thumb hüvelykujj [hewvay^{yuh}koo^{yuh}]
thunderstorm vihar [vihor]
Thursday csütörtök [chewturtuhk]
ticket jegy [yedj]

•••••• DIALOGUE ••••••

a return to Szeged kérek egy menettérti jegyet Szegedre [kayrek edj menettayrti yedjet segedreh]
coming back when? mikor akar visszajönni? [okor visso-yuhnni]
today/next Tuesday ma/kedden
that will be 2,000 forints kétezer forint

ticket office pénztár [paynztar]
tie (necktie) nyakkendő [nyokkendur]
tight (clothes etc) szűk [sewk]
it's too tight túl szűk [tool]
tights harisnyanadrág [horish-nyonodrag]
till (cash desk) pénztár [paynztar], kassza [kosso]
time* (occasion) ...-szer/-szor/-ször [-ser/-sor/-sur]
what time is it? hány óra (van)? [ha^nyuh awro (von)]
this time ezúttal [ezoottol]
last time legutoljára [legootol-yaro]
next time legközelebb [legkuh-zeleb]
three times háromszor [haromsor]
we have plenty of time bőven van időnk [burven von idurnk]
timetable menetrend
tin (can) konzerv
tinfoil sztaniol [stoni-ol]
tin-opener konzervnyitó [konzerv-nyitaw]
tiny pici [pitsi]
tip (to waiter etc) borravaló [borrovolaw]

> A service charge isn't usually included in a restaurant bill and the staff depend on customers tipping: you should leave about 10–15 per cent, as in most other countries, but the etiquette is slightly different. When you ask to pay, the waiter will often come and stand by the table waiting for you to pay. To tip, you tell the waiter how much you are adding on, so that they know how much change to bring back. Do not simply say 'thank you', because 'thank you' means 'keep the change'.
> Taxi drivers also expect tips of 10 per cent or, if you feel certain that you have been badly cheated, round the sum up to the nearest hundred. Should you accept a start-of-journey quotation and the meter isn't used, no tipping is necessary at all.
> Tips are expected in hotels, for the boy who carries your luggage to your room (100 forints is in order), and for anyone who renders a service not charged for by the hotel.

tired fáradt [farodt]
I'm tired fáradt vagyok [vodjok]
tissues papírzsebkendő [popeerJebkendur]
to* (place) ...-ra/-re [-ro/-reh]
(place abroad) ...-ba/-be [-bo/-beh]
(someone) ...-nak/-nek [-nok/-nek]
to Budapest/London Budapestre/Londonba [boodopeshtreh/londonbo]
to Hungary/England Magyarországra/Angliába [modjororsagro/ongli-abo]

to the post office a postára [o poshtaro]
to the receptionist a recepciósnak [o retseptsi-awshnok]
toast (bread) pirított kenyér [pireetot keh-nyayr]
today ma [mo]
toe lábujj [laboo[yuh]]
together együtt [edjewt]
we're together (in shop etc) együtt vagyunk [vodjoonk]
toilet W.C. [vay tsay], mosdó [moshdaw]
where is the toilet? hol van a W.C.? [von o]
I have to go to the toilet a W.C.-re kell mennem [–reh]

> Use public conveniences only as a last resort: they are inconvenient and often filthy to the point of being dangerously unhygienic. Your best bet is a hotel, department store, restaurant, museum or other public building.
> The attendant expects a small tip; your best guide to the sum is the denomination of coins already in the plate which is prominently displayed.

toilet paper W.C. papír [vay tsay popeer]
tomato paradicsom [porodichom]
tomato juice paradicsomlé [porodichomlay]
tomato ketchup kecsup [kechoop]
tomorrow holnap [holnop]
tomorrow morning (9am–noon) holnap délelőtt [holnop daylelurt]
(4–9am) holnap reggel
the day after tomorrow holnapután [holnopootan]
toner (cosmetic) arcfrissítő [ortsfrish-sheetur]
tongue nyelv
tonic (water) 'tonic'
tonight ma este [mo eshteh], ma éjjel [ay-yel]
tonsillitis mandulagyulladás [mondoolo-djoollodash]
too (excessively) túl(ságosan) [tool(shagoshon)]
(also) is [ish]
too hot túl meleg [tool]
too much túl sok [shok]
me too én is [ayn ish]
tooth fog
toothache fogfájás [fogfī-ash]
toothbrush fogkefe [fogkefeh]
toothpaste fogkrém [fogkraym]
top: on top of ... a ... tetején [o ... teta-yayn]
at the top legfelül [legfelewl]
top floor legfelső emelet [legfelshur]
topless 'topless'
torch zseblámpa [Jeblampo]
total (noun) végösszeg [vayguhsseg]
tour (noun) kirándulás [kirandoolash]
is there a tour of ...? lehet ...-ba/-be kirándulni? [-bo/-beh kirandoolni]

tour guide kalauz [kolowz], idegenvezető [idegen-vezetur]
tourist túrista [toorishto]
tourist information office túristairoda [toorishto-eerodo]

In Hungary itself you'll find local tourist agencies in most larger towns and a growing network of Tourinform offices, set up by the Hungarian Tourist Board, which have excellent information on accommodation and activities, although they do not book rooms. Tourinform offices hand out a free monthly magazine, 'Programme', which details tourist events throughout Hungary. There are also four other agencies operating nationwide: Ibusz; Volántourist, which specializes in travel bookings and tour groups; Cooptourist, which deals with car and apartment rental for relatively upmarket travellers; and the 'youth travel' agency, Express, which no longer confines itself to the under-35s and will now book anyone into its stable of hotels and campsites, or college hostels, which are vacant at weekends and during school holidays.

towards felé [felay]
towel törülköző [tuhrewl-kuhzur]
town város [varosh]
in town a városban [o varoshbon]
just out of town a város közelében [o varosh kuhzelayben]
town centre belváros [belvarosh], város központ [varosh kuhzpont]
town hall városháza [varoshhazo]
toy játék [yatayk]
track (US) vágány [vaga^{nyuh}]
(where passengers wait) peron
which track is it for Miskolc? melyik vágányról indul a miskolci vonat? [may-yik vaga^{nyuh}rawl indool o mishkoltsi vonot]
tracksuit melegítő [melegeetur]
traditional hagyományos [hodjoma-nyosh]
traffic forgalom [forgolom]
traffic lights forgalmi lámpa [forgolmi lampo]
trailer (for carrying tent etc) utánfutó [ootanfootaw]
(US: caravan) lakókocsi [lokawkochi]
trailer park lakókocsi parkoló [porkolaw]
train vonat [vonot]
by train vonaton

•••••• DIALOGUE ••••••

is this the train for Pécs? ez a vonat megy Pécsre? [o vonot medj paychreh]
sure hogyne [hodjneh]
no, you want that platform there nem, ahhoz a vágányhoz kell mennie [o-hoz o vaga^{nyuh}hoz kel menni-eh]

The centralization of the **MÁV** rail network means that many cross-country journeys are easier if you travel via Budapest rather than on branch lines. Timetables are in yellow (for departures) and white (for arrivals), with the different types of fast trains picked out in red. The fastest are the **Intercity** (**IC**) trains, which run express services between Budapest and Miskolc, Szeged and other larger towns; and **Express** trains (**Ex**), stopping at major centres only, and costing ten per cent more than **gyorsvonat** [djorshvonot] and **sebesvonat** [shebeshvonot] services, which stop more regularly. The slowest trains (**személyvonat** [semay^yuh^vonot]) halt at every hamlet along the way, and since the fare is the same as on a gyorsvonat, you might as well opt for the latter.

All trains have first- and second-class sections, and many also feature a buffet car (indicated on timetables). International services routed through Budapest have sleeping cars and couchettes (**hálókocsi** [halawkochi] and **kusett** [kooshet]), for which tickets can be bought at MÁV offices in advance, or sometimes on the train itself.

Finding out travel information (**információ** [informatsi-aw]) can be your biggest problem, since transport staff rarely speak anything but Hungarian, which is the only language used for notices and announcements (except around Lake Balaton, where German is widely spoken).

Tickets for domestic train services can be bought at the station on the day of departure, although it's possible to reserve them up to sixty days in advance. You can break your journey once between the point of departure and the final destination, but must get your ticket validated within an hour of arrival at the interim station. Most Hungarians purchase one-way tickets (**egy útra** [edj ootro]), so specify a **retur** [retoor] or **oda-vissza** [odo-vissa] if you want a return ticket.

Seat bookings (**helyjegy** [hay-yedj]), in the form of a separate numbered bit of card, are obligatory for services marked R in a square on the timetable and optional on those designated by an R in a circle. They can be made up to two months in advance at any MÁV or Volántourist office. Fares on Intercity trains automatically include reservations.

It's best to buy tickets for international trains (**nemzetközi gyorsvonat** [nemzetkuhzi djorshvonot]) at least 36 hours in →

advance, since demand is heavy. MÁV issues various train passes, valid on domestic lines nationwide for a week or ten days, but you'd need to travel fairly extensively to make savings. There's also a short-term Hungarian Flexipass, which you must buy at home before departure.

trainers (shoes) tornacipő [tornotsipur]
train station vasútállomás [voshoot-allomash]
tram villamos [villomosh]
see **bus**
Transdanubia Dunántúl [doonantool]
translate lefordítani [lefordeetoni]
could you translate that? legyen szíves, fordítsa ezt le nekem [ledjen seevesh fordeetsho ezt leh]
translation fordítás [fordeetash]
translator fordító [fordeetaw]
trash szemét [semayt]
trashcan szemétláda [semaytlado]
travel utazni [ootozni]
we're travelling around utazgatunk [ootozgotoonk]
travel agent's utazási ügynökség [ootozashi ewdj-nuhkshayg], utazási iroda [ootozashi irodo]
traveller's cheque utazó csekk [ootozaw chek], travellercsekk [travellerchek]

Although a modest amount of low-denomination US dollar bills or Deutschmarks can be useful, it's safest to carry the bulk of your money in traveller's cheques. Traveller's cheques issued by American, British, Dutch, Norwegian and German banks are all accepted; but for speedy refunds in case of loss, American Express is by far the most reliable brand.

tray tálca [taltso]
tree fa [fo]
trendy divatos [divotosh]
trim: just a trim please (to hairdresser) csak kiigazítást kérek [chok ki-igozeetasht kayrek]
trip (excursion) kirándulás [kirandoolash]
I'd like to go on a trip to ... szeretnék ...-ba/be kirándulni [seretnayk ...-bo/beh kirandoolni]
trolley tolókocsi [tolawkochi]
trolley bus troli(busz) [troli(boos)]
see **bus**
trouble (noun) baj [boy]
I'm having trouble with ... meggyűlt a bajom ...-val/-vel [megdjewlt o bo-yom ...-vol/-vel]
trousers nadrág [nodrag]
truck teherautó [teher-owtaw]
true igaz [igoz]
that's not true az nem igaz [oz

trunk (US: of car) csomagtartó [chomogtortaw]
trunks (swimming) fürdőnadrág [fewrdurnodrag]
try (verb) megpróbálni [megprawbalni]
can I try it? kipróbálhatom? [kiprawbal-hotom]
try on felpróbálni [felprawbalni]
can I try it on? felpróbálhatom? [felprawbal-hotom]
T-shirt alsóing [olshawing]
Tuesday kedd
tunnel alagút [ologoot]
Turkish baths gőzfürdő [gurzfewrdur]
turn: turn left/right forduljon balra/jobbra [fordool-yon bolro/yobbro]
turn off: where do I turn off? hol kell befordulnom? [befordoolnom]
can you turn the heating off? lenne szíves kikapcsolni a fűtést? [lenneh seevesh kikopcholni o fewtaysht]
turn on: can you turn the heating on? lenne szíves bekapcsolni a fűtést? [bekopcholni]
turning (in road) kanyar [ko-nyor]
TV tévé [tayvay]
tweezers csipesz [chipes]
twice kétszer [kaytser]
twice as much kétszer annyi [on-nyi]
twin beds két külön ágy [kayt kewluhn adj]
twin room kétágyas szoba [kaytadjosh sobo]
twist: I've twisted my ankle kificamodott a bokám [kifitsomodot o bokom]
type (noun) típus [teepoosh]
another type of ... másfajta ... [mashfoyto]
typical tipikus [tipikoosh]
tyre gumi [goomi]

U

ugly csúnya [choo-nyo]
UK UK [oo-ka], EK [eh-ka]
Ukraine Ukrajna [ookroyno]
Ukrainian ukrán [ookran]
umbrella esernyő [esher-nyur]
uncle nagybácsi [nodjbachi]
unconscious eszméletlen [esmayletlen]
under (in position) alatt [olot]
(less than) nem egészen [egaysen]
underdone (meat) angolosan [ongoloshon]
underground (railway) metró [metraw]

The underground railway in Budapest is called the Metro, although the Hungarian word **földalatti** (underground) exists and is also used. The ticket is the same as on buses, trolley buses and trams, and has to be validated in the machines set up at the top of the escalators. As on other forms of transport, the →

standard ticket is for one journey only, but it's possible to buy transfer tickets which allow transfer to another Metro line.

underpants alsónadrág [olshawnodrag]
understand: I understand értem [ayrtem]
I don't understand nem értem
do you understand? Ön érti? [uhn ayrti]
unemployed munkanélküli [moonkonaylkewli]
unfashionable nem divatos [divotosh]
United States Egyesült Államok [edjeshewlt allomok]
university egyetem [edjetem]
unleaded petrol ólommentes benzin [awlommentesh]
unlimited mileage távolságkorlátozás nélkül [tavolshagkor-latozash naylkewl]
unlock kinyitni [ki-nyitni]
unpack kicsomagolni [kichomogolni]
until ...-ig
unusual szokatlan [sokotlon]
up fel
up there odafenn [odofenn]
he's not up yet (not out of bed) még nincs fenn [mayg ninch]
what's up? (what's wrong?) mi baj? [boy]
upmarket (restaurant, hotel) elegáns [elegansh]
upset stomach gyomorrontás [djomorrontash]
upside down fejjel lefelé [fay-yel lefelay]
upstairs az emeleten [oz]
up-to-date naprakész [noprokays]
urgent sürgős [shewrgursh]
us* minket
for us, to us nekünk [nekewnk]
with us velünk [velewnk]
USA USA [oosho], Egyesült Államok [edjeshewlt allomok]
use (verb) használni [hosnalni]
may I use ...? használhatom a ...-t? [hosnalhotom o]
useful hasznos [hosnosh]
usual szokásos [sokashosh]
the usual (drink etc) a szokásosat [o sokashoshot]

V

vacancy: do you have any vacancies? (hotel) van kiadó szobájuk? [von ki-odaw sobī-ook]
see **room**
vacation (from university) vakáció [vokatsi-aw]
(US: holiday) szabadság [sobod-shag], ünnep [ewnnep]
on vacation szabadságon [sobod-shagon]
vaccination oltás [oltash]
vacuum cleaner porszívó [porsee-vaw]
valid (ticket etc) érvényes [ayrvay-nyesh]
how long is it valid for?

meddig érvényes?
valley völgy [vuhldj]
valuable (adj) értékes [ayrtaykesh]
can I leave my valuables here? itt hagyhatom az értéktárgyaimat? [hodj-hotom oz ayrtayk-tardjo-eemot]
value (noun) érték [ayrtayk]
van furgon [foorgon]
vanilla vanília [voneeli-o]
a vanilla ice cream vaníliafagylalt [–fodjlolt]
vary: it varies változó [valtozaw]
vase váza [vazo]
veal borjúhús [bor-yoo-hoosh]
vegetables zöldség [zuhldshayg]
vegetarian (noun) vegetariánus [veg-etori-anoosh]

Despite the emergence of **vegetariánus** restaurants in Budapest, and a growing understanding of the concept, the outlook for vegetarians remains poor: most Hungarians are amazed that anyone might forgo meat willingly. Apart from cooked vegetables (notably **rántott gomba**, mushrooms in breadcrumbs), the only meatless dish that's widely available is eggs: **tükörtojás** [tewkuhr-to-yash] (fried, literally 'mirror'), **lágy tojás** [ladj to-yash] (soft-boiled), **tojásrántotta** [to-yash-rantotto] (scrambled), or **kaszinótojás** [kasinawto-yash] in (in mayonnaise). Even innocuous vegetable soups may contain meat stock, and the pervasive use of sour cream and animal fat in cooking means that avoiding animal products or by-products is difficult.

vending machine automata [owtomoto]
very nagyon [nodjon]
very little for me nagyon keveset kérek [keveshet kayrek]
I like it very much nagyon szeretem [seretem]
vest (under shirt) trikó [trikaw]
via ... útján [oot-yan]
video 'video'
Vienna Bécs [baych]
view kilátás [kilatash]
village falu [foloo]
vinegar ecet [etset]
vineyard szőlő [surlur]
violin hegedű [hegedew]
visa vízum [veezoom]
visit (verb) meglátogatni [meglatogotni]
I'd like to visit ... szeretnék elmenni a ...-ba/-be [seretnayk elmenni o ...-bo/-beh]
vital: it's vital that ... létfontosságú, hogy ... [laytfontosh-shagoo hodj]
vodka 'vodka'
voice hang [hong]
volleyball röplabda [ruhplobdo]
voltage feszültség [fesewltshayg]
vomit (verb) hányni [ha^{nyuh}ni]

W

waist derék [derayk]
waistcoat mellény [mellay[nyuh]]
wait várni
wait for me várjon meg [varyon]
don't wait for me ne várjon rám [neh]
can I wait until my wife gets here? megvárhatom, amíg a feleségem megérkezik? [megvar-hotom omeeg o feleshaygem megayrkezik]
can you do it while I wait? meg tudja csinálni, amíg itt vagyok? [tood-yo chinalni omeeg it vodjok]
could you wait here for me? legyen szíves, várjon meg [ledjen seevesh var-yon]
waiter pincér [pintsayr]
waiter! legyen szíves! [ledjen seevesh]
waitress pincérnő [pintsayrnur]
waitress! kisasszony! [kishosso[nyuh]], legyen szíves! [ledjen seevesh]
wake: can you wake me up at 5.30? legyen szíves fél hatkor felkelteni [ledjen seevesh – felkelteni]
wake-up call keltés [keltaysh]
Wales Wales [vels]
walk: is it a long walk? hosszú gyalogút? [hossoo djologoot]
it's only a short walk csak rövid séta [chok ruhvid shayto]
I'll walk én gyalog megyek [ayn djolog medjek]
I'm going for a walk megyek sétálni [shaytalni]
wall fal [fol]
wallet levéltárca [levayl-tartso]
wander: I like just wandering around szeretek barangolni [seretek borongolni]
want: I want a ... egy ...-t szeretnék [edj – seretnayk]
I don't want any ... nem kell ...
I want to go home haza akarok menni [hozo okorok]
I don't want to ... nem akarok ...
he wants to ... ... akar [okor]
what do you want? mit akar?
ward (in hospital) kórterem [kawrterem]
warm meleg
I'm so warm melegem van [von]
was* volt
wash (verb) mosni [moshni]
(oneself) mosakodni [moshokodni]
can you wash these? lenne szíves kimosni ezeket? [lenneh seevesh kimoshni ezeket]
washer (for bolt etc) alátét [olatayt]
washhand basin mosdókagyló [moshdawkodj-law]
washing (clothes) mosott ruha [moshott roo-ho]
washing machine mosógép [moshawgayp]
washing powder mosópor

[moshawpor]
washing-up: to do the washing-up mosogatni [moshogotni]
washing-up liquid mosogatószer [moshogotawser]
wasp darázs [doraJ]
watch (wristwatch) karóra [korawro]
will you watch my things for me? lenne szíves vigyázni a holmimra? [lenneh seevesh vidjazni o holmimro]
watch out! vigyázzon! [vidjazzon]
watch strap óraszíj [awrosee^yuh]
water víz [veez]
may I have some water? kaphatnék egy kis vizet? [kop-hotnayk edj kish]

> Tap water is safe everywhere, while potable springs (**forrás** [forrash]) and streams are designated on maps, and with signs, as **ivóvíz** [ivawveez].

waterproof (adj) vízhatlan [veez-hotlon]
waterskiing vízisíelés [veezisheh-eelaysh]
wave (in sea) hullám [hoollam]
way: it's this way erre tessék [erreh tesh-shayk]
it's that way arra tessék [orro tesh-shayk]
is it a long way to ...? messze van ide ...? [messeh von ideh]
no way! szó sem lehet róla! [saw shem lehet rawlo]

••••• DIALOGUE •••••

could you tell me the way to ...? meg tudná mondani, hogy kell ...-hez menni? [toodna mondoni hodj]
go straight on until you reach the traffic lights menjen egyenesen előre a forgalmi lámpáig [men-yen edjeneshen elurreh o forgolmi lampo-eeg]
turn left forduljon balra [fordool-yon bolro]
take the first on the right forduljon jobbra az első sarkon [yobbro oz elshur shorkon]
see **where**

we* mi
weak gyenge [djengeh]
weather idő [idur]

••••• DIALOGUE •••••

what's the weather forecast? milyen időt jósoltak? [mi-yen idurt yawsholtok]
it's going to be fine szép idő lesz [sayp idur les]
it's going to rain esni fog [eshni fog]
it'll brighten up later később kiderül [kayshurb kiderewl]

wedding esküvő [eshkewvur]
wedding ring jegygyűrű [yedj-djewrew]
Wednesday szerda [serdo]
week hét [hayt]
this week a héten [o hayten]
a week (from) today mához egy hétre [edj haytreh]

a week (from) tomorrow holnaphoz egy hétre [holnop-hoz]
weekend hétvég [haytvayg]
at the weekend a hét végén [o hayt vaygayn]
weight súly [shoo^yuh]
weird hátborzongató [hatborzongotaw]
weirdo különös figura [kewluhnuhsh figooro]
welcome: you're welcome (don't mention it) szívesen [seeveshen]
well: I don't feel well rosszul érzem magam [rossool ayrzem mogom]
she's not well nincs jól [ninch yawl]
you speak English very well Ön nagyon jól beszél angolul [uhn nodjon yawl besayl ongolool]
well done! kitűnő! [kitewnur]
this one as well ezt is, kérem [ish kayrem]
well well! (surprise) lám, lám!

•••••• DIALOGUE ••••••

how are you? hogy van? [hodj von]
very well, thanks, and you? köszönöm, nagyon jól, és Ön? [kuhsuhnuhm nodjon yawl aysh uhn]

well-done (meat) jól átsütve [yawl atshewtveh]
Welsh walesi [velsi]
I'm Welsh walesi vagyok [velsi vodjok]
were*: we were voltunk [voltoonk]
you were (sing, formal) volt
(sing, fam) voltál [teh]
(pl, formal) voltak [unuk voltok]
(pl, fam) voltatok [voltotok]
they were voltak [urk]
west Nyugat [nyoogot]
in the west nyugaton [nyoogoton]
western nyugati [nyoogoti]
West Indian nyugat-indiai [nyoogot-indi-o-ee]
wet nedves [nedvesh]
what? mi?
what's that? mi az? [oz]
what's happening? mi van? [von]
(what's going on?, what's on?) mi a program? [o progrom]
what should I do? mit csináljak? [chinal-yok]
what a view! micsoda kilátás! [michodo kilatash]
what bus do I take? melyik autóbuszra szálljak? [meh-yik owtawboosro sal-yok]
wheel kerék [kerayk]
wheelchair tolószék [tolawsayk]
when? mikor?
when we get back amikor visszajön [omikor visso-yuhn]
when does it leave? (train, bus etc) mikor indul? [indool]
where? hol?
I don't know where it is nem tudom, hol van [toodom hol von]

•••••• DIALOGUE ••••••

where is the cathedral? hol a székesegyház?
it's over there ott
could you show me where it is on the map? meg tudná mutatni a térképen? [toodna moototni o tayrkaypen]
it's just here éppen itt van [ayppen it von]
see **way**

which: which bus? melyik autóbusz? [meh-yik owtawboos]

•••••• DIALOGUE ••••••

which one? melyik?
that one az ott [oz]
this one? ez?
no, that one nem, az

while: while I'm here amíg itt vagyok [omeeg it vodjok]
whisky viski
white fehér [fehayr]
white wine fehérbor [fehayrbor]
who? ki?
who is it? ki az? [oz]
the man who ... az a férfi, aki ... [oz o fayrfi oki]
whole: the whole week az egész hét [egays hayt]
the whole lot az egész
whose: whose is this? kié ez? [ki-ay ez]
why? miért? [mi-ayrt]
why not? miért ne? [neh]
wide széles [saylesh]
wife feleség [feleshayg]
will*: will you do it for me? megtenné nekem? [megtennay]
wind (noun) szél [sayl]
window ablak [oblok]
near the window az ablak mellett [oz]
in the window (of shop) a kirakatban [o kirokotbon]
window seat ablak melleti ülés [ewlaysh]
windscreen szélvédő [saylvaydur]
windscreen wiper ablaktörlő [obloktur-lur]
windsurfing hullámlovaglás [hoollam-lovoglash]
windy: it's windy fúj a szél [foo[yuh] o sayl]
wine bor
can we have some more wine? kaphatnánk még egy kis bort? [kop-hotnank mayg edj kish]

Hungarian red wines (**vörös bor** [vuruhsh]) can be divided into light-bodied and full-bodied varieties. Examples of the former are **Villányi burgundi**, **Vaskúti kadarka** and **Egri pinot noir**; in the full-bodied category are **Villányi medoc noir**, **Tihanyi merlot**, **Soproni kékfrankos** and the famous **Egri bikavér**, or 'Bull's Blood of Eger'. White wines (**fehér bor** [fehayr]) are classified as sweet (**édes** [aydesh]) or dry (**száraz** [saroz]) or **furmint** [foormint]. **Olasz riszling** wines tend to be sweet, →

ENGLISH ❖ HUNGARIAN **Wh**

with the exception of the 'Sand Wines' produced on the sandy soil between the Tisza and the Danube. Other sweet white wines include **Balatonfüredi szemelt**, **Akali zöldszilváni** and the richest of the Tokaj wines, **Tokaji aszú**. In the dry category are two wines from the Badacsony vineyards, **Szürkebarát** and **Zöldszilváni**; **Egri Leányka** from the Gyöngyös region; and two varieties of Tokaj, **furmint** and **szamorodni**. **Tököly** and **Pannonia** are sparkling wines. Wine bars (**borozó**) are ubiquitous and generally far less pretentious than in the West; true devotees of the grape make pilgrimages to the extensive wine cellars (**borpince**) that honeycomb towns like Tokaj and Eger. Some of these serve **borkóstoló** [borkawshtolaw] (a 'wine-tasting meal'), which typically consists of cold meats and sausages with a variety of pickles and breads. The meal begins with a **pálinka** (Hungarian brandy) apéritif, and continues with, typically, five or six different wines, progressing from the driest to the sweetest. By day, people often drink wine with water or soda water, specifying a **fröccs** [fruhch] or a yet more diluted **hosszú lépés** [hossoo laypaysh] (literally, a 'long step'). Hungarians enjoy the ritual of toasting, so the first word to get your tongue round is '**egészségedre!**' [egayshay-gedreh] ('cheers!'). When toasting more than one other person, it's grammatically correct to change this to '**egészségünkre!**' [egayshay-gewnkreh] ('cheers to us!'). Hungarians only consider it appropriate to toast with wine or spirits.

wine bar borozó [borozaw]
wine cellar borpince [borpintseh]
wine list borlista [borlishto], itallap [itollop]
winter tél [tayl]
in the winter télen [taylen]
winter holiday téli vakáció [tayli vokatsi-aw]
wire drót [drawt]
(electric) villanyvezeték [villo[nyuh]vezetayk]
wish: best wishes fogadja legjobb kívánságaimat [fogodyo leg-yobb keevanshago-eemot]
with ...-val/-vel [-vol/-vel]
I'm staying with ... ...-nál/-nél lakom [-nal/-nayl lokom]
without nélkül [naylkewl]
witness tanu [tonoo]
will you be a witness for me? tanúskodik mellettem? [tonoosh-kodik]
woman nő [nur]

women
Sexual harassment can be a problem for women travelling alone. 'Provocative' clothing may encourage unwelcome male attention if you visit rural or working-class **italbolt** (bars); hitch-hiking alone is not recommended. It's also advisable to avoid travelling on one of the Friday-night trains taking migrant workers home for the weekend, and walking around Budapest's VIII district or in Miskolc after dark.

wonderful remek
won't*: it won't start nem akar beindulni [okor beh-indoolni]
wood (material) fa [fo]
woods (forest) erdő [erdur]
wool gyapjú [djop-yoo]
word szó [saw]
work (noun) munka [moonko]
  it's not working nem működik [mewkuhdik]
  I work in ... ...-ban/-ben dolgozom [-bon/-ben]
world világ
worry: I'm worried aggódom [oggawdom]
worse: it's worse rosszabb [rossob]
worst legrosszabb [legrossob]
worth: is it worth a visit? érdemes megnézni? [ayrdemesh megnayzni]
would: would you give this to ...? lenne szíves átadni ezt ...-nak/-nek? [lenneh seevesh atodni ezt ...-nok/-nek]
wrap: could you wrap it up? legyen szíves becsomagolni [ledjen seevesh bechomogolni]
  could you gift-wrap it? kaphatnám ajándék csomagolásban? [kop-hotnam o-yandayk chomogolashbon]
wrapping paper csomagoló papír [chomogolaw popeer]
wrist csukló [chooklaw]
write írni [eerni]
  could you write it down? lesz szíves leírni? [les seevesh leh-eerni]
  how do you write it? hogy kell írni? [hodj]
writing paper levélpapír [levaylpopeer]
wrong: it's the wrong key ez nem a megfelelő kulcs [o megfelelur koolch]
  this is the wrong train ez nem a mi vonatunk [vonotoonk]
  the bill's wrong ez a számla téves [o samlo tayvesh]
  sorry, wrong number (when answering a call) sajnálom, téves kapcsolás [shoynalom tayvesh kopcholash]
  (when making a call) bocsánat téves kapcsolás [bochanot]
  sorry, wrong room bocsánat, nem ez a szoba [o sobo]
  there's something wrong with ... valami baja van a ... [volomi bo-yo von o]

what's wrong? mi baj van? [boy von]

X

X-ray röntgen [ruhntgen]

Y

yacht jacht [yot]
year év [ayv]
yellow sárga [shargo]
yes igen
yesterday tegnap [tegnop]
yesterday morning tegnap reggel
the day before yesterday tegnapelőtt [tegnopelurt]
yet még [mayg]

•••••• DIALOGUE ••••••

is it here yet? itt van már? [von]
no, not yet nem, még nincs itt [ninch]
you'll have to wait a little longer yet még egy kicsit várnia kell [edj kichit varni-o]

yoghurt joghurt [yog-hoort]
you* (sing, pol) Ön [uhn]
(sing, fam) te [teh]
(pl, pol) Önök [uhnuhk]
(pl, fam) ti
this is for you (sing, pol) ez az Öné [oz uhnay]
with you (sing, pol) Önnel [uhnnel]
to you (sing, pol) Önnek [uhnnek]
see **The Basics** pages 18-21

young fiatal [fi-otol]
your* (sing, pol) az Ön ...-a/-e/-ai/-ei [oz uhn ...-o/-eh/-o-ee/-eh-i]
(sing, fam) a te ...-d/-id [o teh]
yours* (sing, pol) az Öné [oz uhnay]
(sing, fam) a tiéd [o ti-ayd]
youth hostel ifjúsági szálló [if-yooshagi sallaw]

Z

zero nulla [noollo]
zip cipzár [tsipzar]
could you put a new zip on? lenne szíves új cipzárat tenni rá? [lenneh seevesh oo[yuh] tsipzarot]
zip code irányítószám [ira-nyeetawsam]
zoo állatkert [allotkert]
zucchini cukkini [tsookkini]

Hungarian-English

COLLOQUIALISMS

The following are words you may well hear. You shouldn't be tempted to use any of the stronger ones unless you are sure of your audience.

a fene egye meg! [o feneh edjeh] damn!
bedöglött [beduhgluht] it's given up the ghost, it's broken down
csaj [choy] woman, broad
dög [duhg] bitch
halvány fogalmam sincs [holva^{nyuh} fogolmom shinch] I haven't the foggiest
homokos [homokosh] gay
hülye! [hew-yeh] idiot!
kajálni [koyalni] to eat (slang)
klozet [klozet] WC, lavvy
krapek [kropek] bloke
megáll az eszem [megal oz esem] you amaze me
megfúrni [megfoorni] to scupper (literally: to drill)
ne fogdosson! [neh fogdosh-shon] keep your hands to yourself!
nyomás! [nyomash] get a move on!
pali [poli], **pasas** [poshosh] bloke, guy
strici [shtritsi], **strigó** [shtrigaw] pimp, bastard
szia(sztok)! [si-o(stok)] hi!
te tróger [teh trawger] you bastard
tele van a hócipôm [teleh von o hawtsipurm] I'm fed up (literally: my snowboots are full)
tragacs [trogoch] broken-down old car
zsaru [Joroo] cop

A/Á

a [o] the
-a his; her; your
-abb comparative suffix
ablak [oblok] window
  az ablakon kihajolni tilos do not lean out of the window
ablaktörlő [oblokturlur] windscreen wiper
abroncsnyomás [obronch-nyomash] tyre pressure
-ad [-od] your
adni [odni] to give
agglegény [ogglegay[nyuh]] bachelor
aggódni ... miatt [oggawdni miot] to worry about
ágy [adj] bed; cot
-aid [-o-eed] your (pl)
-aim [-o-eem] my (pl)
-aink [-o-eenk] our (pl)
-aitok [-o-eetok] your (pl)
ajak [oyok] lip
ajándék [oyandayk] present, gift
ajándékbolt [oyandaykbolt] souvenir shop, gift shop
  ajándékcsomagolásban parancsolja? would you like it gift-wrapped?
ajánlani [oyanloni] to offer; to recommend
ajánlott küldemény [oyanlot kewldemay[nyuh]] registered mail
ajánlott levél [levayl] registered letter
ajtó [oytaw] door
  az ajtónak támaszkodni veszélyes it is dangerous to lean against the doors
-ak [-ok] plural ending
akárhol [okarhol] anywhere; wherever
akárki [okarki] anyone; whoever
akármelyik [okarmeh-yik] either of them
akármi [okarmi] anything; whatever
akarni [okorni] to want
  akarsz ...? [okors] do you want ...?
akasztó [okostaw] hanger
akié [oki-ay] whose
akkor [okkor] then
  akkor is [ish] anyway
akkumulátor [okkoomoolator] battery (for car)
aktatáska [oktotashko] briefcase
alacsony [olocho[nyuh]] low; small
alagsor [ologshor] basement
alagút [ologoot] tunnel
aláírni [ola-eerni] to sign
alapozó krém [olopozaw kraym] foundation
alatt [olot] below, under; during
albérleti szoba [olbayrleti sobo] room usually let for longer periods
alföld [olfuhld] lowland
Alföld: az Alföld [oz] Great Plain
alkatrész [olkotrays] spares
alkohol árusításra jogosult [olkohol arooshee-tashro yogoshoolt] licensed to sell alcohol
alkohol tartalmú contains alcohol

áll chin; fit (verb); he/she stands
áll. State, State-owned
állam [allom] state
állampolgár [allompolgar] citizen
állampolgárság [allompolgarshag] nationality
állandó használatban in constant use
állapot [allopot] condition
állapotos [allopotosh] pregnant
állás [allash] job
állat [allot] animal
  az állatok etetése tilos do not feed the animals
állatkert [allotkert] zoo
állj! [al^{yuh}] stop!
állkapocs [alkopoch] jaw
állni [alni] to stand
állóhely standing room
állomás [allomash] station
állomásfőnök [allomash-furnuhk] station master
állomásfőnökség [allomash-furnuhkshayg] stationmaster's office
álmodni to dream
álmos [almosh] sleepy
alpinizmus [olpinizmoosh] rock climbing
alsó [olshaw] lower
  az alsó szinten [oz olshaw sinten] on the lower floor
alsóing [olshawing] vest
alsónadrág [olshawnodrag] underpants
alsónemű [olshawnemew] underwear
ált. general
által [altol] by
általában [altolabon] generally
általános [altolanosh] ordinary
aludni [oloodni] to sleep
alul [olool] underneath
aluljáró [olool-yaraw] underpass
alva [olvo] asleep
-am [-om] my
amely [omeh^{yuh}] which
amerikai [omeriko-ee] American
ami [omi] what
amikor [omikor] when
amint [omint] as soon as
-an [-on] adverbial suffix
Anglia [onglio] England
angol [ongol] English
  az angolok [oz ongolok] the English
  angolul [ongolool] in English
angolosan [ongoloshon] rare (steak)
annyi [on-nyi] so much, so many
annyira [on-nyiro] so much
antik üzlet [ontik ewzlet] antique shop
antikvárium [ontikvarioom] second-hand bookshop/bookstore
anya [o-nyo] mother
anyag [o-nyog] material
anyós [o-nyawsh] mother-in-law
anyu [o-nyoo] mum
apa [opo] father
ápoló/ápolónő [apolaw/apolawnur] nurse (man/woman)
após [opawsh] father-in-law
április [aprilish] April
aprópénz [oprawpaynz] change

apu [opoo] dad
ár [ar] price
árak [arok] charges
áram [arom] current
arany [oro^{nyuh}] gold
aranyozott [oro-nyozot] gold-plated
arc [orts] face
arcápolás [ortsapolash] beauty salon
arcbőrtisztító krém [ortsbur-tisteetaw kraym] cleansing cream
arcfesték [ortsfeshtayk] mascara
arckifestés [ortski-feshtaysh] make-up
arclemosó [ortslemoshaw] skin cleanser
arcvíz [ortsveez] aftershave
arcszínező [orchzeenezur] make-up
árengedmény [arengedmay^{nyuh}], **árleszállítás** [arlesalleetash] discount
árlista [arlishto] charges
árnyék [ar-nyayk] shade; shadow
arra [orro] that way
ártalmas [artolmosh] harmful
ártalmatlan [artolmotlon] harmless
áru [aroo] goods
áruház [aroohaz] department store
áruhoz: az áruhoz hozzányúlni tilos please do not touch
árvíz [arveez] flood
asszony [osso^{nyuh}] married woman; Mrs; Madam
Asszonyom [osso-nyom] Madam
asztal [ostol] table
asztali edények [ostoli eday-nyek] crockery
asztali tenisz [ostoli tenis] table tennis
asztalkendő [ostolkendur] napkin
át [at] via
átkelni ...-n to cross
átkelőjárat [atkelur-yarot] passenger ferry service
átmenni to go through; to pass
-atok [-otek] your (pl)
átöltözni [atuhltuhzni] to get changed
átszállás [atsallash] change
átszállni [atsallni] to change (bus, train)
augusztus [owgoostoosh] August
Ausztria [owstrio] Austria
autó [owtaw] car
autóbérlés [owtawbayrlaysh] car hire, car rental
autóbusz [owtawboos] bus
autóbuszállomás [owtawboos-allomash] bus station
autóbuszbérlet [owtawboos-bayrlet] bus pass; pass for public transport
autóbuszmegálló [owtawboos-megallaw] bus stop
autóbusz pályaudvar [owtawboos pa-yowdvor] bus station
autógumi [owtawgoomi] tyre
autójavító [owtaw-yoveetaw] car repairs
autójavitóműhely [owtaw-yovitaw-mewheh^{yuh}] garage (for repairs)

automata [owtomoto] automatic
autómentő [owtawmentur] breakdown service
autópálya [owtawpa-yo] motorway, (US) highway, freeway
autópályafeljárat [owtawpa-yo-fel-yarot] motorway junction
autóstop [owtawshtop] hitch-hiking
autóstoppal utazni [owtawshtoppol ootozni] to hitch-hike
autóstoppolni [owtawshtoppolni] to hitch-hike
autószerelő [owtawserelur] mechanic
az [oz] the; it; that; that one
  az a, az az that
aznap [oznop] that day
azok [ozok] those
  azok a, azok az those
azonnal [ozonnol] immediately
  azonnal adom [odom] I'll put you through immediately
azt [ozt] that; that one
  azt hiszem ... [hisem] I think that ...
aztán [oztan] then

B

-ba [-bo] in; into; to
baba [bobo] doll; baby
baj [boy] trouble
  mi a baj? what's the matter?
bajusz [boyoos] moustache
bakancs [bokonch] boot, ankle boot
bal [bol] left (not right)
bál dance
baleset [boleshet] accident; emergency
balesetbejelentés emergency call
baleseti osztály [bolesheti osta[yuh]] casualty department
baloldalt [bololdolt] on the left
balra [bolro] on the left; to the left
-ban [-bon] in
bankautomata [bonk-owtomoto] cash dispenser, ATM
bankjegy [bonk-yedj] banknote, (US) bill
bár although; bar
barát [borat] friend (male); boyfriend
barátnő [boratnur] friend (female); girlfriend
barátságos [boratshagosh] friendly
barátságtalan [boratshagtolon] unfriendly; bleak
barlang [borlong] cave
barna [borno] brown
bárpult [barpoolt] bar; counter
bársony [barsho[nyuh]] velvet
bástya [bash-tyo] bastion
bátya [ba-tyo] brother (elder)
-bb comparative suffix
-be [-beh] in; into; to
bébiruházat [baybiroo-hazot] baby clothes
Bécs [baych] Vienna
becsomagolni [bechomogolni] to wrap

beengedni [beh-engedni] to let in
befejezni [befayezni] to finish
behajtani tilos no entry for motor vehicles
beindítani [beh-indeetoni] to switch on
bejárat [bayarot] way in, entrance
bejárat a másik ajtón entry at the next door
bejáró betegek [bayaraw] outpatients
bejárónő [bayarawnur] cleaning woman, daily help
bejelentkezés [bayelent-kezaysh] (making an) appointment
bejutni [bayootni] to get in
bekapcsolni [bekopcholni] to switch on
bekapcsolva [bekopcholvo] on, switched on
beleértve [beleh-ayrtveh] included
belépés [belaypaysh] entry
belépés csak érvényes jeggyel admission with valid ticket only
belépés csak meghívóval admission with invitation only
belépés díjtalan [belaypaysh dee^{yuh}tolon], **belépés ingyenes** [indjenesh] admission free
belépni [belaypni] to enter
belépni tilos no entry
belépődíj [belaypurdee^{yuh}] admission fee
belépődíj nincs [ninch] admission free
belépőjegy [belaypuryedj] ticket
belföldi díjszabás [belfuhldi dee^{yuh}sobash] inland postage
belföldi információ local and national enquiries
belföldi távhívás [belfuhldi tavheevash] domestic long-distance call
belső [belshur] inside; inner tube
belül [belewl] inside; within
belváros [belvarosh] town centre
bélyeg [bay-yeg] stamp
bélyegárusítás [bay-yegaroosheetash] stamps
bemenni to go in
bemutatni [bemoototni] to introduce
bemutató [bemoototaw] show
-ben in
benn inside
benneteket you
bennünket [bennewnket] us
benzin petrol, (US) gas
benzinkút [benzinkoot] petrol station, (US) gas station
bér [bayr] rent
berakás [berokash] set
bérelhető [bayrelhetur] for hire, to rent
bérelni [bayrelni] to rent, to hire
bérelt gép [bayrelt gayp] charter flight
bérlakás [bayrlokash] self-catering apartment

bérlet [bayrlet] pass for public transport
bérmentesítés [bayrmen-tesheetaysh] postage
bérmentesített postage prepaid
beszállás boarding
beszállni [besallni] to get in
beszállóhely [besallaw-heh^{yuh}] gate
beszállókártya [besallawkar-tyo] boarding card
beszárítás [besareetash] blow-dry
beszéd [besayd] speech
beszélni [besaylni] to speak; to talk
  beszél ...? do you speak ...?
  nem beszélek ... [nem besaylek] I don't speak ...
beteg ill, sick; patient
betegellátás [betegellatash] health service
beteggondozó [beteggondozaw] nurse (man)
betegség [betegshayg] disease
betörő [beturur] burglar
beváltani [bevaltoni] to change (money)
beváltás [bevaltash] exchange
bevásárló központ [bevasharlaw kuhzpont] shopping centre
bevásárló szatyor [so-tyor] shopping bag
bevásárolni [bevasharolni] to do one's shopping, to go shopping
bezárni to close; to lock up
bézs [bayJ] beige
bíbor [beebor] purple
bicikli [bitsikli] bicycle
bika [biko] bull
birka [birko] sheep
bírság [beershag] fine
bisztró [bistraw] snack bar
biztonság [biztonshag] safety, security
biztonsági öv [biztonshagi uhv] seatbelt
biztonságos [biztonshagosh] safe, secure
biztos [biztosh] sure
  biztos? are you sure?
biztosítás [biztosheetash] insurance
BKVRt Budapest Public Transport Network
blokk receipt
blúz [blooz] blouse
bocsánat! [bochanot] sorry!, excuse me!
bocsánatot kérek! [bochanotot kayrek] excuse me!
bocsásson meg! [bochashshon] would you excuse me, please?
boka [boko] ankle
boldog happy
boldog születésnapot! [sewletaysh-nopot] happy birthday!
bolha [bolho] flea
bolond idiot
bolt shop
bonyolult [bo-nyoloolt] complicated
borbély [borbay^{yuh}] barber
borda [bordo] rib
boríték [boreetayk] envelope

borotva [borotvo] razor
borotvahab [borotvo-hob] shaving foam
borotválás [borotvalash] shave
borotválkozás [borotval-kozash] shave
borotválkozni [borotvalkozni] to shave
borotvapenge [borotvopengeh] razor blade
borozó [borozaw] wine bar
borpince [borpintseh] wine cellar
borravaló [borrovolaw] tip (payment)
borzalmas [borzolmosh] horrible
borzasztó [borzostaw] awful
bosszantani [bossontoni] to annoy
bosszantó [bossontaw] annoying
botrányos [botra-nyosh] shocking
bő [bur] loose, too big
bögre [buhgreh] mug
bőr [bur] leather; skin
bőráru [buraroo] leather goods
bőrdíszmű [burdeesmew] leather goods
bőr felsőrész [bur felshurays] leather upper
bőrönd [bur-ruhnd] suitcase
bőrtisztító krém [burtisteetaw kraym] skin cleanser
börtön [burtuhn] prison
brit British
brosúra [broshooro] brochure
bugyi [boodji] panties
bukkanó uneven road surface
busz [boos] bus
buszmegálló [boos-megallaw] bus stop
buszsáv bus lane
buta [booto] stupid
butángáz [bootangaz] camping gas
butik [bootik] boutique
bútor [bootor] furniture
büdös [bewduhsh] stinking; bad smell
büfé [bewfay] snack bar
büfékocsi [bewfaykochi] buffet car

C

camping campsite
cégkártya [tsaygkar-tyo] business card
centrum [tsentroom] town centre
cérna [tsayrno] thread
ceruza [tseroozo] pencil
cigány [tsiga^{nyuh}] gypsy
cigányzene [tsiga^{nyuh}zeneh] gypsy music
cigányzenekar [tsiga^{nyuh}zenekor] gypsy band
cím [tseem] address; title
cimke [tsimkeh] label
címzett [tseemzet] addressee
cipész [tsipays] shoemaker, shoe repairer
cipő [tsipur] shoe
cipőbolt [tsipurbolt] shoe shop
cipőfűző [tsipurfewzur] shoelace
cipőkrém [tsipurkraym] shoe polish
cipzár [tsipzar] zip

comb [tsomb] thigh
cukorka [tsookorko] sweet, candy
cukrászda [tsookrasdo] confectionery; patisserie shop, cake shop
cumi [tsoomi] dummy (for baby)

CS

csak [chok] just; only
csak egy kicsit [edj kichit] just a little
csak 6 személyre room for 6 persons only
csak autóbuszoknak buses only
csak egy pillanatra! [pillonotro] just a moment!
csak hétköznapokon weekdays only
csak munkanapokon workdays only (not on Sundays or holidays)
csak munkaszüneti napokon bank holidays only
csak oda jegy [odo yedj] single ticket, one-way ticket
csak személyzet részére staff only
csak ünnepnapokon public holidays only
család [cholad] family
családi family (adj)
családnév [choladnayv] surname
csalni [cholni] to cheat
csalódott [cholawdot] disappointed
csap [chop] tap, faucet
csapat [chopot] team
csapos [choposh] barman
csárda [chardo] country inn
csatlakozás [chotlokozash] connection
csatorna [chotorno] canal
csecsemő [chechemur] baby
cseh [cheH] Czech, Bohemian
Cseh Köztársaság [cheH kuhztarshoshag] Czech Republic
Csehország [cheH-orsag] Bohemia
csekk [chek] cheque
csekkbefizetés cheque deposits
csekk-füzet [chek-fewzet] cheque book
csekk kártya [chek kar-tyo] cheque card
csekk-könyv [chek-kuh[nyuh]v] cheque book
csemege(bolt) [chemegeh(-bolt)] delicatessen
csend [chend] silence
csendet kérünk! [kayrewnk] quiet please!
csendes [chendesh] quiet
csengetni [chengetni] to ring the bell
csengő [chengur] door bell
csepp [chep] drop
cseppkőbarlang [chepkur-borlong] stalagtite cave
cserélni [cheraylni] to exchange
csésze [chayseh] cup
csillag [chillog] star
csinálni [chinalni] to make; to do
csinos [chinosh] handsome; pretty

csípés [cheepaysh] bite; sting
csipke [chipkeh] lace
csipkeáru [chipkeh-aroo] laces
csípni [cheepni] to pinch; to sting
csípő [cheepur] hip
csípős [cheepursh] hot
csizma [chizmo] boot (footwear)
csók [chawk] kiss
csokoládé [chokoladay] chocolate
csókolni [chawkolni] to kiss
csókolózni [chawkolawzni] to kiss each other
csomag [chomog] parcel, package; luggage, baggage
csomag feladás [felodash] parcels
csomagfelvétel [chomog-felvaytel] parcels counter
csomagkuli [chomog-kooli] luggage trolley
csomagmegőrző [chomog-megurzur] left luggage, baggage checkroom
csomagmegőrző automata [owtomoto] left-luggage locker
csomagolás [chomogolash] package
csomagolni [chomogolni] to pack; to wrap
csomagolópapír [chomogolaw-popeer] wrapping paper
csomagtargonca [chomog-torgontso] luggage van
csomagtartó [chomog-tortaw] boot, (US) trunk; roof rack; luggage rack
csomó [chomaw] many; lump; knot
csónak [chawnok] boat
csont [chont] bone
csonttörés [chontturaysh] fracture
csoport [choport] group, party
cső [chur] pipe (for gas/liquid)
csúcs [chooch] tip (end)
csukló [chooklaw] wrist
csúnya [choo-nyo] ugly
csúszni [choosni] to skid
csúszós [choosawsh] slippery
csütörtök [chewturtuhk] Thursday

D

-d your
dagadt [dogot] swollen
dal [dol] song
dalest [dolesht] song recital
dán Danish
Dánia [danio] Denmark
darab [dorob] piece
darabja [dorob-yo] each, apiece
darázs [doraJ] wasp
dátum [datoom] date
dauer [dower] perm
de [deh] but
d.e. am
defekt breakdown; puncture
defektes [defektesh] flat (tyre)
defektet kapni [kopni] to break down
deka(gr) [deko(gr)] 10 grammes
dél [dayl] noon; south
Dél-Afrika [dayl-ofriko] South Africa

délben [daylben] at noon
délelőtt [daylelurt] morning; am
délután [daylootan] afternoon; pm
derék [derayk] waist; decent
dezodor deodorant
diák [diak] student
diapozitív [diopoziteev] slide
díj [dee^{yuh}] charge(s); fare(s)
diszko [disko] disco
disznó [disnaw] pig
divat [divot] fashion
divatáru [divotaroo] confectionery
divatos [divotosh] fashionable
dízel(olaj) [deezel(oloy)] diesel
djami [d-yomi] mosque
dkg. 10 grammes
dobni to throw
doboz box; packet
dohány [doha^{nyuh}] tobacco
dohányáru [doha-nyaroo], **dohánybolt** [doha^{nyuh}bolt] tobacconist
dohányos [doha-nyosh] smoker
dohányozni [doha-nyozni] to smoke
dohányozni tilos no smoking
dohányzó [doha-nyzaw] smoking room/area; smoking
dohányzók részére (fenntartott hely) area reserved for smokers
doktor/doktornő [doktornur] doctor (man/woman)
dolgok things
dolgozni to work
dolog thing; work
domb hill
dönteni [duhnteni] to decide
drága [drago] expensive
drapp beige
drótkötélpálya kocsi [drawt-kuhtaylpa-yo kochi] cable car
d.u. pm
duda [doodo] horn (car)
dugaszhüvely [doogoshew-veh^{yuh}] socket
dugó [doogaw] plug; cork
dugóhúzó [doogaw-hoozaw] corkscrew
Duna [doono] Danube
Dunakanyar [doono-ko-nyor] Danube Bend
Dunántúl [doonantool] Transdanubia
dunyha [doo^{nyuh}ho] quilt; duvet
duplaágyas szoba [dooplo-adjosh sobo] double room
dühös [dewhuhsh] angry; furious
dzsessz [dJess] jazz
dzsogging [dJogging] jogging

E/É

-e [-eh] his; her; your
eb dog
-ebb comparative suffix
ebéd [ebayd] lunch
ebédidő [ebaydidur] lunchtime
ebédlő [ebaydlur] dining room
ébren [aybren] awake
ébresztőóra [aybrestur-awro] alarm clock
-ed your
edények [eday-nyek] cooking utensils

édes [aydesh] sweet
édesség [aydeshshayg] dessert, sweet
édességbolt [aydesh-shaygbolt] confectionery shop
ég [ayg] sky
egér [egayr] mouse
égés [aygaysh], **égési seb** [aygayshi sheb] burn
egész [egays] whole
egész nap [nop] all day
egészen [egaysen] completely; quite, fully
egészség [egayshayg] health
egészségedre! [egayshay-gedreh], **egészségére!** [egayshay-gayreh] cheers!; bless you!
egészséges [egayshay-gesh] fit, healthy
egészségügyi tampon [egayshay-gewdji tompon] sanitary towel/ napkin
egészségünkre! [egayshay-gewnkreh] cheers!; bless you!
éghajlat [ayghoylot] climate
égni [aygni] to burn
egy [edj] a; one
egyágyas szoba [edjadjosh sobo] single room
egyedül [edjedewl] alone
egyedülálló [edjedew-lallaw] single, unmarried
egyenesen [edjeneshen] straight on
egyenleg [edjenleg] balance
Egyesült Államok [edjeshewlt allomok] United States
Egyesült Királyság [kirayshag] United Kingdom
egyetem [edjetem] university
egyetemi hallgató [edjetemi hollgotaw] student (male/female)
egyetemi hallgatónő [hollgotawnur] student (female)
egyetlen [edjetlen] single, one
egyház [edjhaz] church
egyikük sem [edjikewk shem] neither of them
egyszemélyes ágy [edjsemay-yesh adj] single bed
egyszemélyes szoba [sobo] single room
egyszer [edjser] once
egyszerre [edjserreh] suddenly; all together at the same time
egyszerű [edjserew] simple
egy útra [edj ootro] single ticket, one-way ticket
együtt [edjewt] together
együttes [edjewttesh] band (musicians)
éhes [ay-hesh] hungry
-ei [-eh-i] his/her; your (pl)
-eid [-eh-id] your (pl)
-eik [-eh-ik] their; your (pl)
-eim [-eh-im] my (pl)
-eink [-eh-ink] our (pl)
-eitek [-eh-itek] your (pl)
éjfél [ay-fayl] midnight
éjjel [ay-yel] at night
éjjeli lámpa [ay-yeli lampo] bedside lamp
éjjeli mulató [moolotaw] nightclub
éjjel-nappali [ay-yel-noppoli] shop open 24 hours
éjszaka [ay^{yuh}soko] night

éjszakai mulató [ay^{yuh}soko-ee moolotaw] nightclub
éjszakai portás [portash] night porter
éjszakai ügyelet [ewdjelet] overnight service
éjszakánként [ay^{yuh}sokan-kaynt] nightly, per night
-ek plural ending
EK [eh-ka] UK
ékszer [aykser] jewellery
ékszerész [ayksersays] jeweller's
ékszerüzlet [ayksrewzlet] jeweller's
el away
eladás [elodash] sale
eladási határidő sell by date
eladni [elodni] to sell
eladó [elodaw] for sale
elágazás [elagozash] fork (in road)
eldobni to throw away
eldugult [eldoogoolt] blocked
elég [elayg] enough
  elég lesz [les] that's enough
elégedett [elaygedet] contented
eléggé [elayggay] quite, fairly, pretty
eleje [elayeh] the front of
elektromos [elektromosh] electric
élelemmel with food
élelmiszeráruház [aylel-miser-aroohaz] supermarket
élelmiszerbolt [aylel-miser-bolt] grocery store
elem [elem] battery (for radio etc)
élet [aylet] life
életmentő mellény [ayletmentur mellay^{nyuh}] lifejacket
eleven alive
elfelejteni [elfelayteni] to forget
elfogadni [elfogodni] to accept
elfoglalt [elfoglolt] busy, occupied
elfogni to catch
elfogyott [elfodjot] there's none left
elhagyni [elhodjni] to leave
elhozni to get, to fetch
elismervény [elish-mervay^{nyuh}] receipt
eljegyzett [el-yedj-zet] engaged (couple)
elképesztő [elkaypestur] astonishing
elkések [elkayshek] I'll be late
elkésni [elkayshni] to be late
elkészíteni [elkayseeteni] to prepare
elkísérni [elkeeshayrni] to accompany
elköltözni [elkuhl-tuhzni] to move (house)
ellen against
ellenkező [ellenkezur] opposite
  ellenkező irányban [ira^{nyuh}bon] in the opposite direction
ellenőrizni [ellenur-rizni] to check
ellopni to steal
elmenni to go away; to leave
elmosogatni [elmoshogotni] to do the washing-up
elnézést (kérek)! [elnayzaysht (kayrek)] sorry!
élni [aylni] to live

elnök [elnuhk] chairman
elosztó [elostaw] adaptor; distributor
élő [aylur] alive
előadás [elur-odash] performance, show
előhívni [elur-heevni] to develop (film)
előleg [elurleg] down payment
előre [elur-reh] in advance
előtt [elurt] before; in front of
elővétel [elurvaytel] advance booking
elővételi pénztár [elurvayteli paynztar] till for advance booking
előzetes [elurzetesh] prior
előzni [elurzni] to overtake
előzni tilos no overtaking
elrejteni [elrayteni] to hide
elreteszelni [elreteselni] to bolt
elseje [elseh-yeh] first (of month)
első [elshur] first
elsőbbség [elshurbbshayg] right of way
első emelet [elshur emelet] first floor, (US) second floor
elsőosztály [elshur-osta^{yuh}] first class
elsősegély [elshur-shegay^{yuh}] first aid
elsősegélyhely [elshur-shegay^{yuh}heh^{yuh}] first-aid post
eltörni [elturni] to break
eltört [elturt] broken
eltűnni [eltewnni] to disappear
elvált divorced
elvenni to take away; to marry (of man)
elveszteni to lose
elviselhetetlen [elvishel-hetetlen] unbearable
em. floor
-em my
ember man
  az ember one; you
emberek people
emelet floor
  az emeleten upstairs
emésztési zavar [emaystayshi zovor] indigestion
emlékezni [emlaykezni] to remember
  nem emlékszem [emlayksem] I don't remember
emlékmű [emlaykmew] monument
emléktárgy [emlayktardj] souvenir(s)
-en on; in; at; adverbial suffix
én [ayn] I
  én is [ish] me too
  az én ...-im/-m my
ének [aynek] song
énekelni [aynekelni] to sing
énekes/énekesnő [aynekesh/aynekeshnur] singer (male/female)
engedély [engeday^{yuh}] licence, permit
engem me
enni to eat
enyém: az enyém [oz eh-nyaym] mine
éppen [ayppen] just; right now
épület [aypewlet] building
ér [ayr] be worth; vein
érdek [ayrdek] interest

érdekes [ayrdekesh] interesting
Erdély [erday^{yuh}] Transylvania
erdő [erdur] forest
eredj innen! [ered^{yuh}] go away!
érett [ayret] ripe
érezni [ayrezni] to feel; to smell
érinteni [ayrinteni] to touch
erkély [erkay^{yuh}] balcony
érkezés [ayrkezaysh] arrival(s)
érkező járatok [ayrkezur yarotok], **érkező vonatok** [ayrkezur vonotok] arrivals
érme [ayrmeh] coin
erős [erursh] strong
erre [erreh] this way
erszény [ersay^{nyuh}] purse
-ért [-ayrt] for
értekezlet [ayrtekezlet] meeting
értékmegőrző [ayrtayk-megurzur] safe deposit
értelmes [ayrtelmesh] intelligent
értem [ayrtem] for me
  nem értem I don't understand
  értem már! I see!
érteni [ayrteni] to understand
érti [ayrti] clear, obvious
érvényes [ayrvay-nyesh] valid
érzékeny [ayrzaykeh^{nyuh}] sensitive
és [aysh] and
esernyő [esher-nyur] umbrella
esernyőjavítás [esher-nyur-yoveetash] umbrella repairs
esik [eshik] it's raining
esküvő [eshkewvur] wedding
esni [eshni] to fall; to rain
eső [eshur] rain
esőház [eshurhaz] shelter
esőkabát [eshurkobat] raincoat
este [eshteh] evening
este 10 után felszállás csak az első ajtón after 10pm entry through the front door only
estélyi ruha [eshtay-yi rooho] nightdress
észak [aysok] north
eszköz [eskuhz] means; tool
eszpresszó [espressaw] coffee bar
-etek your
étel [aytel] food
ételbár [aytelbar] snack bar
ételkülönlegességek specialities
ételmérgezés [aytel-mayrgezaysh] food poisoning
étkezés [aytkezaysh] meal
étkezés előtt before meals
étkezés után after meals
étkezőkocsi [aytkezur-kochi] restaurant car
étlap [aytlop] menu
étrend [aytrend] diet
étterem [aytterem] restaurant; dining room
éttermek [ayttermek] restaurants
étvágy [aytvadj] appetite
Európa [eoorawpo] Europe
európai [eoorawpo-ee] European
év [ayv] year
  ... éves vagyok [ayvesh vodjok] I'm ... years old
evangélikus [evongaylikoosh] Lutheran
evezés [evezaysh] rowing
evezős csónak [evezursh chawnok] rowing boat

évforduló [ayvfordoolaw] anniversary
évi [ayvi] annual
evőeszközök [evures-kuhzuhk] cutlery
évszak [ayvsok] season
évszázad [ayvsazod] century
Ex express train
expressz [ekspres] special delivery; express train
expresszvonat [ekspressvonot] express train
extra [ekstro] four-star, premium, 98-octane petrol/gas
ez it; this, this one
  mi ez? what's this?
  ez a, ez az this
ezek these
  ezek a, ezek az these
ezelőtt [ezelurt] ago
ezer thousand
ezüst [ezewsht] silver (metal)
ezüstözött [ezewsht-uhzuht] silver-plated

F

fa [fo] tree; wood
fagy [fodj] frost
fagyásgátló [fodjashgatlaw] antifreeze
fagyasztott [fodjostot] frozen
fagylalt [fodjlolt] ice cream
fagylaltos [fodjloltosh] ice-cream vendor
fagylaltozó [fodjloltozaw] ice-cream parlour
faház [fohaz] bungalow
fáj [fī] it hurts
fájdalmas [fīdolmosh] painful
fájdalom [fīdolom] ache, pain
fájdalomcsillapító [fīdolom-chillopeetaw] painkiller
fal [fol] wall
falatozó [folotozaw] snack-bar
falevél [folevayl] leaf
falragasz [folrogos] poster
falu [foloo] village
fáradt [farot] tired
farmernadrág [formernodrag] jeans
fazék [fozayk] saucepan
fázni to be cold
február [febroo-ar] February
fedél [fedayl] cover
fedélzet [fedaylzet] deck
fedő [fedur] lid
fehér [fehayr] white
fehérítő [fehayreetur] bleach
fej [fay] head
fejest ugrani tilos no diving
fejfájás [fayfī-ash] headache
fejkendő [faykendur] headscarf
fejleszteni [faylesteni], **fejlődni** [faylurdni] to develop
fék [fayk] brake (noun)
fekete [feketeh] black
fékezni [faykezni] to brake
feküdni [fekewdni] to lie
fel up
fél [fayl] half
feladni [felodni] to post, to mail
feladó [felodaw] sender
felár surcharge
felborítani [felboreetoni] to knock over
felé [felay] towards

felébredni [felaybredni] to wake up
felelős [felelursh] responsible
félemelet [faylemelet] mezzanine
félénk [faylaynk] shy
feleség [feleshayg] wife
felfelé [felfelay] upwards
félfogadás [faylfogodash] office hours
felhívni [felheevni] to ring, to call
felhő [felhur] cloud
felhős [felhursh] cloudy
feliratos with subtitles
felismerni [felishmerni] to recognize
felkelni to get up
felkelteni to wake up
felmenni to go up
félni [faylnee] to be afraid
felnőtt [felnurt] adult
felnyitás után hűtőszekrényben tartandó refrigerate after opening
félóra [faylawro] half an hour
fél panzió [fayl ponziaw], **fél penzió** [penziaw] half board
felpróbálni [felprawbalni] to try on
félreértés [faylreh-ayrtaysh] misunderstanding
felső: a felső szinten [o felshur sinten] on the upper floor
felszállás [felsallash] take-off
felszállás az első ajtón/hátsó ajtón entry at the front/rear
felszállni [felsallni] to get in
felszeletelni [felseletelni] to chop; to cut
felszíni küldemény [felseeni kewldemay^{nyuh}] surface mail, overland mail
feltétel [feltaytel] condition
feltételes megálló request stop
felvilágosítás [felvilagosheetash] information
felvonó [felvonaw] lift, elevator
felvonószék [felvonawsayk] chairlift
fém [faym] metal
fenék [fenayk] bottom
fenekén [fenekayn] at the bottom of
fenn upstairs
fény [fay^{nyuh}] light
fénykép [fay^{nyuh}kayp] photograph
fényképész [fay^{nyuh}kaypays] photographer
fényképészeti bolt [fay^{nyuh}kaypayseti bolt] shop selling photographic equipment
fényképezni [fay^{nyuh}kaypezni] to photograph
fényképezőgép [fay^{nyuh}kaypezurgayp] camera
fényszóró [fay^{nyuh}sawraw] headlights
férfi [fayrfi] man
férfiak [fayrfiok] men; gents' toilet, men's room
férfiáru [fayrfi-aroo] menswear
férfidivat [fayrfi-divot] men's fashion
férfi fodrász [fayrfi fodras] men's hairdresser
férfi napozó [nopozaw] sunbathing area for men only

férfi osztály [osta^{yuh}] men's department
férfi öltöző [uhltuhzur] men's changing room
férfiruha [fayrfi-rooho] men's clothing
férfi WC [vay tsay] gents' (toilet), men's room
férj [fayr^{yuh}] husband
férjes [fayr-yesh], **férjezett** [fayr-yezet] married (woman)
férjhez menni [fayr^{yuh}hez] to get married (of woman)
fertőtlenítő [ferturt-leneetur] antiseptic; disinfectant
Fertő tó [fertur taw] Lake Neusiedlersee
fertőzés [fertur-zaysh] infection
festmény [fesht-may^{nyuh}] painting
festő [feshtur] painter, artist
fésű [fayshew] comb
fia [fio] son
fiatal [fiotol] young
fiatalok [fiotolok] young people
figyelem caution
figyelmet kérek! attention please!
figyelmeztetés [fidjelmez-tetaysh] warning
figyelni [fidjelni] to watch; to pay attention
fillér [fillayr] one hundredth of a forint
finom delicious
fiú [fi-oo] boy
fiúja [fi-oo-yo] her boyfriend
fiúm [fi-oom] my boyfriend
fivér [fivayr] brother
fiz. paying guest service, private accommodation
fizetés [fizetaysh] payment; wage
fizetni to pay
fizetővendégszolgálat [fizetur-vendaygsolgalot] paying guest service, private accommodation
fodrászszalon [fodrassolon] hairdressing salon
fodrász [fodras] hairdressing; hairdresser
fodrászat [fodrasot] hairdresser's
fog tooth; he/she will
fogadás [fogodash] reception
fogadni [fogodni] to receive
fogadó [fogodaw] bed and breakfast accommodation
fogamzásgátló [fogom-zashgatlaw] contraceptive
fogantyú [fogon-tyoo] handle
fogfájás [fogfī-ash] toothache
fogja [fog-yo] he/she will
fogják [fog-yak] they will
fogjátok [fog-yatok] you will
fogjuk [fog-yook] we will
fogkefe [fogkefeh] toothbrush
fogkrém [fogkraym] toothpaste
foglalás [foglolash] reservation
foglalj(on) helyet please, take a seat
foglalni [foglolni] to book; to reserve
foglalt [foglolt] reserved; engaged, occupied
fognak [fognok] they will
fogod you will
fogok, fogom I will

fogorvos [fogorvosh] dentist (man)
fogorvosi rendelő [fogorvoshi rendelur] dentist's surgery
fogorvosnő [fogorvoshnur] dentist (woman)
fogsz [fogs] you will
fogtok, fogunk [fogoonk] we will
fogyasztó [fodjostaw] consumer
fogyni [fodjni] to lose weight
folt stain; spot
folyadékkal nyelje le take with water
folyó [foyaw] river
folyóirat [foyaw-irot] magazine
folyóiratok [fo-yaw-irotok] newspaper kiosk
folyosó [foyoshaw] aisle; corridor
folyószámla [fo-yawsamlo] current account
font pound (money)
fontos [fontosh] important
font sterling [shterling] pound sterling
fordítani [fordeetoni] to turn; to translate
forduljon balra [fordool-yon bolro] turn left
forduljon jobbra [yobbro] turn right
forduljon vissza [visso] turn back
fordulni [fordoolni] to turn
forgalmas [forgolmosh] busy
forgalmi dugó [forgolmi doogaw] traffic jam
forgalmi lámpa [lampo] traffic lights
forgalmi rendőr [rendur] traffic policeman
forgalom [forgolom] traffic; turnover; sales
forgalomelterelés traffic diversion
forint unit of currency
forrás [forrash] potable spring; fountain
forró [forraw] hot
fő [fur] main
föld [fuhld] earth; land
földalatti [fuhldolotti] underground, (US) subway
földszint [fuhldsint] ground floor, (US) first floor; stalls
fölé [fuhlay] over, above
fölösleges [fuhluhsh-legesh] unnecessary
fölött [fuhluht] above
főnök [furnuhk] boss; manager
főpályaudvar [furpa-yowdvor] central station
főszezon [fursezon] high season
főváros [furvarosh] capital
fővárosi [furvaroshi] metropolitan; of Budapest
főzni [furzni] to cook; to boil
főzőeszköz [furzur-eskuhz] cooking utensils
francia [frontsio] French
Franciaország [frontsi-oorsag] France
friss [frish-sh] fresh
frissen mázolva wet paint
frufru [froo-froo] fringe (hair)
fszt. ground floor, (US) first floor
furcsa [foorcho] funny, odd

furgon [foorgon] van
futballmeccs [footbol-metsch] football match
futballpálya [footbol-pa-yo] football pitch, football ground
futni [footni] to run
fű [few] grass
függeni: attól függ [ottawl fewg] it depends
független [fewggetlen] independent
függöny [fewgguh^{nyuh}] curtain
fül [fewl] ear(s)
fülbevaló [fewl-bevolaw] earrings
fülfájás [fewlfī-ash] earache
fülke [fewlkeh] compartment
fülledt [fewllet] close, stuffy
fürdő [fewrdur] bath; bathroom; baths
fürdőkád [fewrdur-kad] bathtub
fürdőkúra [fewrdur-kooro] water cures
fürdőnadrág [fewrdur-nodrag] swimming trunks
fürdőruha [fewrdur-rooho] swimming costume
fürdősapka [fewrdur-shopko] bathing cap
fürdősó [fewrdur-shaw] bath salts
fürdőszoba [fewrdur-sobo] bathroom
fűre: a fűre lépni tilos keep off the grass
fürödni tilos no swimming
füst [fewsht] smoke
füstmentes járat flight reserved for non-smokers
fűszeres [fewseresh] grocer
fűszerüzlet [fewser-ewzlet] grocery store
fűtés [fewtaysh] heating
fűtőtest [fewtur-tesht] radiator

G

gallér [gollayr] collar
garancia [gorontsio] guarantee
garantálni [gorontalni] to guarantee
garázs [goraJ] garage (at home)
gazda [gozdo] farmer
gazdag [gozdog] rich
gazdaság [gozdoshag] farm
gázolaj [gazoloy] diesel
gázpedál accelerator
gépkocsi bérlés [gaypkochi bayrlaysh] car hire, car rental
gépkocsival behajtani tilos no entry for cars
golfpálya [golfpa-yo] golf course
golyóstoll [goyawshtol] ballpoint pen
gomb button
gombostű [gomboshtew] pin
gondatlan [gondotlon] careless
gondolkozni, gondolni to think
gondos [gondosh] careful
goromba [gorombo] rude
gömb [guhmb] ball
görögkatolikus [guruhg-kotolikoosh] Uniate
görögkeleti [guruhg-keleti] Orthodox
gőz [gurz] steam
gőzfürdő [gurz-fewrdur] Turkish bath

gratulálok! [grotoolalok] congratulations!
gratulálok születésnapjára! [sewletayshnop-yaro] happy birthday!
gumi [goomi] rubber; tyre, (US) tire; elastic
gumidefekt puncture

GY

gyakran [djokron] often
gyalog [djolog] on foot
gyalogjáró [djolog-yaraw] pedestrian; pavement
gyalogjáróknak for pedestrians
gyalogjáróknak fenntartott utca pedestrian zone
gyaloglás [djolog-lash] walking
gyalogolni [djologolni] to walk
gyalogos [djologosh] pedestrian
gyalogos átkelőhely [atkelurheh^{yuh}] pedestrian crossing
gyalogosforgalom a túloldalon pedestrians cross over
gyalogosforgalom a bal oldalon pedestrians keep to the left
gyalogösvény [djologuhsh-vay^{nyuh}] footpath
gyapjú [djop-yoo] wool
gyapot [djopot] cotton
gyár [djar] factory
gyémánt [djaymant] diamond
gyenge [djengeh] weak
gyep [djep] lawn
gyerek [djerek] child
gyerekek [djerekek] children
gyerekjegy [djerek-yedj] children's ticket
gyerekkocsi [djerek-kochi] pram; pushchair
gyermek [djermek] child
gyermekadag [djermekodog] children's portion
gyermekek elől elzárva tartani keep out of the reach of children
gyermekosztály [djermek-osta^{yuh}] children's department
gyermekruha [djermek-rooho] children's clothing
gyertya [djer-tyo] candle; sparkplug
gyerünk! [djerewnk] come on!
gyógyfürdő(hely) [djawdj-fewrdurheh(^{yuh})] thermal baths, medicinal baths
gyógyszer [djawdjser] medicine
gyógyszertár [djawdj-sertar] pharmacy, dispensing chemist's
gyomor [djomor] stomach
gyomorfájás [djomorfī-ash] stomachache
gyomorrontás [djomorrontash] indigestion
gyors [djorsh] quick; fast
gyorsan [djorshon] quickly
gyorsvonat [djorsh-vonot] fast train with a few main stops
gyöngy [djuhndj] pearl
gyufa [djoofo] match
gyűjtemény [djew^{yuh}temay^{nyuh}] collection
gyűjteni [djew^{yuh}teni] to collect, to gather

gyümölcs [djewmuhlch] fruit
gyümölcskereskedés [djewmuhlch-keresh-kedaysh] fruit shop
gyűrű [djew-rew] ring

H

ha [ho] if
háború [haboroo] war
hagyni [hodjni] to let; to allow; to leave behind
hagyomány [hodjoma^{nyuh}] tradition
hagyományos [hodjoma-nyosh] traditional
haj [hoy] hair
hajadon [hoyodon] unmarried (woman)
hajbalzsam [hoy-bolJom], **hajkondicionáló** [hoy-konditsionalaw] conditioner
hajkrém [hoy-kraym] hair gel
hajlakk [hoy-lok] hairspray
hajmosás [hoy-moshash] wash
hajó [hoyaw] ship; boat
hajrögzítő zselatin [hoyruhg-zeetur Jelotin] styling mousse
hajszárító [hoy-sareetaw] hairdryer
hajvágás [hoy-vagash] haircut
hajvágószalon [hoy-vagawsolon] hairdressing salon
hal [hol] fish
halál [holal] death
halárus [holaroosh], **halas** [holosh] fishmonger's
hálás [halash] grateful
halász [holas] fisherman
hall [hol] foyer; lounge; he/she hears
hallani [holloni] to hear
hallgatni [hollgotni] to listen to
háló [halaw] net
hálóing [halaw-ing] nightdress
hálókabát [halaw-kobat] dressing gown
hálókocsi [halaw-kochi] sleeping car
hálószoba [halaw-sobo] bedroom
halott [holot] dead
hálóvendég [halaw-vendayg] overnight guest
hálózsák [halaw-Jak] sleeping bag
halvány [holva^{nyuh}] faint; pale
hamar [homor] soon
hamis [homish] false
hamis fogsor [fogshor] dentures
hamutálca [homootaltso], **hamutartó** [homootortaw] ashtray
hang [hong] voice
hanglemez [honglemez] record
hangos [hongosh] loud
hanglemezbolt [honglemezbolt] record shop
hangverseny [hongversheh^{nyuh}] concert
hangya [hondjo] ant
hány? [ha^{nyuh}] how many?
hány óra van? [awro von] what time is it?
harang [horong] bell (church)
harapás [horopash] bite (by dog)
harapnivaló [horopnivolaw] snack

harapós kutya beware of the dog
harisnya [horish-nyo] stockings
harisnyanadrág [horish-nyonodrag] tights, pantyhose
harmadik [harmodik] third
harmadika [hormodiko] third (of month)
harminc [hormints] thirty
harmincadika [hormints-adiko] thirtieth (of month)
harmincegyedike [hormints-edjeh-dikeh] thirty-first (of month)
három three
háromnegyedóra [harom-nedjedawro] three quarters of an hour
háromszáz [harom-saz] three hundred
has [hosh] belly
hashajtó [hosh-hoytaw] laxative
hasmenés [hosh-menaysh] diarrhoea
hasonló [hoshonlaw] similar
használat [hosnalot] use
használat előtt felrázandó shake before use
használati határidő use by date
használati utasítás directions for use
használni [hosnalni] to use
használt [hosnalt] second-hand
hasznos [hosnosh] useful
haszon [hoson] profit
hat [hot] six
hát [hat] back (of body)
hat.eng. licensed
határ [hotar] border
hátfájás [hatfī-ash] backache
hátizsák [hatiJak] rucksack
hatodik [hotodik] sixth
hatodika [hotodiko] sixth (of month)
hátráló sebesség [hatralaw shebesh-shayg] reverse gear
hátsó [hatshaw] rear, back
hátsólámpa [hatshaw-lampo] rear lights
hátsólépcső [hatshaw-laypchur] back stairs
hatszáz [hutsaz] six hundred
hatvan [hotvon] sixty
havi bérlet [hovi bayrlet] monthly pass
ház house
hazamenni [hozomenni] to go home
házas [hazosh] married (man, couple)
házasodni [hazoshodni] to get married (of man)
házaspár [hazoshpar] married couple
háztartási bolt [haztortashi] household goods shop
hazudni [hozoodni] to lie, tell a lie
hegedű [hegedew] violin
hegy [hedj] mountain; point (of knife etc)
hely [heh^{yuh}] seat; place; room, space
helyes [heh-yesh] correct, right
helyfoglalás [heh^{yuh}foglolash] seat reservation; flight reservation
helyfoglalás kötelező seats must be reserved

helyi beszélgetés [heh-yi besaylgetaysh] local call
helyi járat [yarot] local train
helyjegy [heh^{yuh}yedj] seat reservation
helység [heh^{yuh}shayg] place
hentes [hentesh] butcher's
hentesáru [hentesharoo] meat and meat products
hentesüzlet [henteshewzlet] butcher's
herceg [hertseg] prince
hercegnő [hertsegnur] princess
hét [hayt] seven; week
  hetenként [hetenkaynt] per week
  a héten [o hayten] this week
hetedik [hetedik] seventh
hetedike [hetedikeh] seventh (of month)
hétfő [haytfur] Monday
heti weekly
hetibérlet [heti-bayrlet] weekly pass
hetijegy [heti-yedj] weekly ticket
hétköznapokon [hayt-kuhz-nopokon] weekdays
hétszáz [haytsaz] seven hundred
hétvége [hayt-vaygeh] weekend
hetven seventy
HÉV Suburban Trains
-hez to (just outside); near to, beside
hiba [hibo] mistake; fault
hibabejelentő [hibo-bayelentur] faults service; engineer
hibás [hibash] wrong; faulty
hibás úttest bad surface
hibát elkövetni [elkuhvetni] to make a mistake
híd [heed] bridge
hidak [hidok] bridges
hideg cold
hidratáló [hidrotalaw] moisturizer
hihetetlen incredible
hímvessző [heemvessur] penis
hímzés [heemzaysh] embroidery
hinni to believe
hintőpor [hinturpor] talcum powder
hír [heer] news
hirdetés [hirdetaysh] advertisement
hírek [heerek] news
híres [heeresh] famous
hirtelen suddenly
hitelkártya [hitelkar-tyo] credit card
hitelkártyával fizetett beszélgetés call paid by credit card
hiv. office; official
hiv.sz. reference no.
hívás [heevash] call
hivatal [hivotol] office
hívják: hogy hívják? [hodj heev-yak] what's it called?
hívni [heevni] to call
hívógomb call button
hívott: a hívott fél fizet [o heevot fayl fizet] reverse charge call, collect call
hó [haw] snow
hogy(an)? [hodj(on)] how?
  hogy vagy? [vodj], **hogy van?** [von] how are you?

hogy-hogy? how's that?, how can it be?
hol? where?
hold [holld] moon
holnap [holnop] tomorrow
holnap délelőtt [daylelurt] tomorrow morning (10am–noon)
holnap éjjel [ay-yel] tomorrow night (late)
holnap este [eshteh] tomorrow night (early)
holnap reggel tomorrow morning (4–10am)
holnapután [holnop-ootan] the day after tomorrow
hólyag [haw-yog] blister; bladder; stupid person
homok sand
homokbuckák [homok-bootskak] sand dunes
homoszexuális [homoseksoo-alish] gay
hónap [hawnop] month
honnan? [honnon] where from?
hordár porter
horgászás [horgasash] fishing
horgászbot [horgasbot] fishing rod
horgászni [horgasni] to go fishing
horgászni tilos no fishing
horvát [horvat] Croatian
Horvátország [horvatorsag] Croatia
hossz(a) [hoss(o)] length
hosszú [hossoo] long
hosszúlejáratú [hossoo-layarotoo] long-term
hova? [hovo] where?
-hoz to (just outside); near to, beside
hozni to bring
hozzá to him
hő [hur] heat
hölgy [huhldj] lady
hölgyek [huhldjek] ladies' toilet, ladies' room
hőmérő [hurmayrur] thermometer
hőmérséklet [hurmayr-shayklet] temperature
-höz [-huhz] to (just outside); near to, beside
húg [hoog] sister (younger)
hulladék [hoollodayk] litter
hullámlovagló [hoollam-lovoglaw] sailboard
húr [hoor] string
hús [hoosh] meat
húsbolt [hooshbolt] butcher's
Húsvét [hooshvayt] Easter
húsz [hoos] twenty
huszadika [hoosodiko] twentieth (of month)
huszonegy [hooson-edj] twenty-one
huszonegyedike [hooson-edjeh-dikeh] twenty-first (of month)
huszonharmadika [hooson-hormodiko] twenty-third (of month)
huszonhatodika [hooson-hotodiko] twenty-sixth (of month)
huszonhetedike [hooson-heteh-dikeh] twenty-seventh (of month)

huszonkét [hooson-kayt] twenty-two
huszonkettedike [hooson-ketteh-dikeh] twenty-second (of month)
huszonkettő [hooson-kettur] twenty-two
huszonkilencedike [hooson-kilentseh-dikeh] twenty-ninth (of month)
huszonnegyedike [hooson-nedjeh-dikeh] twenty-fourth (of month)
huszonnyolcadika [hooson-nyoltso-diko] twenty-eighth (of month)
huszonötödike [hooson-uhtuh-dikeh] twenty-fifth (of month)
huzat [hoozot] draught
húzni [hoozni] to pull; pull
hülye [hew-yeh] idiot
hűtőszekrény [hewtur-sekray[nyuh]] fridge
hűtőszekrényben tartani keep in refrigerator
hűtve kell fogyasztani served chilled
hűvös [hewvuhsh] cool
hűvös helyen tartandó, hűvös helyen tartani keep in a cool place

I/Í

-i his/her; your (pl)
IC Intercity train
-id your (pl)
ide [ideh] here
idegen stranger; strange
idegennyelvű könyvüzlet [idegen-nyelvew kuh[nyuh]vewzlet] foreign language bookshop/bookstore
ideges [idegesh] nervous
ideiglenes [ideh-iglenesh] temporary
ideiglenes sebességkorlátozás temporary speed limit
idén [idayn] this year
idő [idur] time; weather
mennyi az idő? [men-nyi oz] what's the time?
időjárás [idur-yarash] weather
időjárásjelentés [idur-yarash-yelentaysh] weather forecast
időnként [idurnkaynt] occasionally
időszak [idursok] period
ifjúsági szálló [if-yooshagi sallaw] youth hostel
-ig until; up to, as far as
öt óráig until 5 o'clock
igaz [igoz] true
igaza(d) van [igozo(d) von] you're right
igazán [igozan] really
igazán nagyon sajnálom [nodjon shoynalom] I'm really sorry
igazgató [igozgotaw] director; manager
igazi [igozi] genuine
igazolás [igozolash], **igazolvány** [igozolva[nyuh]] certificate
igazságos [igoJagosh] fair, just
igen yes
igen sürgős beszélgetés [shewrgursh besaylgetaysh] very

urgent call
így [eedj] thus
-ik their; your (pl)
illat [illot] smell
illatszertár [illot-sertar] non-dispensing chemist's
-im my (pl)
index indicator
indokolatlan használatért bírság róható ki penalty for misuse
indulás [indoolash] departure(s)
induló járatok [indoolaw yarotok] departures
indulóváró [indoolaw-varaw] departure lounge; departure gate
induló vonatok [vonotok] departures
infarktus [inforktoosh] heart attack
információ [informatsiaw] information
ing shirt
ingyen(es) [indjen(esh)] free (of charge)
injekció [i-nyektsiaw] injection
-ink our (pl)
inkább rather
inni to drink
interurbán hívás [interoorban heevash] long-distance call
ír [eer] Irish; he/she writes
irány [ira^{nyuh}] direction
irányítószám [ira-nyeetawsam] postcode, zip code
irányjelző [ira^{nyuh}yelzur] indicator
iránytű [ira^{nyuh}tew] compass
irat(ok) [irot(ok)] document(s)
írni [eerni] to write
író [eeraw] writer
iroda [irodo] office
írországi [eerorsagi] Irish
is [ish] also; too
iskola [ishkolo] school
ismerni [ishmerni] to know
ismét [ishmayt] again
ismételni [ishmaytelni] to repeat
Isten [ishten] God
Isten hozta! [hozto] welcome!
istentisztelet [ishtentistelet] mass, church service
iszappakolás [isoppokolash] mudpack
ital [itol] drink
italbolt [itolbolt] off-licence, liquor store
-itek, -itok your (pl)
itt here
itt van/vannak [von/vonnok] here is/are
ivóvíz [ivaw-veez] drinking water
íz [eez] flavour
ízesítő flavouring
ízesítve: ...-val/vel ízesítve flavoured with ...
izgalmas [izgolmosh] exciting
ízlés [eezlaysh] taste

J

-ja [-yo] his; her; your
-jai [-yo-ee] his/her; your (pl)
-jaik [-yo-eek] their; your (pl)
január [yonoo-ar] January
járat [yarot] flight

járatszám [yarotsam] flight number
járda [yardo] pavement, sidewalk
jármű [yarmew] vehicle
járókelő [yarawkelur] passer-by; pedestrian
játék [yataykl] game; toy
játékbolt toy shop
játszani [yatsoni] to play
javítani [yoveetoni] to improve; to mend
javítás [yoveetash] repair
javítóműhely [yoveetaw-mewheh^{yuh}] garage
javulni [yovoolni] to improve
-je [-yeh] his; her; your
jég [yayg] ice
jégeső [yaygeshur] hail
jégpálya [yaygpa-yo] ice rink
jegy [yedj] ticket
  a jegyeket kérem [o yedjeket kayrem] tickets please
jegyeladás ticket sales
jegy- és poggyászkezelés [yedj-aysh pogdjas-kezelaysh] ticket and baggage check-in
jegyezve: **el van jegyezve** [von yedjezveh] engaged
jegyiroda [yedj-irodo] box office; ticket office
jegykalauz [yedj-kolowz] ticket collector
jegykezelés [yedj-kezelaysh] check-in
jegykezelőpult [yedj-kezelurpoolt] check-in desk
jegypénztár [yedj-paynztar] ticket office, booking office
jegyszedő [yedj-sedur] conductor
jegyváltás [yedj-valtash] ticket office
jegyzet [yedj-zet] note
jegyzetfüzet [jedj-zet-fewzet] notebook
jelenteni [yelenteni] to mean; to report
jó [yaw] good
jobb [yob] better; right
jobban szeretni [yobbon seretni] to prefer
jobboldalt [yobboldolt], **jobbra** [yobbro] on the right
jó éjszakát [yaw ay^{yuh}sokat], **jó éjt** [ay^{yuh}t] good night
jó estét (kívánok) [eshtayt (keevanok)] good evening
jó étvágyat (kívánok)! [aytvadjot] enjoy your meal!
jog [yog] right; law
jogosítvány [yogosheetva^{nyuh}] driving licence; authorisation
jóízű [yaw-eezew] nice
jóképű [yaw-kaypew] handsome
jól [yawl] well
  jól van [von] OK
jó napot (kívánok) [yaw nopot (keevanok)] hello; good afternoon; good morning
jó reggelt (kívánok) good morning
jó utat! [ootot] have a good journey!
jó vásár [vashar] bargain
jöjjön ide! [yuh-yuhn ideh] come here!

jönni [yuhnni] to come
jövő [yuhvur] future; next
 jövő héten [hayten] next week
jövőre [yuhvurreh] next year
-juk [-yook] their; your
 van ...-juk? [von] have you got ...?
július [yooli-oosh] July
június [yooni-oosh] June
-jük [-yewk] their; your

K

-k plural ending
kabát [kobat] coat; jacket
kábítószer [kabeetawser] drug
kagyló [kodjlaw] receiver; shell
kajak [koyok] canoe
kajakozás [koyokozash] canoeing
kalap [kolop] hat
kamaraszínház [komoro-seenhaz] small-stage theatre
kamarazene [komoro-zeneh] chamber music
kamat [komot] interest
kanál [konal] spoon
kanyar [ko-nyor] bend
kapcsolat [kopcholot] connection
kapcsoló [kopcholaw] switch
kaphatnék: kaphatnék ...? [kop-hotnayk] can I have ...?
kapni [kopni] to get; to receive
kar [kor] arm
kár damage; it's a pity
Karácsony [koracho[nyuh]] Christmas
karambol [korombol] crash
karcsú [korchoo] slim
karkötő [korkuhtur] bracelet
karóra [korawro] watch
Kárpátok Carpathian Mountains
karperec [korperets] bracelet
karton [korton] cotton; cardboard
kártya [kar-tyo] card
karzat [korzot] gallery
kassza [kosso] cash desk
katolikus [kotolikoosh] Catholic
kávéház [kavayhaz] coffee house
kávéskanál [kavayshkonal] teaspoon
kazettás magnó [kozettash mognaw] cassette player
kb. approximately
kedd Tuesday
kedv mood; humour
kedvelni to like
kedvenc [kedvents] favourite
kedves [kedvesh] kind
kedvezményes utazás travel concessions
kefe [kefeh] brush
kék [kayk] blue
kelet east
kell must, have to; need
 nem kell there's no need
kellemes [kellemesh] nice; pleasant
kellemes karácsonyi ünnepeket! [koracho-nyi ewnnepeket] merry Christmas!
kellemetlen unpleasant; embarrassing
kellett had to
kemény [kemay[nyuh]] hard

kemény lencse [lencheh] hard lenses
kemping camping
kenőcs [kenurch] ointment
kenu [kenoo] canoe
kenuzás [kenoozash] canoeing
kényelmes [kay-nyelmesh] comfortable
kenyér [keh-nyayr] bread
kép [kayp] picture
képes folyóirat [kaypesh foyaw-irot] magazine
képeslap [kaypeshlop] picture postcard
képtár [kayptar] art gallery
ker. district
kérdés [kayrdaysh] question
kérdezni [kayrdezni] to ask
kerek round
kerék [kerayk] wheel
kerekek wheels
kerékpár [keraykpar] bicycle
kerékpáros [keraykpar-osh] cyclist
kerékpározás [keraykpar-ozash] cycling
kerékpárösvény [keraykpar-uhsh-vay^{nyuh}] cycle path
kerékpártúra [keraykpar-tooro] cycling; cycling trip
kérem [kayrem] please
kérem, hogy tartsa a vonalat please, hold the line
kérem tartani [kayrem tortoni] please hold
kérem, tegye le a kagylót please, hang up
keresni [kereshni] to look for; to earn
kereső [kereshur] viewfinder
keresztény [kerestay^{nyuh}] Christian
keresztnév [kerestnayv] first name
keresztül [kerestewl] through
kerítés [kereetaysh] fence
kert garden
kerthelyiség [kert-heh-yishayg] open-air restaurant
kerület [kerewlet] district
kerülni [kerewlni] to cost
mennyibe kerül? [men-nyibeh] how much is it?
kés [kaysh] knife
keserű [kesherew] bitter
késés [kayshaysh] delay
keskeny [keshkeh^{nyuh}] narrow
késni [kayshni] to be late
késő [kayshur] late
későre jár [kayshurreh yar] it's getting late
később [kayshurb] later on
kész [kays] over; finished; ready
készpénz [kayspaynz] cash
készpénz automata [owtomoto] cash dispenser, ATM
készpénzben fizetni to pay cash
kesztyű [kes-tyew] gloves
két [kayt] two
kétágyas szoba [kaytadjosh sobo] room with twin beds
kétezer [kaytezer] two thousand
két hét [kayt hayt] fortnight
kétszáz [kaytsaz] two hundred
kétszemélyes ágy [kaytsemay-yesh adj] double bed
kettő [kettur] two

kettős [kettursh] double
kettős megállóhely double stop
kevés [kevaysh] few, a little
kevesebb [kevesheb] less
kéz [kayz] hand
kézbesítés [kayz-besheetaysh] delivery
kezdeni to begin; to start
kezdet beginning
kezdő [kezdur] beginner
kezek hands
kezelési díj [kezelayshi dee^{yuh}] handling charge, commission
kezelni to treat, to handle
kézi [kayzi] manual
kézifék [kayzifayk] handbrake
kézi kapcsolással through the operator
kézileg mosni wash by hand
kézimunka [kayzi-moonko] embroidery
kézipoggyász [kayzi-pogdjas] hand luggage/baggage
kézitáska [kayzi-tashko] handbag, (US) purse
kezitcsókolom [kezit-chawkolom] hello (very polite)
kézműipar [kayzmew-ipor] crafts
kéztörlő [kayzturlur] serviette, napkin
ki? who?
kiállítás [kialleetash] exhibition
kiárúsítás [kiaroosheetosh] sale
kiárusítási vásár closing down sale
ki beszél? [besayl] who's calling?

kicsi [kichi] small, little
(egy) kicsit [edj] a little bit
kicsomagolni [kichomogolni] to unpack; to unwrap
kié: kié ez? [kiay] whose is this?
kificamodott [kifitsomodot] sprained
kifogyott [kifodjot] out of stock, sold out
kifőzés [kifurzaysh] takeaway
kígyó [keedjaw] snake
kihajolni veszélyes és tilos do not lean out
kihúzó ceruza [ki-hoozaw tseroozo] eyeliner
kijárat [ki-yarot] way out, exit; gate
kijárat a vonatokhoz to the trains
kijutni [ki-yootni] to get out
kikapcsolni [kikop-cholni] to switch off
kikapcsolva [kikop-cholvo] off, switched off
kikötőhely [kikuh-turheh^{yuh}] jetty, pier
kilátás [kilatash] view; prospect
kilenc [kilents] nine
kilencedik [kilentseh-dik] ninth
kilencedike [kilentseh-dikeh] ninth (of the month)
kilencven [kilentsven] ninety
kilencszáz [kilents-saz] nine hundred
kilincs [kilinch] door handle
kimenni to go out
kínai [keeno-ee] Chinese
kínos [keenosh] embarrassing

kint outside
kinyitni [ki-nyitni] to open
kipufogó [kipoofogaw] exhaust
kipufogócső [kipoofogaw-chur] exhaust pipe
király [kira^{yuh}] king
királyné [kira^{yuh}nay] queen (wife of king)
királynő [kira^{yuh}nur] queen (in own right)
kirándulás [kirandoolash] trip, excursion
kiránduló hajó [kirandoolaw hoyaw] excursion boat
kis [kish] little; some
egy kis ... [edj] some ...
kisasszony [kishosso^{nyuh}] Miss
kisbaba [kishbobo] baby
kísérleti színház [keeshayrleti seenhaz] experimental theatre
kisétálni [kishaytalni] to go for a walk
kishajójárat [kish-hoyaw-yarot] passenger ferry service
kistányér [kishta-nyayr] saucer
kiszállni [kisallni] to get off
kiszolgálás [kisolgalash] service; service charge
kiszolgálási díj [kisolgalashi dee^{yuh}] service charge
kiszolgáló [kisolgalaw] shop assistant
kiszolgálólány [kisolgalaw-la^{nyuh}], **kiszolgálónő bárban** [kisolgalaw-nur barbon] barmaid
kitölteni [kituhlteni] to fill in
kitűnő [kitewnur] excellent
kiürítés ideje [ki-ewreetaysh idayeh] collection times
kivált especially
kívánni [keevanni] to wish
kívánság [keevanshag] wish
fogadja legjobb kívánságomat [fogod-yo leg-yobb keevanshagomot] best wishes
kivel beszélek? [besaylek] who's speaking?
kivéve [kivayveh] except
kivéve célforgalom access only
kívül [keevewl] outside
klasszikus zene [klossikoosh zeneh] classical music
klinika [kliniko] specialist department; teaching hospital
kocogni [kotsogni] to jog
kocsi [kochi] carriage; car; trolley
kocsiállás [kochiallash] bus stand, departure bay
kocsira felvenni valakit [kochiro felvenni volokit] to give a lift to
kollégium [kollaygi-oom] college
komoly [komoy] serious
komp ferry
kompakt lemez [kompokt] compact disc
Komturist tourist information office
koncert [kontsert] concert
konfekció [konfektsi-aw] clothing shop
konnektor socket
kontaktlencse [kontoktlencheh] contact lenses

konyha [ko^{nyuh}ho] kitchen
konyhaeszközök [ko^{nyuh}ho-eskuhzuhk] cooking utensils
konyharuha [ko^{nyuh}horooho] tea towel
konzerv can, tin
konzervnyitó [konzerv-nyitaw] tin-opener
konzulátus [konzoolatoosh] consulate
kor age
kora(i) [koro(-ee)] early (adj)
korán early (adverb)
korcsolya [korcho-yo] skates
korcsolyapálya [korcho-yo-pa-yo] skating rink
korcsolyázni [korcho-yazni] to skate
korcsoport age group
kórház [kawrhaz] hospital
korlátozott várakozás limited waiting
kormány [korma^{nyuh}] government
kormánymű [korma^{nyuh}mew] steering
korsó [korshaw] jug; half-litre beer mug
korszerű [korserew] modern
kosár [koshar] basket
kóstolni [kawshtolni] to taste
kosztüm [kostewm] suit (woman's)
kozmetika [kozmetiko], **kozmetikai szerek** [kozmetiko-ee serek] cosmetics
kozmetikus [kozmetikoosh] skin-care specialist; beautician
kő [kur] stone
köd [kuhd] fog; mist
ködös [kuhduhsh] foggy; dim; confusing
köhögés [kuh-huhgaysh] cough
köhögni [kuh-huhgni] to cough
kölcsönadni [kuhlchuhn-odni] to lend
kölcsönvenni [kuhlchuhn-venni] to borrow
kölni [kuhlni] perfume
kölni férfiaknak [fayrfioknok] aftershave
kölni víz [veez] eau de toilette
költeni [kuhlteni] to spend
költség [kuhltshayg] cost
könnyű [kuhn-nyew] easy; light
könyök [kuh^{nyuh}k] elbow
könyv [kuh^{nyuh}v] book
könyvesbolt [kuh^{nyuh}veshbolt] bookshop, bookstore
könyvtár [kuh^{nyuh}vtar] library
könyvüzlet [kuh^{nyuh}vewzlet] bookshop, bookstore
kör [kuhr] circle
köralakú [kuhr-olokoo] round
körbehajtás [kuhr-behoytash] roundabout
körmök [kuhr-muhk] nails
köröm [kuhruhm] nail
körömlakk [kuhruhmlok] nail polish
körömlakk tisztító [tisteetaw] nail polish remover
körömreszelő [kuhruhm-reselur] nailfile
körte [kurteh] pear; light bulb
körút [kurroot] boulevard
körül [kurewl] round, around
körülbelül [kurewl-belewl], **körüli** about, approximately

körzethívószám [kurzet-heevawsam] code
körzeti orvos [kurzeti orvosh] panel doctor
körzeti orvosi rendelő [rendelur] GP's surgery, doctor's office
kösz [kuhs] ta, thanks
köszönöm [kuhsuhnuhm] thank you
köszönöm nem no thank you
köszönöm szépen [saypen] thank you very much
kötél [kuhtayl] rope
kötés [kuhtaysh], **kötszer** [kuhtser] bandage
köv. next
kövér [kuhvayr] fat
követelés [kuhvetelaysh] demand; claim, credit balance
következő [kuhvet-kezur] next
következő megálló [megallaw] next stop
követni [kuhvetni] to follow
köz [kuhz] lane; space
közben [kuhzben] meanwhile
közbenső állomásokon nem áll meg does not stop at stations in between
közel [kuhzel] near, close
közép [kuhzayp] middle
közepén [kuhzepayn] in the middle
közepes nagyságú [kuhzepesh nodjshagoo] medium-sized
közlekedés [kuhzlekedaysh] traffic
közlekedési lámpa [lampo] traffic lights
közönség [kuhzuhnshayg] audience; public
között [kuhzuht] among; between
közp., központ [kuhzpont] centre; central
központi fűtés [fewtaysh] central heating
központi jegyiroda [yedjirodo] central booking office
közvetett [kuhzvetet] indirect
közvetlen direct
közvetlen járat [yarot] direct flight
közvetlen tárcsázás [tarchazash] direct dialling
kp/k.p. cash
krém [kraym] face cream
kresz. traffic regulations, highway code
kulcs [koolch] key
kulcsra zárni [koolchro] to lock
kupak [koopok] cap (of bottle)
kuplung [kooploong] clutch
kusett [kooshet] couchette
kutya [koo-tyo] dog
küldeni [kewldeni] to send
küldönc [kewlduhnts] messenger, courier
külföldi [kewlfuhldi] foreign; foreigner
külföldi díjszabás [dee^{yuh}sobash] postage abroad
külföldön [kewlfuhlduhn] abroad
külön [kewluhn] separate; separately; extra

különálló [kewluhn-allaw] separate
különben otherwise
különböző [kewluhn-buhzur] different
különbül [kewluhn-bewl] better
különélő [kewluhn-aylur] separated (couple)
különleges ajánlat [kewluhn-legesh oyanlot] special offer
különös [kewluhn-uhsh] strange; funny, amusing
különösen [kewluhn-uhshen] especially
külső vágányokhoz to outside platforms/tracks
külváros(ok) [kewlvarosh(ok)] suburb(s)

L

láb leg; foot
lábas [labosh] saucepan
labda [lobdo] ball
labdarúgás [lobdo-roogash] football
labdarúgó pálya [lobdo-roogaw pa-yo] football ground
labdázásra kijelölt terület area reserved for ball games
labdázni tilos no ball games
lábfej [labfay] foot
lábujj [laboo^{yuh}] toe
lágy lencse [ladj lencheh] soft lenses
lakás [lokash] flat, apartment
lakni [lokni] to live, to dwell
lakó [lokaw] tenant; inhabitant
lakodalom [lokodolom] wedding feast
lakókocsi [lokawkochi] caravan, (US) trailer
lakókocsi parkoló [porkolaw] caravan site, trailer park
lakosztály [lokostay] suite
lakótelep [lokawtelep] high-rise housing estate
lámpa [lampo] light
lánc [lants] chain
langyos [londjosh] lukewarm
lány [la^{nyuh}] girl; daughter
lánya [la-nyo] his/her daughter
lányom [la-nyom] my daughter
lánynév [la^{nyuh}nayv] maiden name
lánytestvér [la^{nyuh}teshtvayr] sister
lap [lop] card; sheet; page; newspaper
lapos [loposh] flat (level)
lassan [losh-shon] slowly
lassan (hajts)! slow!
lassú [losh-shoo] slow
látni to see
látnivalók [latnivolawk] the sights
látogatás [latogotash] visit
látogatási idő [idur] visiting hours
látogató [latogotaw] visitor
látszani [latsoni] to appear
látszerész [latserays] optician
látvány [latva^{nyuh}] view
láz fever
le [leh] down

leállítani [leh-alleetoni] to switch off
lecke [letskeh] lesson
ledőlni [ledurlni] to lie down; to collapse
leégés [leh-aygaysh] sunburn
leértékelés [leh-ayrtay-kelaysh] discount, sale
leértékelt reduced
lefeküdni [lefekewdni] to go to bed; to lie down; to go to sleep
lefoglalni [lefoglolni] to book
lefordítani [lefordeetoni] to translate
leg- the most
legalább [legolab] at least
legalsó [legolshaw] the lowest, the bottom
legfelső [legfelshur] the highest, the top
legfelül [legfelewl] at the top
légikisasszony [laygiki-shosso^{nyuh}] stewardess
légiposta [laygi-poshto] airmail; by airmail
légipostán [laygi-poshtan] by airmail
légitársaság [laygi-tarshoshag] airline
légiutaskisérő [laygi-ootosh-kishayrur] steward
legjobb [leg-yob] best
legkevesebb [legkevesheb] least
légkondicionálás [layg-konditsionalash] air-conditioning
légkondicionáló [layg-konditsionalaw] air-conditioning
légkondicionált air-conditioned
legközelebb [legkuhzeleb] next
  a legközelebbi ... the nearest ...
legrosszabb [legrossob] worst
légszárítás [laygsareetash] blow-dry
legtöbb [legtuhb] most, most of
legtöbben most people
légy [laydj] fly
legy(en) szíves! [ledj(en) seevesh] excuse me!; would you please ...
legyen szíves hangosabban beszélni please, speak up
lehet maybe; possible
  lehet beszélni you can speak with the number now
lehetetlen impossible
lehetséges [lehet-shaygesh] possible
lék [layk] leak
lekésni [lekayshni] to miss
lemenni to go down
lencse [lencheh] lens; lentils
lengyel [lendjel] Polish
Lengyelország [lendjel-orsag] Poland
lenn, lent downstairs
lenyelni [leh-nyelni] to swallow
lépcső [laypchur] stairs
lépcsőház staircase
lepedő [lepedur] sheet
lepihenni to take a rest
lerobbanni [lerobbonni] to break down

lesikló pálya [leshiklaw pa-yo] ski slope
lesülés [leshewlaysh] suntan
lesülni [leshewlni] to tan
lesz [les] he/she/it will be
ez jó lesz that will be fine
leszállás [lesallash] exit
leszállítás [lesalleetash] delivery
leszállított árak reduced prices
leszállni [lesallni] to get off; to get out; to land
leszek [lesek] I will be
leszel [lesel] you will be
lesznek [lesnek] they will be
lesztek [lestek] you will be
leszünk [lesewnk] we will be
lesz szíves [les seevesh] excuse me!; would you please
letartóztatni [letortawz-totni] to arrest
letét [letayt] deposit
létra [laytro] ladder
leülni [leh-ewlni] to sit down
levegő [levegur] air
levegőfrissítő [levegur-frishsheetur] air-freshener
levegőnyomás [levegur-nyomash] air pressure
levél [levayl] letter; leaf
levelek letters; leaves
levelesláda [levelesh-lado] letterbox, mail box
levelező barát [levelezur borat] penfriend
levelezőlap [levelezurlop] postcard
levélfelvétel [levayl-felvaytel] letters counter
levélpapír [levayl-popeer] writing paper
levéltárca [levayl-tartso] wallet
levenni to take off
levetkőzni [levetkurzni] to get undressed
lift lift, elevator
a lift nem működik the lift is out of order
liget park
lila [lilo] purple
lista [lishto] list
ló [law] horse
lopás [lopash] theft
lopni to steal
lovaglás [lovoglash] horseriding
lovaglóiskola [lovoglaw-ishkolo] riding school
lovagolni [lovogolni] to go horse-riding
lovarda [lovordo] riding school
lovasbemutató [lovosh-bemootataw] equestrian show
lóversenypálya [lawver-sheh[nyuh]pa-yo] race course
lusta [looshto] lazy

LY

lyuk [yook] hole

M

-m my
ma [mo] today
macska [mochko] cat
macskajaj [mochkoyoy] hangover
madár [modar] bird

ma délután [mo daylootan] this afternoon
ma éjjel [ay-yel] tonight; this morning (midnight–4am)
ma este [eshteh] this evening, tonight
maga [mogo] you; ...-self
magam [mogom] myself
magamtól [mogom-tawl] by myself; from myself
magán(lakás) [mogan(lokash)] private
magánterület private grounds
magántulajdon private property
magánút [moganoot] private road
magas [mogosh] high; tall
magasföldszint [mogosh-fuhldsint] mezzanine
maguk(at) [mogook(ot)] you
magyar [modjor] Hungarian
a magyarok the Hungarians
magyarul [modjorool] in Hungarian
magyar gyártmány made in Hungary
Magyarország [modjororsag] Hungary
Magyar Posta [poshto] Hungarian Post Office
magyarul beszélő ... film ... film dubbed into Hungarian
máj [mī] liver
majdnem [moydnem] almost
május [mī-oosh] May
MALÉV [molayv] Hungarian national airline
már already
maradék [morodayk] rest, remainder
maradni [morodni] to stay
március [martsi-oosh] March
ma reggel this morning (4–10am)
márvány [marva^{nyuh}] marble
más: az más [oz mash] that's different
valami más [volomi] something else
máshol [mash-hol] elsewhere
másik [mashik] other; another, different
másikat [mashikot] another one, a different one
másnap [mashnop] the next day
második [mashodik] second
másodika [mashodiko] second (of month)
másodosztály [mashod-osta^{yuh}] second class
másodperc [mashod-perts] second
mással beszél [mash-shol besayl] engaged (phone)
mást nem parancsol will there be anything else?
másvalaki [mashvoloki] someone else
másvalami [mashvolomi] something else
matrac [motrots] mattress
MÁV Hungarian State Railways
maximális súly maximum weight
meccs [metsch] match (sport)
medence [medentseh] pool

medencében: a medencében az úszósapka használata kötelező bathing caps must be worn in the pool
medencében: a medencében labdázni tilos no ball games in the pool
még [mayg] still, yet; even more; some more
még mindig still
még nem not yet
még egy [edj] another, one more
megakadt [megokot] stuck
megállni to stop
megállni tilos no stopping
megálló [megallaw] bus stop; tram stop
megborotválkozni [megborotvalkozni] to shave
megcsúszni [megchoosni] to skid
megdöbbentő [megduhb-bentur] appalling
megégetni [megaygetni] to burn
megelőzni [megelurzni] to overtake
megengedni to allow
megérkezni [megayrkezni] to arrive, to get in
megerősíteni [megerursheeteni] to confirm
megerőszakolni [megerursokolni] to rape
megérteni [megayrteni] to understand
megfázás [megfazash] cold
megfelelni to suit
ez megfelel? will this do?
megfürödni [megfewruhdni] to have a bath
meggyújtani [meg-djoo[yuh]toni] to light
meghalni [megholni] to die
meghívás [megheevash] invitation
meghívni [megheevni] to invite
megígérni [megeegayrni] to promise
megint again
megjavítani [meg-yoveetoni] to repair
megkóstolni [megkaw-shtolni] to taste
megköszönni [megkuh-suhnni] to thank
meglátogatni [meglatogotni] to visit
meglepetés [meglepetaysh] surprise
meglepő [meglepur] surprising
megmagyarázni [megmodjorazni] to explain
megnyugodni [meg-nyoogodni] to calm down; to relax
megosztani [megostoni] to share
megőrző [megurzur] left luggage, baggage checkroom
megőrzőben hagyott poggyász [hodjot podjas] left luggage
megpróbálni [megprawbalni] to try
megrendelés [megrendelaysh] order
megrendelni to order
megrongálni to damage

megszakítás nélkül [megsokeetash naylkewl] direct (flight etc)
megszállni [megsallni] to stay
megszúrni [megsoorni] to sting
megtartani [megtortoni] to keep
megtelt no vacancies; full
megtéríteni [megtayreeteni] to refund
megváltani [megvaltoni] to book
megvenni to buy
méh [mayH] bee; womb
meleg warm
melegedő [melegedur] rest lounge
mell chest; breast
mellék [mellayk] extension (phone)
melléklet supplement
mellett next to, beside, by
mellkas [melkosh] chest
melltartó [meltortaw] bra
melltű [meltew] brooch
mély [may^{yuh}] deep
mélyhűtő [may^{yuh}hewtur] freezer
melyik? [meh-yik] which?
mélytányér [may^{yuh}ta-nyayr] bowl
menetdíj [menet-dee^{yuh}] fare
menetjegy [menet-yedj] ticket
menetjegykiadás [menet-yedj-kiodash] ticket counter
menet közben a vezetővel beszélni tilos do not speak to the driver while vehicle is in motion
menetrend timetable, (US) schedule
menetrendszerinti járat [menetrend-serinti yarot] scheduled flight
menettérti jegy [menettayrti yedj] return ticket, round-trip ticket
menjen át a túloldalra cross the road
menj(en) innen! [men(-yen)] go away!
menni to go
mennydörgéses vihar [men^{nyuh}dur-gayshesh vihor] thunderstorm
mennyezet [men-nyezet] ceiling
mennyi? [men-nyi] how many?
mennyi az idő? [oz idur] what's the time?
mennyibe kerül? [men-nyibeh kerewl] how much is it?
mentacukor [mento-tsookor] peppermints
mentőautó [mentur-owtaw] ambulance
mentők [menturk] ambulance service
meny [meh^{nyuh}] daughter-in-law
menyasszony [meh-nyosso^{nyuh}] fiancée
meredek steep
méreg [mayreg] poison
méret [mayret] size
merev lencse [lencheh] hard lenses
mérföld [mayrfuhld] mile
mérkőzés [mayrkurzaysh] match
merni to dare
mérnök [mayrnuhk] engineer
mert because
messze [messeh] far, far away

mesterséges [meshter-shaygesh] artificial
metró [metraw] underground, (US) subway
mező [mezur] field
meztelen naked
mi we
mi? what?
miatt [miot] because of
miénk: **a miénk** [o miaynk] ours
miért? [mi-ayrt] why?; what for?
miféle ...? [mifayleh] what kind ...?
míg [meeg] while
mikor? when?
millió [milli-aw] million
milyen ...? [mi-yen] what is ... like?
mind all
  mind ... mind ... both ... and...
mindegyik [mindedjik] each, every
minden all; every; everything
  ez minden that's all
  ez minden? will this be all?
mindenhol everywhere
mindenki everyone
minden nap [nop] every day
mindenütt [mindenewt] everywhere
mindig always
mindketten, mindkettő [mindkettur] both
mindkettőnk both of us
minket us
minőség [minurshayg] quality
minőségi áru quality product
mint like; as; than
mit? what?
mivel as; since
  mivel? with what?
  mivel szolgálhatok? how can I help you?
mocsok [mochok] filth
mohamedán [mohomedan] Muslim
móló [mawlaw] quay, pier, jetty
mondani [mondoni] to say
  ne mondd! [neh], **ne mondja!** [mond-yo] you don't say!
mosakodni [moshokodni] to wash
mosás-berakás [moshash-berokash] wash and set
mosdó [moshdaw] toilet, lavatory, rest room; hand basin
mosdók toilets, lavatories, rest rooms
mosdókagyló [moshdaw-kodjlaw] basin, sink
mosni [moshni] to wash, to do the washing
mosoda [moshodo] laundry
mosogatás [moshogotash] washing-up
mosogató [moshogotaw] kitchen sink
mosogatógép [moshogotaw-gayp] dishwasher
mosogatószer [moshogotaw-ser] washing-up liquid
mosógép [moshawgayp] washing machine
mosógépben mosható machine washable
mosoly [mosho[yuh]] smile

mosolyogni [mosho-yogni] to smile
mosópor [moshawpor] washing powder
mosott ruha [moshott rooho] washing
most [mosht] now
mostoha anya [moshtoho o-nyo] stepmother
mostoha apa [opo] stepfather
most tessék bedobni a pénzt please, insert the money now
most tessék bedugni a kártyát please, push the card in now
motor [mo-tor] engine
motorcsónak [mo-tor-chawnok] motorboat
motorháztető [mo-tor-haztetur] bonnet, (US) hood
motorkerékpár [mo-tor-keraykpar] motorbike
mozdony [mozdo^{nyuh}] engine
mozgólépcső [mozgaw-laypchur] escalator
mozi cinema, movie theater
mozogni to move
mögött [muhguht] behind
mulató [moolotaw] nightclub
mulatságos [moolot-shagosh] funny, amusing
múlt [moolt] past; last
  múlt éjjel [ay-yel] last night
  tíz perccel múlt egy ten past one
múlva: három nap múlva [nop moolvo] in three days
mumsz [mooms] mumps
munka [moonko] work; job
munkanapokon (hetfőtől péntekig) weekdays, Monday to Friday
munkanélküli [moonkonayl-kewli] unemployed
munkaszüneti napok kivételével naponta daily, except on public holidays
munkaszüneti napokon on bank holidays, Sundays and public holidays
múzeum [moozeh-oom] museum
muzulmán [moozoolman] Muslim
műanyag [mewo-nyog] plastic
műanyagszatyor [mewo-nyogso-tyor] plastic bag
műanyag talp [tolp] synthetic sole
műanyag zacskó [zochkaw] plastic bag
műbőr [mewbur] artificial leather
műemlék [mewemlayk] monument
műfogsor [mewfogshor] dentures
működik: nem működik [nem mewkuhdik] it's not working
működni [mewkuhdni] to function
műsor [mewshor] programme; brochure
műszaki áruk [mewsoki arook] household goods and DIY
műszaki hiba [hibo] technical fault, breakdown

műtét [mewtayt] operation; surgery
művész [mewvays] artist (man)
művészet [mewvayset] art
művésznő [mewvaysnur] artist (woman)

N

-n on; in; at; adverbial suffix
nadrág [nodrag] trousers, (US) pants
na és? [no aysh] so what?
nagy [nodj] big
nagyanya [nodj-nyo] grandmother
nagyapa [nodj-opo] grandfather
nagybácsi [nodj-bachi] uncle
Nagy-Britannia [nodj-britonnio] Great Britain, Britain
nagyítás [nodj-eetash] enlargement
nagykövetség [nodj-kuhvetshayg] embassy
nagymama [nodj-momo] grandmother
nagyméretű [nodj-mayretew] large
nagynéni [nodj-nayni] aunt
nagyon [nodjon] very; very much
nagypapa [nodj-popo] grandfather
nagypéntek [nodj-payntek] Good Friday
nagyszerű [nodj-serew] excellent
-nak [-nok] to; for
-nál at; by
nálam [nalom] at my place
nap [nop] sun; day
napibérlet [nopibayrlet] day pass
napló [noplaw] diary
napolaj [nopoloy] suntan lotion
naponta [noponto] daily
naponta háromszor three times a day
naponta kétszer twice a day
napos [noposh] sunny
napozni [nopozni] to sunbathe
nappal [noppol] during the day
nappali living room
napsütés [nopshewtaysh] sunshine
napszemüveg [nopsemewveg] sunglasses
naptár [noptar] diary; calendar
narancssárga [noronch-shargo], **narancsszinű** [noronts-sinew] orange (colour)
nászút [nasoot] honeymoon
nátha [nat-ho] cold
-né [-nay] Mrs
Molnárné Mrs Molnár
Molnár Péterné Mrs Péter Molnár
ne ... [neh] do not ...
nedves [nedvesh] wet; damp
négy [naydj] four
negyed [nedjed] quarter
negyed kettő quarter past one
negyedik [nedjeh-dik] fourth
negyedike [nedjeh-keh] fourth (of the month)
negyedóra [nedjeh-dawro] quarter of an hour
négyszáz [naydjsaz] four hundred

negyven [nedjven] forty
néha [nayho] sometimes
néhány [nayha^{nyuh}] some; a few
nehéz [nehayz] hard, difficult; heavy; rich (food)
-nek to; for
neked for you; to you
nekem for me; to me
  nekem nincs ... [ninch] I don't have ...
  nekem nem kell ... I don't have to ...; I don't need ...
  nekem szól [sawl] for me; to me
neki to him/her; for him/her
  neki szól for him/her/it; to him/her/it to it
nekik to them; for them
nektek for you; to you
nekünk [nekewnk] for us; to us
-nél [-nayl] at; by
nélkül [naylkewl] without
nem no; not; sex
nem bejárat no entry
nem-dohányzó [nem-dohan^{yuh}zaw] area for nonsmokers, nonsmoking
nem dohányzóknak for non-smokers
nem-dohányzók részére [raysayreh] area for non-smokers
német [naymet] German
Németország [naymet-orsag] Germany
nem működik [mewkuhdik] out of order
nemsokára [nemshokaro] soon
nem tudom [toodom] I don't know
nemzetiség [nemzetishayg] nationality
nemzetközi expresszvonat [nemzetkuhzi ekspressvonot] international train
nemzetközi hívás [heevash] international call
nemzetközi információ international enquiries
nemzetközi jegypénztár [yedjpaynztar] international ticket desk
nép [nayp] people, nation
népi tánc [tants] folk dance
népművészet [nayp-mewvayset] folk art
népművészeti bolt craft shop selling folk art
népszerű [nayp-serew] popular
népzene [nayp-zeneh] folk music
nettó súly net weight
név [nayv] name
a nevem ... my name is ...
nevetni to laugh
nevetséges [nevet-shaygesh] ridiculous
névjegy [nayv-yedj] business card, visiting card
nézni [nayzni] to look (at)
nincs [ninch] there's no; there aren't any
nincs otthon he's out
nincsenek [ninchenek] there are no
-nk our
non-stop open 24 hours

normál two-star, 86 octane petrol/gas
normális [normalish] normal
notesz [not-es] notebook; address book
nő [nur] woman
női [nuh-i] women's, ladies'
női divat [divot] ladies' fashion
női fodrászszalon [fodrassolon] ladies' salon
női fodrász [fodras] ladies' hairdresser
női napozó [nopozaw] sunbathing area for women only
női öltöző [uhltuhzur] women's changing cabins
női ruha [rooho] ladies' clothing
női ruha osztály [ostayuh] ladies' wear
női WC [vay tsay] ladies' toilet, ladies' room
nők [nurk] women; ladies' toilet, ladies' room
nős [nursh] married (man)
nőtlen [nurtlen] unmarried (man)
növény [nuhvaynyuh] plant
nővér [nurvayr] sister
nudista strand [noodishto shtrond] naturist beach
nulla [noollo] zero

NY

nyak [nyok] neck
nyakkendő [nyok-kendur] tie, necktie
nyaklánc [nyok-lants] necklace
nyalóka [nyolawko] lollipop; ice lolly
nyár summer
nyaraló [nyorolaw] holidaymaker; summer cottage
nyári szünet closed for summer vacation
nyári vakáció [vokatsiaw] summer holidays/vacation
nyári vásár [vashar] summer sale
nyél [nyayl] handle
nyelv tongue; language
nyelviskola [nyelv-ishkolo] language school
nyerni to win
nyers [nyersh] raw
nyílt [nyeelt] open
nyílvános [nyeelvanosh] public
nyilvánvaló [nyilvanvolaw] obvious
nyirkos [nyirkosh] damp
nyitott, nyitva [nyitvo] open
nyitvatartási idő [nyitva-tortashi idur] opening hours
nyolc [nyolts] eight
nyolcadik [nyolts-odik] eighth
nyolcadika [nyolts-odiko] eighth (of the month)
nyolcvan [nyolts-von] eighty
nyolcszáz [nyolts-saz] eight hundred
nyomni press; to press
nyomtatvány [nyomtotvanyuh] printed matter; form
nyomtatványként to be charged at printed matter rate

nyugágy [nyoogadj] deckchair
Nyugat [nyoogot] west
nyugdíjas [nyoog-dee-yosh] pensioner
nyugodt [nyoogot] quiet
nyugta [nyoogto] receipt

O/Ó

-od your
oda [odo] there
odaát over there
odafenn up there
odalenn down there
oda-vissza [odo-visso] there and back; return, round-trip
ok cause
-ok plural ending
okmány [okma^nyuh] document
okos [okosh] clever; sensible
oktatás [oktotash] education
oktatni [oktotni] to instruct; to train
oktató [oktotaw] instructor
október [oktawber] October
olaj [oloy] oil
olajszint [oloysint] oil level
olasz [olos] Italian
Olaszország [olos-orsag] Italy
olcsó [olchaw] cheap, inexpensive
oldal [oldol] side; page
olló [ollaw] scissors
ólommentes benzin [awlommentesh] unleaded petrol/gas
olvasni [olvoshni] to read
olvasó [olvoshaw] reader
olyan [oyon] so
olyan nagy mint [nodj] as big as
olyan mint ... it's like ...
-om my
-on on; in; at
operáció [operatsiaw] operation
optikus [optikoosh] optician
óra [awro] hour; clock, watch
... órakor [awrokor] at ... o'clock
órajavítás [awro-yoveetash] watch repair
órás- és ékszerész [awrash- aysh aykserays] watchmaker and jeweller
orosz [oros] Russian
Oroszország [oros-orsag] Russia
orr nose
ország [orsag] country, state
országút [orsagoot] trunk road, highway
országúti lámpa [lampo] headlights
orvos [orvosh] doctor (man)
orvosi kivizsgálás [kiviJgalash] check-up
orvosi rendelő [rendelur] doctor's surgery
orvosi utasítás szerint follow doctor's instructions
orvosnő [orvoshnur] doctor (woman)
orvosság [orvosh-shag] medicine
osztály [osta^yuh] class
osztrák [ostrak] Austrian
Osztrák-Magyar Monarchia [ostrak-modjor monorHio] Austro-Hungarian Empire
óta: ... óta [awto] since ...

-otok your
ott there; over there
ott van/vannak [von/vonnok] there is/are
otthon [ot-hon] at home
óvakodjunk a zsebtolvajoktól beware of pickpockets
óvatos [awvotosh] careful
légy óvatos! [laydj] be careful!
óvatosan hajts drive with caution
óvszer [awvser] condom
oxigénáteresztő lencse [oksigayn-aterestur lencheh] gas-permeable lens

Ö/Ő

ő [ur] he; she
ő az [oz] it's him
öcs [uhch] brother (younger)
-öd [-uhd] your
ők [urk] they
ők azok [ozok] it's them
-ök plural ending
őket [urket] them
ölni [uhlni] to kill
öltöny [uhltuh^nyuh] suit (man's)
öltözködni [uhltuhzkuhdni] to get dressed
öltözők [uhltuhzurk] locker rooms
-öm [-uhm] my
Ön [uhn] you
-ön on; in; at
Önért [uhnayrt] for you
öngyújtó [uhndjoo^yuh taw] lighter
öngyújtógáz lighter fuel
önindító [uhn-indeetaw] starter (of car)
önkiszolgálás [uhn-kisolgalash] self-service
önkiszolgáló [uhn-kisolgalaw] self-service
önkiszolgáló mosoda [moshodo] launderette, laundromat
Önnek [uhnnek] for you; to you
Önök [uhnuhk] you
Önöké: az Önöké [oz uhnuhkay] yours
Önökért [uhnuh-kayrt] to you; for you
Önöket [uhnuhket] you
Önöknek [uhnuhknek] to you
Önt [uhnt] you
öreg [uhreg] old
örülni [urewlni] to be glad
örülök [urewluhk] I'm glad, I'm pleased
örülök hogy megismerhettem [hodj megish-merhettem] pleased to meet you
őrült [urrewlt] mad
őrültség [urrewlt-shayg] madness
örvendek [urvendek] how do you do, nice to meet you
ősbemutató [ursh-bemoototaw] first night
ősi [urshi] ancient
ősszel [urssel] in the autumn/ fall
összes [uhssesh] all the
összesen [uhsseshen] all-inclusive; all; altogether
ösvény [uhshvay^nyuh] path
ősz [urs] autumn, (US) fall; grey (hair)

őt [urt] her; him
öt [uht] five
ötödik [uhtuh-dik] fifth
ötödike [uhtuh-dikeh] fifth (of the month)
-ötök [-uhtuhk] your
ötszáz [uhtsaz] five hundred
ötven [uhtven] fifty
ötvösmester [uhtvuhsh-meshter] gold- and silversmith
öv [uhv] belt
övé: az övé [oz uhvay] his; hers
övék: az övék [uhvayk] theirs
özvegy [uhzvedj] widowed; widow
özvegyasszony [urzvedj-osso^{nyuh}] widow
özvegyember widower

P

pad [pod] bench
padló [podlaw] floor
páholy [paho^{yuh}] box
palota [poloto] palace
pályaudvar [pa-yowdvor] railway station
pamut [pomoot] cotton
panasz [ponos] complaint
panasziroda [ponos-irodo] complaints desk
panaszkodni to complain
panzió [ponziaw] guesthouse, bed and breakfast accommodation
pap [pop] priest
papír [popeer] paper
papír- és írószer [aysh eerawser] stationery and office supplies
papír- és írószerbolt stationery and office supplies shop
papírszalvéta [popeer-solvayto] paper napkin
papírüzlet [popeer-ewzlet] stationery shop
papírzsebkendő [popeer-Jebkendur] tissues, Kleenex®
papucs [popooch] slipper; henpecked husband
pár pair; some, a few
parancsolni [poroncholni] to order
parkolni [porkolni] to park
parkolni tilos no parking
parkoló [porkolaw] car park, parking lot
parkolóház [porkolaw-haz] multistorey car park
parkolóhely [porkolaw-heh^{yuh}] parking place, parking bay
párna [parno] pillow
part [port] coast; shore
párt party (political)
parti [porti] party (celebration)
patak [potok] stream
patika [potiko] pharmacy, dispensing chemist's
pázsit [paJit] lawn
pék [payk] baker
pékség [payk-shayg] bakery
péküzlet [payk-ewzlet] baker's
példa [payldo] example
például [paylda-ool] for example
pelenka [pelenko] nappy, diaper
péntek [payntek] Friday

pénz [paynz] money
penzió [penziaw] guesthouse, bed and breakfast accommodation
pénztár [paynztar] till, cash desk; ticket office; booking office
a pénztárnál tessék fizetni please pay at the cashier's desk
pénztárca [paynztartso] purse; wallet
pénztári órák [awrak] cash desk opening times
pénzt bedobni insert money
pénzt vissza nem adunk, pénzt vissza nem térítünk no refunds
pénzutalvány [paynz-ootolva^{nyuh}] money orders
pénzváltás [paynz-valtash], **pénzváltó [paynz-valtaw]** currency exchange
perc [perts] minute
peron platform, (US) track
perselyes telefon [persheh^{yuh}esh] pay-phone
persze [perseh] of course
piac [piots] market
pihenni to rest
pihenő [pihenur] lay-by
pillanat [pillonot] moment
pillanatnyilag [pillonot-nyilog] at the moment
pilula [piloolo] pill
pince [pintseh] basement, cellar
pincér [pintsayr] waiter
pincérnő [pintsayrnur] waitress
pipa [pipo] pipe (for smoking)
piros [pirosh] red
piros csatorna [chotorno] red Customs channel
piszkos [piskosh] dirty
piszok [pisok] dirt
pisztoly [pistoy] gun, pistol
pizsama [piJomo] pyjamas
plakát [plokat] poster
plébánia csengője vicarage bell
poggyász [podjas] luggage, baggage; baggage claim
poggyászkiadás [podjas-kiodash] baggage claim
poggyászmegőrző [podjas-megurzur] left luggage, baggage checkroom
poggyászt leadni (repülőtéren) [leh-odni (repewlurtayren)] check-in
poggyász túlsúly [toolshoo^{yuh}] excess baggage
pohár glass
poharak [pohorok] glasses, eyeglasses
pók [pawk] spider
pokróc [pokrawts] rug, blanket
pongyola [pondjolo] dressing gown
pontosan [pontoshon] on time
popzene [popzeneh] pop music
por powder
porrongy [porrondj] duster
porszívó [porseevaw] vacuum cleaner
porta [porto] reception
portás [portash] receptionist; porter
portó [portaw] postage

portörlő [porturlur] duster
posta [poshto] post office; mail
postafiók [poshto-fiawk] PO box
postahivatal [poshto-hivotol] post office
postai díjszabás [poshto-ee dee^{yuh}sobash] postage rates
postaláda [poshto-lado] letterbox, mail box
postás [poshtash] postman, mailman
postatakarék [poshto-tokorayk] post office bank
postázni to post, to mail
pótalkatrész [pawtolkotrays] spare part
pótdíj [pawtdee^{yuh}] supplement
pótkerék [pawtkerayk] spare wheel
próbafülke [prawbofewlkeh] fitting rooms
probléma [problaymo] problem
protestáns [proteshtansh] Protestant
púder [pooder] talcum powder
p.u. railway station
puha [pooho] soft
pulóver [poolawver] jumper
pult [poolt] counter
puska [pooshko] gun, rifle

R

-ra [-ro] on; onto; to; for; by
radír [rodir] rubber
ragasztószalag [rogostawsolog] Sellotape®, Scotch tape®
rágja meg mielőtt lenyelné chew before swallowing
rágógumi [ragawgoomi] chewing gum
ragtapasz [rogtopos] plaster, Bandaid®
rajongó [royongaw] fan (enthusiast)
rák cancer; lobster; crab
rakott layered
rakpart [rokport] quay; embankment
rándulás [randoolash] sprain
R-beszélgetés [ayr-besaylgetaysh] reverse charge call, collect call
-re [-reh] on; onto; to; for; by
recepció [retseptsiaw] reception
recepciós [retseptsiawsh] receptionist
recept [retsept] recipe; prescription
redőny [redur^{nyuh}] shutters
református [reformatoosh] Reformed; Calvinist
regény [regay^{nyuh}] novel
reggel morning; am
reggeli breakfast
reggeli nélkül [naylkewl] without breakfast
reggelivel breakfast included
régi [raygi] old
régiségkereskedés [raygi-shaygkeresh-kedaysh] antique shop
reklám advertisement
remek first-rate
remélni [remaylni] to hope
rendben van [von] all right
rendelés [rendelaysh] surgery hours

rendelni to order
rendelő [rendelur] surgery
rendetlen untidy
rendetlenség [rendetlen-shayg] mess
rendház monastery
rendőr [rendur] policeman
rendőrkapitányság [rendur-kopitanyuhshag] police station
rendőr őrszoba [ursobo] police station
rendőrség [rendur-shayg] police
rendszám [rendsam] registration number
rendszámtábla [rendsam-tablo] number plate
rendszerint [rendserint] usually
rep(ülő)téri buszjárat [rep(ewlur)tayri boos-yarot] airport bus
repülés [repewlaysh] flight
repülési idő [idur] flight time
repülési útvonal [ootvonol] flight route
repülni [repewlni] to fly
repülőgép [repewlurgayp] plane, airplane
repülőgéppel by air
repülőjárat [repewlur-yarot] flight
repülőtér [repewlurtayr] airport
repülőtéri buszjárat [boos-yarot] airport coach service
repülőtéri minibusz járat [miniboos yarot], **repülőtéri minibusz szolgálat** [miniboos solgalot] airport minibus
rész [rays] part
részeg [rayseg] drunk
részegeket nem szolgálunk ki drunks will not be served
retesz [retes] bolt (on door)
retikül [retikewl] handbag, (US) purse
rettenetes [rettenetesh] terrible
retúr(jegy) [retoor(-yedj)] return ticket, round-trip ticket
rév [rayv] ferry (service)
révhajó [rayv-hoyaw] ferry (boat)
R-hívás [ayr-heevash] reverse-charge call, collect call
ritka [ritko] rare, uncommon
rock-zene [rok-zeneh] rock (music)
roham [rohom] attack; fit
rokkant [rokkont] disabled
rokkantak részére fenntartott ülőhely seat reserved for the handicapped
rokon relative
rokonság [rokon-shag] relatives
rokonszenves [rokon-senvesh] nice, likeable
rom ruin
román Romanian
romok ruins
róseibni [rawsheh-ibni] crisps, (US) chips
rossz [ross] bad; wrong
rosszabb [rossob] worse
rosszul [rossool] badly
rothadt [rothot] rotten
rovar [rovor] insect
rovarcsípés [rovor-cheepaysh] insect bite
rovarirtó [rovor-irtaw] insecticide
rózsaszín [rawJoseen] pink
röpcédula [ruhptsaydoolo] leaflet

röpirat [ruhpirot] leaflet
röplabda [ruhplobdo] volleyball
röplabda pálya [pa-yo] volleyball court
rövid [ruhvid] short, brief
rövidlátó [ruhvid-lataw] shortsighted
rövidnadrág [ruhvid-nodrag] shorts
rugalmas [roogolmosh] elastic
ruha [rooho] clothes; dress
ruha akasztó [okostaw] coathanger
ruhaanyag [rooho-o-nyog] material, cloth
ruhaszárító csipesz [rooho-sareetaw chipes] clothes peg
ruhaszekrény [rooho-sekray[nyuh]] wardrobe
ruhatár [roohotar] cloakroom
ruhatisztító [rooho-tisteetaw] laundry (place)
rúzs [rooJ] lipstick

S

saját [shoyat] own (adj)
sajnálom [shoynalom] I'm sorry
nagyon sajnálom I'm very sorry
sajnos [shoynosh] unfortunately
sakk [shok] chess
sál [shal] scarf
sampon [shompon] shampoo
sapka [shopko] cap, hat; bonnet
sárga [shargo] yellow
Sárga Angyal [ondjol] 'Yellow Angels', 24-hour breakdown service
sarok [shorok] corner; heel
sátor [shator] tent
sátrak [shatrok] tents
savanyú [shovo-nyoo] sour
seb [sheb] wound
sebes [shebesh] rapid
sebesség [shebeshshayg] speed
sebességek gears
sebességhatár, sebességkorlátozás speed limit
sebességváltó [shebeshayg-valtaw] gear box
sebességváltókar [shebeshayg-valtawkor] gear lever
sebesvonat [shebeshvonot] slow long-distance train with fewer stops than local trains
sebtapasz [shebtopos] plaster, Bandaid®
segély [shegay[yuh]] aid
segíteni [shegeeteni] to help
segíthetek? [shegeet-hetek] may I help?
segítség [shegeetshayg] help
sehol [sheh-hol] nowhere
selyem [sheh-yem] silk
sem [shem] negative
sem ... sem ... neither ... nor ...
semmi [shemmi] nothing
senki [shenki] nobody
seprő [sheprur] broom
sérteni [shayrteni] to hurt; to insult
sértő [shayrtur] insulting
sérülés [shayrewlaysh] injury

sérült [shayrewlt] injured
séta [shayto] walk, stroll
sétahajó [shayto-hoyaw] river cruise, pleasure boat
sétálni [shaytalni] to go for a walk
sétálómagnó [shaytalaw-mognaw] personal stereo
sétány [shayta^{nyuh}] promenade
sí [shee] ski
sícipő [sheetsipur] ski boots
síelni [shee-elni] to ski
siess(en)! [shiesh(en)] hurry up!
sietni [shietni] to hurry
siker [shiker] success
sílift [sheelift] ski-lift
sincs [shinch] there isn't one either
sízés [sheezaysh] skiing
s.k. signed
só [shaw] salt
sógor [shawgor] brother-in-law
sógornő [shawgor-nur] sister-in-law
soha [sho-ho] never
sok [shok] much; many, a lot, a lot of
  nem sok not much
  ne túl sokat [neh tool shokot] not too much
soká [shoka] for a long time
sokkal [shokkol] by much, by a lot
  sokkal jobb much better
sok szerencsét! [shok serenchayt] good luck!
sor [shor] queue; row
sorbaállni [shorbo-allni] to queue
sorszám [shorsam] row number; serial number
sós [shawsh] salty
sovány [shova^{nyuh}] thin
sör [shur] beer
sörkert [shurkert] garden pub-restaurant
sörnyitó [shur-nyitaw] bottle opener
söröző [shuruhzur] beer hall; pub-restaurant
sötét [shuhtayt] dark
spanyol [shpo-nyol] Spanish
Spanyolország [shpo-nyol-orsag] Spain
spiritusz [shpiritoos] methylated spirit
sportáru [shportaroo] sportswear and equipment
sportcsarnok [shport-chornok] sports hall
sportkocsi [shport-kochi] pushchair; sportscar
sportközpont [shport-kuhzpont] sports centre
stadion [shtodion] stadium
stb. etc.
Stomatológiai Intézet emergency dental service
strand [shtrond] beach; open-air swimming pool
súly [shoo^{yuh}] weight
súlyhatár, súlykorlátozás weight limit
surf [shoorf] sailboard
surfelés [shoorfelaysh] windsurfing
süket [shewket] deaf
sürgős [shewrgursh] urgent

sütni [shewtni] to bake; to fry
sütő [shewtur] oven
sütőde [shewturdeh] bakery
svábbogár [shvabbogar] cockroach

SZ

szabad [sobod] free; vacant; allowed; for hire, to rent; one is allowed
szabad! come in!
szabad kemping campsite free of charge
szabadság [sobod-shag] holiday, vacation; freedom
szabadság miatt zárva closed for holiday period
szabó [sobaw] tailor
szag [sog] smell
szagolni [sogolni] to smell
szagtalanító [sogtoloneetaw] deodorant
száj [sī] mouth
szájon keresztül orally
szájsebész [sīshebays] dental surgeon
szakács [sokach] chef; cook
szakáll [sokal] beard
szakrendelő [sokrendelur] clinic
szállás [sallash] accommodation
szálláshelyfoglalás [sallash-heh^{yuh}foglolash] accommodation reservation
szállítás [salleetash] delivery; shipment
szálló [sallaw], **szálloda** [sallodo] hotel
szalon [solon] lounge
szalvéta [solvayto] serviette
szám [sam] number
a szám átmenetileg nem működik the number is temporarily out of order
ezt a számot nem lehet megkapni it is impossible to reach this number
számítógép [sameetaw-gayp] computer
számla [samlo] bill, (US) check; invoice
számológép [samolaw-gayp] calculator
számtábla [samtablo] number plate
szandál [sondal] sandals
szándékosan [sanday-koshon] deliberately
szántóföld [santaw-fuhld] field
szappan [soppon] soap
száraz [saroz] dry
szárítani [sareetoni] to dry
szárny [sar^{nyuh}] wing
szárnyashajó [sar-nyosh-ho-yaw] hydrofoil
szarvas [sorvosh] deer
szarvasbőr [sorvoshbur] suede
szauna [sowno] sauna
száz [saz] hundred
százalék [sazolayk] per cent
szebb [seb] more beautiful
széf [sayf] safe (for valuables)
szegény [segay^{nyuh}] poor
szégyenlős [saydjenlursh] shy
szék [sayk] chair
székesegyház [saykeshedj-haz] cathedral

székrekedés [saykrekedaysh] constipation
szekrény [sekray^{nyuh}] cupboard; wardrobe
szél [sayl] wind; edge
széle [sayleh] side, edge
széles [saylesh] wide
szélvédő [saylvaydur] windscreen
szélvédő ablaktörlő [oblokturlur] windscreen wipers
szem [sem] eye(s)
szemben [semben] opposite
szemcsepp(ek) [semchepp(ek)] eye drops
személy [semay^{yuh}] person
személyi igazolvány [semay-yi igozolva^{nyuh}] ID card
személyvonat [semay^{yuh}vonot] slow train with frequent stops
személyzet [semay^{yuh}zet] personnel; crew
személyzet staff only
szemét [semayt] rubbish, trash; litter
szemeteszsák [semet-eshak] bin liner
szemétláda [semayt-lado] dustbin, trashcan
szemhéjfestő ceruza [semhay^{yuh}feshtur tseroozo] eye shadow
szemöldök [semuhlduhk] eyebrow
szempillafesték [sempillofeshtayk] mascara
szemüveg [semewveg] glasses, eyeglasses
szénanátha [saynonatho] hayfever
szendvics [sendvich] sandwich
szennyes [sen-nyesh] laundry (dirty clothes)
szennyezett [sen-nyezet] polluted
szénsavas [saynshovosh] fizzy
szenteste [senteshteh] Christmas Eve
szép [sayp] beautiful; pretty
szeptember [september] September
-szer [-ser] times
négyszer [naydjser] four times
szerda [serdo] Wednesday
szerelmes [serelmesh] in love
szerelő [serelur] mechanic
szerencse [serencheh] luck
szerencsére [serenchayreh] fortunately
szerencsétlenség [serenchayt-lenshayg] disaster
szeretek ... [seretek] I like ...
szeretkezni [seretkezni] to make love
szeretnék [seretnayk] I would like
szeretni [seretni] to love; to like
szerető [seretur] lover
szerezni [serezni] to get, to obtain
szerkezet [serkezet] device
szerszám [sersam] tool
szertartás [sertortash] church service
szervezni [servezni] to organize
szervíz [serveez] garage, service station

szervusz(tok) [servoos(tok)] hello
szerződés [serzurdaysh] contract
szia(sztok)! [si-o(stok)] hi!
sziget [siget] island
szíj [seeyuh] belt
szikla [siklo] rock, stone; cliff
szilveszter [silvester] New Year's Eve (the whole day)
Szilveszter este [eshteh] New Year's Eve (evening and night only)
szimpatikus [simpotikoosh] nice
szín [seen] colour
színdarab [seendorob] play (in theatre)
színes film [seenesh film] colour film
színezés [seenezaysh] tint
színező [seenezur] colouring
színház [seenhaz] theatre
szinkronizált [sinkronizalt] dubbed
színpad [seenpod] stage
szintén [sintayn] too, also; likewise
szintetikus [sintetikoosh] man-made
szív [seev] heart
szivar [sivor] cigar
szivattyú [sivot-tyoo] pump
szívesen [seeveshen] gladly, with pleasure; you're welcome
szívroham [seevrohom] heart attack
szó [saw] word
szoba [sobo] room
szoba kiadó [sobo kiodaw] rooms to let, rooms to rent
szobalány [sobolanyuh] chambermaid
szobapincér [sobopintsayr] room service
szobor [sobor] statue
szokás [sokash] custom; habit
szokásos [sokashosh] usual
szokatlan [sokotlon] unusual
szoknya [sok-nyo] skirt
szolárium [solari-oom] sunbed
szolga [solgo] steward; servant
szolgálat [solgalot] service
szolgálni [solgalni] to serve
szombat [sombot] Saturday
szombaton és vasárnap zárva closed on Saturdays and Sundays
szomjas [som-yosh] thirsty
szomorú [somoroo] sad
szomszéd/szomszédasszony [somsayd/somsaydossonyuh] neighbour (male/female)
-szor [-sor] times
szórakozás [sawrokozash] entertainment
szórakozni [sawrokozni] to have fun
szóra sem érdemes [sawro shem ayrdemesh] you're welcome, don't mention it
szórólap [sawrawlop] leaflet
szótár [sawtar] dictionary
szóval [sawvol] well; as I was saying
szőke [surkeh] blond
szőkítés [surkeetaysh] bleach
szőlő [surlur] grape(s); vineyard
szőlőzsír [surlurJeer] lip salve

szőnyeg [sur-nyeg] carpet
szőrmeáru [surmeh-aroo] fur shop
sztár [star] film star
szúnyog [soo-nyog] mosquito
szuper [sooper] three-star, 92 octane petrol/gas
szupermárket [soopermarket] supermarket
szurkoló [soorkolaw] fan (sports enthusiast)
szuvenír [sooveneer] souvenir
szűcs [sewch] furrier's
szűk [sewk] tight; narrow
szükséges [sewkshaygesh] necessary
születésnap [sewletayshnop] birthday
szülő [sewlur] parent
szünet [sewnet] interval
szürke [sewrkeh] grey

T

-t accusative suffix
tábla csokoládé [tablo chokoladay] bar of chocolate
tabletta [tobletto] tablet
táborozás [taborozash] camping
táborozni [taborozni] to camp
tág wide
táj [tī] scenery
tájkép [tīkayp] landscape
takaró [tokoraw] blanket
tál dish
találkozni [tolalkozni] to meet
találkozó [tolalkozaw] appointment; meeting
találkozót megbeszélni [megbesaylni] to make an appointment
találni [tolalni] to find
talált tárgyak [tolalt tardjok] lost property
talán [tolan] maybe, perhaps
tálca [taltso] tray
talp [tolp] sole (of foot/shoe)
tanár/tanárnő [tonar/tonarnur] secondary school teacher (man/woman)
tánc [tants] dance
táncolni [tantsolni] to dance
tanítani [toneetoni] to teach
tanító/tanítónő [toneetaw/toneetawnur] primary school teacher (man/woman)
tanítvány [toneetva[nyuh]] pupil
tanu [tonoo] witness
tanulni [tonoolni] to learn
tanuló [tonoolaw] learner
tányér [ta-nyayr] plate
tárcsahang [tarchohong] dialling tone
tárcsázás [tarchazash] dialling
tárcsázni [tarchazni] to dial
tárlat [tarlot] special art exhibition
tárolófolyadék [tarolaw-foyodayk] soaking solution
társadalom [tarshodolom] society
társalgó [tarsholgaw] lounge
társaság [tarshoshag] company
társasjáték [tarshosh-yatayk] party game; board game
társasutazás [tarshosh-ootozash] package tour

tartály [tortay] tank
tartani [tortoni] to hold
tartóshullám [tortawsh-hoollam] perm
tartósító preservative
tartozik [tortozik] credit
tartózkodás [tortawzkodash] stay
tartozni [tortozni] to owe; to belong to
tartsa a vonalat hold the line
táska [tashko] bag
tavak [tovok] lakes, ponds
tavaly [tovo^{yuh}] last year
tavasz [tovos] spring
távbeszélő [tavbesaylur] telephone
távhívás [tavheevash] long-distance call
táviratfelvétel [tavirot-felvaytel] telegrams counter
távol far away
távolabb [tavolob] further
távolság [tavolshag] distance
távolsági autóbusz [owtawboos] long-distance bus
távolsági autóbuszállomás [owtawboos-allomash] long-distance bus station
távolsági beszélgetés [besaylgetaysh] long-distance call
távolsági buszjárat [boos-yarot] long-distance bus
taxiállomás [toksi-allomash] taxi rank
te [teh] you
a te ...-d/-id your ...
teáscsésze [teh-ashchayseh] teacup
teáskanna [teh-ashkonno] teapot
téged [tayged] you
tegnap [tegnop] yesterday
tegnap délután [daylootan] yesterday afternoon
tegnapelőtt [tegnop-elurt] the day before yesterday
tehén [tehayn] cow
teherautó [teherowtaw] lorry
teherautók számára fenntartott for heavy vehicles
teherkocsi [teherkochi] van
tej [tay] milk
tej-bár [tay-bar] snack bar serving mainly dairy products
tejbolt [taybolt] shop selling dairy products
tejivó [tayivaw] snack bar serving mainly dairy products
tejtermék [taytermayk] dairy product
-tek your
tél [tayl] winter
tele [teleh] full
telefax [telefoks] fax
telefon telephone
telefonálni [telefonalni] to phone
telefonfülke [telefon-fewlkeh] phone box, phone booth
telefonhívás [telefon-heevash] telephone call
telefon kódszám [telefon kawdsam] dialling code
telefonkönyv [telefon-kuh^{nyuh}v] phone book
telefonközpont [telefon-kuhzpont] telephone exchange

telefonszám [telefon-sam] phone number
televízió [televeeziaw] television
teljes [tel-yesh] entire, complete
teljes ellátás [ellatash] full board
temetés [temetaysh] funeral
temető [temetur] cemetery
templom church
teniszpálya [tenispa-yo] tennis court
tenni to do; to put
tényleg? [taynyuhleg] is that so?
tér [tayr] square; place
térd [tayrd] knee
térdnadrág [tayrdnodrag] shorts
terek [terek] squares; places
terelőút [terelur-oot] diversion
terhes [terhesh] pregnant
terhesanyák számára fenntartott ülőhely seat reserved for pregnant women
térkép [tayrkayp] map
termék [termayk] product
természet [termayset] nature
természetes [termaysetesh] natural
természetesen [termayseteshen] naturally, of course
termosz [termos] vacuum flask
terület [terewlet] area
terv plan; design
tessék [tesh-shayk] please; here you are
tessék? pardon (me)?; can I help you?
tessék parancsolni [poroncholni] here you are
tessék a biztonsági öveket bekapcsolni fasten seat belts
tessék a jegyeket ellenőrzésre előkészíteni please prepare your tickets for control
tessék az útlevél- és vámvizsgálathoz (felkészülni) please prepare for passport and Customs control
tessék befáradni come straight in
tessék beszélni you can speak with the number now
tessék helyet foglalni please, take a seat
tessék kosarat venni please take a basket
tessék várni, mindjárt adom please, wait, I'll put you through
tessék vigyázni! [tesh-shayk vidjazni] look out!
test [tesht] body
testvér [teshtvayr] brother; sister
tető [tetur] roof
tetszik: tetszik nekem [tetsik] I like it
tetszik parancsolni? are you being served?
tévé [tayvay] TV
téved [tayved] you're wrong
tévedés [tayvedaysh] mistake
tévedni [tayvedni] to make a mistake
téves kapcsolás [tayvesh kopcholash] wrong number

téves számot hívott [tayvesh samot heevot] you've got the wrong number
ti you
tiéd: a tiéd [o ti-ayd] yours
tiétek: a tiétek [o ti-aytek] yours
tilos [tilosh] forbidden
tilos a ... no ...
tilos a belépés no admittance
tilos a bemenet no entry; no admittance
tilos a vízbe ugrani no diving
tilos a dohányzás no smoking
tilos a horgászás no angling
tilos az átjárás no trespassing
tinta [tinto] ink
tiszta [tisto] clean; clear
tiszta gyapjú [djop-yoo] pure wool
tisztítani [tisteetoni] to clean
titeket you
tíz [teez] ten
tizedik [tizeh-dik] tenth
tizedike [tizeh-dikeh] tenth (of month)
tizenegy [tizenedj] eleven
tizenegyedike [tizenedjeh-dikeh] eleventh (of month)
tizenharmadika [tizenhormo-dikeh] thirteenth (of month)
tizenhárom [tizenharom] thirteen
tizenhat [tizenhot] sixteen
tizenhat 16 éven aluliakat nem szolgálunk ki no-one under 16 will be served
tizenhatodika [tizenhoto-diko] sixteenth (of month)
tizenhét [tizenhayt] seventeen
tizenhetedike [tizenheteh-dikeh] seventeenth (of month)
tizenkét [tizenkayt] twelve
tizenkettedike [tizenketteh-dikeh] twelfth (of month)
tizenkettő [tizenkettur] twelve
tizenkilenc [tizenkilents] nineteen
tizenkilencedike [tizenkilentseh-dikeh] nineteenth (of month)
tizennégy [tizennaydj] fourteen
tizennegyedike [tizennedjeh-dikeh] fourteenth (of month)
tizennyolc [tizen-nyolts] eighteen
tizennyolcadika [tizen-nyoltsodiko] eighteenth (of month)
tizenöt [tizenuht] fifteen
tizenötödike [tizenuhtuh-dikeh] fifteenth (of month)
tó [taw] lake; pond
-tok your
-tól [-tawl] from, from just outside; by
magamtól [mogomtawl] by myself
toll pen; feather
tollaslabda [tolloshlobdo] badminton
tolmács [tolmach] interpreter
tolni [tolni] to push; push
tolókocsi [tolawkochi] trolley
tolószék [tolawsayk] wheelchair
tolvaj [tolvoy] thief
tornacipő [tornotsipur] trainers; gym shoes
torok throat
torokcukorka [torok-tsookorko] throat pastilles

torokfájás [torokfī-ash] sore throat
torokfájás elleni cukorka [torokfī-ash elleni tsookorko] throat lozenges
torony [toro^{nyuh}] tower
tósztot mond [tawstot] to toast (with drink)
továbbítani [tovabbeetoni] to forward
több [tuhb] more; several
  több mint more than
többi [tuhbbi] the rest
-tök [-tuhk] your
tökéletes [tuhkayletesh] perfect
-től [-turl] from, from just outside; by
tölteni [tuhlteni] to pour; to fill; to charge; to pass
töltőállomás [tuhltur-allomash] petrol station, (US) gas station
töltőtoll [tuhlturto] fountain pen
tőlük [turlewk] from them
tömeg [tuhmeg] crowd
tömegközlekedési térkép [tuhmeg-kuhzlekedayshi tayrkayp] network map
tömés [tuhmaysh] filling (in tooth)
törés [turaysh] fracture
törölni [turuhlni] to cancel
törött [turuht] broken
történelem [turtaynelem] history
történet [turtaynet] story
történni [turtaynni] to happen
törülköző [turewlkuhzur] towel
törve [turveh] broken
törvény [turvay^{nyuh}] law
tréfa [trayfo] joke
tudakozó [toodokozaw] enquiries' office; directory enquiries; directory
tudni [toodni] to know; to be able to
  tudna ... [toodno] could you ...?
  nem tudna ... couldn't you ...?
  nem tudom I don't know
  tudsz ...-ni? [toods] can you ...?
tudomány [toodoma^{nyuh}] science
túl [tool] too; beyond
  ...-n túl past the ...
tulajdonos [tooloydonosh] owner
túlfőtt [toolfurt] overcooked
túlsúlydíj charge for excess weight
túra [tooro] tour
túrista [toorishto] tourist
túristaház [toorishto-haz] chalet-type tourist accommodation in mountains
túristahivatal [toorishto-hivotol] tourist office
túristaszálló [toorishto-sallaw] traditional tourist hostel
túrista szálló [toorishto sallaw] hostel-type accommodation
túristatérkép [toorishto-tayrkayp] hiking map
túsz [toos] hostage
tű [tew] needle
tükör [tewkur] mirror
türelmét kérem, adom just a moment, please, I am putting you through

tűrni [tewrni] to tolerate
tűz [tewz] fire
tűzhely [tewzheh^{yuh}] cooker
tüzijáték [tewzi-yatayk] fireworks
tűzoltóautó [tewzoltaw-owtaw] fire engine
tűzoltók [tewzoltawk] fire brigade
tűzoltókészülék [tewzoltawk-aysewlayk] fire extinguisher
tűzoltóság [tewzoltaw-shag] fire brigade
tűzoltó szerkezet [tewzoltaw serkezet] fire extinguisher

TY

tyúk [tyook] hen

U/Ú

u. street
udvarias [oodvoriosh] polite
ugrani [oogroni] to jump
ugródeszka [oograwdesko] diving board
ugyanaz [oodjonoz] same
ugyanaz(ok) a the same
úgy-úgy [oodj-oodj] so-so
úgy van [oodj von] that's right
új [oo^{yuh}] new
Újév [oo-yayv] New Year
ujj [oo^{yuh}] finger
újság [oo^{yuh}shag] newspaper; news
újságárus [oo^{yuh}shagaroosh] newspaper vendor
újságos [oo^{yuh}shagosh] newsagent's
Új-Zéland [oo^{yuh}zaylond] New Zealand
új-zélandi [oo^{yuh}zaylondi] New Zealand (adj)
-uk [-ook] their; your
Ukrajna [ookroyno] Ukraine
ukrán [ookran] Ukrainian
-ul [-ool] in; adverbial suffix
angolul [ongolool] in English
rosszul [rossool] badly
unalmas [oonolmosh] boring
undorító [oondoreetaw] disgusting
-unk [-oonk] our
unoka [oonoko] grandchild
unokabáty [oonokoba^{tyuh}] cousin (male: elder)
unokahúg [oonoko-hoog] niece; cousin (female: younger)
unokanővér [oonoko-nurvayr] cousin (female)
unokaöcs [oonoko-uhch] nephew; cousin (male: younger)
unokatestvér [oonoko-teshtvayr] cousin
úr [oor] gentleman; Mr
urak [oorok] gentlemen; gents' toilet, men's room
uram [oorom] Sir
úszás [oosash] swimming
úszni [oosni] to swim
uszoda [oosodo] swimming pool
úszónadrág [oosaw-nodrag] swimming trunks
uszószemüveg [oosaw-semewveg] goggles
út [oot] way; road
utak [ootok] ways; roads

után [ootan] after
utána [ootano] afterwards
utánfutó [ootanfootaw] trailer
utas [ootosh] passenger
utasok [ootoshok] passengers
utastájékoztató [ootoshtī-aykoztotaw] travel information
utazás [ootozash] journey
utazási igazolvány [ootozashi igozolva^{nyuh}] travel card
utazási iroda [irodo] travel agent
utazási ügynökség [ewdjnuhkshayg] travel agency
utazni [ootozni] to travel
utazó csekk [ootozaw chek] travellers' cheque
utca [oot-tso] street
útépítés [ootaypeetaysh] roadworks
útépítés miatt zárva closed for roadworks
úthibák bad surface
útikönyv [ootikuh^{nyuh}v] guidebook
útja [oo-tyo] avenue
útkereszteződés [ootkeres-tezurdaysh] crossroads, intersection
útlevél [ootlevayl] passport
útlevelek [ootlevelek] passports
az útleveleket kérem passports please
útlevélvizsgálat [ootlevayl-viJgalot] passport control
útmutatás [ootmoototash] direction
útmutató [ootmoototaw] guidebook
utolsó [ootolshaw] last, final
útvonal [ootvonol] route

Ü/Ű

üdítők [ewdeeturk] refreshments
üdülőház [ewduhlurhaz] bungalow
ügy [ewdj] cause
ügyeletes gyógyszertár [ewdjeletesh djawdj-sertar] duty pharmacy
ügyeleti szolgálat [ewdjeleti solgalot] all-night service
ügyes [ewdjesh] skilful
ügyetlen [ewdjetlen] clumsy
ügyfél [ewdjfayl] client, customer
ügyfelek [ewdjfelek] clients, customers
ügynökség [ewdjnuhk-shayg] agency
ügyvéd [ewdjvayd] lawyer (man/woman)
ügyvédnő [ewdjvaydnur] lawyer (woman)
ügyvezető [ewdjvezetur] manager; executive
ügyvezető igazgató [igozgotaw] managing director
-ük [-ewk] their; your
-ül [-ewl] in; adverbial suffix
németül [naymetewl] in German
ülés [ewlaysh] seat
ülésszám [ewlayssam] seat number

ülni [ewlni] to sit
-ünk [-ewnk] our
ünnepi nyitvatartás bank holiday opening time
ünnepnap [ewnnepnop] holiday, vacation
üres [ewresh] empty
űrlap [ewrlop] form; application form
ütő [ewtur] racket; golf club; bat
üveg [ewveg] glass (material); bottle
üvegnyitó [ewveg-nyitaw] bottle-opener
üzemanyag [ewzemo-nyog] fuel
üzemanyagtöltőállomás [ewzemo-nyog-tuhltur-allomash] petrol station, (US) gas station
üzenet [ewzenet] message
üzlet [ewzlet] shop; business
üzleti órák [awrak] business hours
üzleti út [oot] business trip

V

vacsora [vochoro] dinner, evening meal; supper
vacsorázni [vochorazni] to have dinner
vad [vod] wild; game
vadász [vodas] hunter
vadászat [vodasot] hunt
vadászni [vodasni] to hunt
vadászpuska [vodas-pooshko] shotgun
vadonatúj [vodonotoo^{yuh}] brand-new
vágány [vaga^{nyuh}] platform, (US) track; tracks
a vágányokhoz to the platforms/tracks
vágás [vagash] cut
vágni to cut
vagon [vogon] carriage, coach
vagy [vodj] or; you are
vagy ... vagy [vodj vodj] either ... or ...
vagyok [vodjok] I am
...-i vagyok I come from ...
vagytok [vodjtok] you are
vagyunk [vodjoonk] we are
vajon [voyon] whether
vak [vok] blind
vaku [vokoo] flash
-val [-vol] with
valaha: ... valaha? [voloho] have you ever ...?
valahogy [volohodj] somehow
valahol [volohol] somewhere
valaki [voloki] somebody
valami [volomi] something
válasz [valos] answer
válaszolni [valosolni] to answer
választani [valostoni] to choose
választék [valostayk] choice; parting (in hair)
váll shoulder
vállalat [vallolot] company
vállalatvezető [vallolot-vezetur] general manager
vallás [vollash] religion
vállfa [vallfo] coathanger
vállkendő [vallkendur] shawl
válni to become

valóban [volawbon] really
valószínűleg [volaw-seenewleg] probably
váltani [valtoni] to change
változékony [valtozayko[nyuh]] changeable
valuta [volooto] foreign currency
valutaárfolyam [volooto-arfo-yom] exchange rate
valutabeváltás [volooto-bevaltash] currency exchange
valuta ügyletek [volooto ewdjletek] foreign currency exchange
vám [vam] Customs
vámárunyilatkozat [vamaroo-nyilotkozot] Customs form
vámhivatal [vamhivotol] Customs office
vámkezelés [vamkezelaysh] Customs inspection
vámmentes [vammentesh] exempt from duty, duty-free
vámmentes áruk [arook], **vámmentes üzlet** [ewzlet] duty-free shop
vámnyilatkozat [vam-nyilotkozot] Customs declaration
vámvizsgálat [vamviJgalot] Customs inspection
van [von] there is; he/she/it is
  van ...? is/are there ...?
  van magának ... [moganok] have you got ...?
  van itt ... ? is there ... here?
van elvámolni valója? [von elvamolni volawyo] have you got anything to declare?
vannak [vonnok] they are; you are; there are
  vannak ...? are there ...?
van szerencsém! [von serenchaym] pleased to meet you!
vár castle
várakozni tilos no waiting
várj(on) csak! [var(yon) chok] wait a moment!
várni [varni] to wait
  várjon meg! [var-yon] wait for me!
város [varosh] city; town
város felé to town
városháza [varosh-hazo] town hall
városi lámpa [varoshi lampo] sidelights
városközpont [varosh-kuhzpont] town centre
városközpont felé [felay] to town centre
város-térkép [varoshi-tayrkayp] city map
várószoba [varawsobo], **váróterem** [varawterem] waiting room
varrni [vorni] to sew
vasalni [vosholni] to iron
vasaló [vosholaw] iron (for ironing)
vásár [vashar] market; fair; sale
vásárcsarnok [vashar-chornok] indoor market
vasár- és ünnepnapokon Sundays and public holidays
vásárlás [vasharlash] shopping
vásárló [vasharlaw] customer, shopper

vasárnap [vosharnop] Sunday
vasárnap kivételével Sundays excepted
vásárolni [vasharolni] to buy; to go shopping
vasáru [vosharoo] hardware
vaskereskedés [voshkeresh-kedaysh] hardware store
vastag [voshtog] thick
vasút [voshoot] railway
vasútállomás [voshoot-allomash] railway station
vasúti átjáró [at-yaraw] level crossing
vászon [vason] linen
vatta [votto] cotton wool, absorbent cotton
váza [vazo] vase
védelem [vaydelem] defence
védelmezni [vaydelmezni] to protect
vég [vayg] end
végállomás [vaygallomash] terminus
vége [vaygeh] end
vége a ...-nak/-nek [o ...-nok/-nek] no more ...
végösszeg [vayguhsseg] total
végre [vaygreh] at last
vegyen be egyszerre ... tablettát take ... pills at a time
vegyesvállalkozás [vedjesh-vallolkozash] joint venture
vegytisztító [vedjtisteetaw] dry-cleaner
vékony [vaykonyuh] thin
-vel with
vele [veleh] with him/her/it
veled with you
velem with me
veletek with you
véletlenül [vaylet-lenewl] by chance
velük [velewk] with them
velünk [velewnk] with us
vendég [vendayg] guest
vendégfogadó [vendayg-fogodaw] inn
vendéglő [vendayg-lur] restaurant
vendégség [vendayg-shayg] party
vendégszeretet [vendayg-seretet] hospitality
venni to take; to buy
ventillátor fan
ventillátorszíj [ventillatorsyuh] fanbelt
vény [vaynyuh] prescription
vér [vayr] blood
véres [vayresh] bloody; rare (steak)
vese [vesheh] kidney
vészcsengő alarm bell
veszély [vesayyuh] danger
veszélyes [vesay-yesh] dangerous
veszélyes útszakasz dangerous stretch of road
vészfék [vaysfayk] emergency brake
vészhelyzet [vayshehyuhzet] emergency
vészjelző [vays-yelzur] emergency cord
vészkijárat [vayski-yarot] emergency exit
vevő [vevur] buyer

vezetéknév [vezetayk-nayv] surname
vezetni to drive; to lead
vezető [vezetur] leader; driver; manager
vezetői jogosítvány [vezetuh-i yogosheetva^nyuh] driving licence
vézna [vayzno] skinny
vicc [vits] joke
vicces [vits-tsesh] funny, amusing
vidámpark [vidampork] funfair
vidék [vidayk] country; countryside
video készülék [kaysewlayk] video recorder
Vietnámi balzsam [bolJom] insect repellent and ointment for bites
vigyázat! [vidjazot] look out!; danger!
vigyázz! look out!; caution!
vihar [vihor] storm
viharkabát [vihor-kobat] cagoule
világ world
világítás lighting; press for light
világos [vilagosh] clear, obvious; bright; light; simple
villa [villo] fork; villa
villamos [villomosh] tram
villamosbérlet [villomosh-bayrlet] travel pass for tram, bus and Métro
villamosjegy [villomosh-yedj] tram ticket
villamosmegálló [villomosh-megallaw] tram stop
villamosság [villomosh-shag] electricity
villanás [villonash] flash
vinni to carry; to take
virág flower
virágkereskedés [virag-keresh-kedaysh] flower shop
virágüzlet [virag-ewzlet] florist's
visszaadni [visso-odni] to give back, to return
visszahívom [visso-heevom] I'll call back
visszajönni [visso-yuhnni] to come back, to get back, to return
visszakapni valamit [vissokopni volomit] to get something back
visszapillantótükör [visso-pillontaw-tewkur] rear view mirror
visszatérni [vissotayrni] to get back
viszketés [visketaysh] itch
viszontlátásra [visontlatashro] goodbye
vitorlás [vitorlash] sailing boat
vitorlás (csónak) [chawnok] sailing boat
vitorláshajó [vitorlash-hoyaw] yacht
vitorlázás [vitor-lazash] sailing
víz [veez] water
vízbe: a vízbe ugrani tilos no diving
vízcsap [veezchop] water tap/faucet
vízesés [veezeshaysh] waterfall

vízhatlan [veezhotlon] waterproof
vizibusz [viziboos] river-bus
vízisí [veezishee] waterskis
vízisíelés [veezishee-elaysh] waterskiing
vizisí-lecke [vizishee-letskeh] waterskiing lessons
vízisízés [veezishee-zaysh] waterskiing
vízisport [veezishport] water sports
vízum [veezoom] visa
vízvezetékszerelő [veezvezetayk-serelur] plumber
vízzel nyelje le take with water
vizsgálat [viJgalot] examination
volán steering wheel
volt he/she/it was; you were
Ön volt [uhn] you were
voltak: ők voltak [urk voltok] they were
Önök voltak [uhnuhk] you were
voltál: te voltál [teh voltal] you were
voltam [voltom] I was
voltatok: ti voltatok [voltotok] you were
voltunk: mi voltunk [voltoonk] we were
vonal [vonol] line
vonat [vonot] train
vonzó [vonzaw] attractive
vő [vur] son-in-law
vödör [vuhdur] bucket
vőlegény [vurlegay^{nyuh}] fiancé; bridegroom
völgy [vuhldj] valley
vörös [vuruhsh] red

W

WC-papír [vay-tsay-popeer] toilet paper

Z

zaj [zoy] noise
zajos [zoyosh] noisy
zakó [zokaw] jacket
zápor shower (of rain)
zár shutter (of camera); lock
zárni to lock
zárva [zarvo] closed
zászló [zaslaw] flag
zavarni [zovorni] to disturb
zene [zeneh] music
zenekar [zenekor] orchestra
zeneműbolt [zenemew-bolt] music shop
zenész [zenays] musician
zokni sock
zongora [zongoro] piano
zöld [zuhld] green
zöld csatorna [chotorno] green Customs channel
zöld kártya [kar-tyo] green card (insurance)
zöldség [zuhldshayg] vegetable
zöldséges [zuhldshaygesh], **zöldség(es)bolt** [zuhldshayg-(-esh)bolt] greengrocer's, fruit and vegetable shop
zöldség és gyümölcs [zuhldshayg aysh djewmuhlch] fruit and vegetables

zuhany [zoohonyuh] shower (in bathroom)
zuhanyozó [zooho-nyozaw] shower room
a zuhanyozó használata kötelező use of the showers is obligatory

ZS

zsák [Jak] bag
zsákutca no through road, dead end
zseb [Jeb] pocket
zsebkendő [Jebkendur] handkerchief
zsebkés [Jebkaysh] penknife
zseblámpa [Jeblampo] torch, flashlight
zsebtolvaj [Jebtolvoy] pickpocket
zsidó [Jidaw] Jewish
zsinagóga [Jinogawgo] synagogue
zsír [Jeer] fat (on meat)
zsíros [Jeerosh] fat; greasy
zsöllye [Juhl-yeh] stalls seat
zsúfolt [Joofolt] crowded

Menu Reader:

Food

ESSENTIAL TERMS

bread kenyér [keh-nyayr]
butter vaj [voy]
cup csésze [chayseh]
dessert édesség [aydesh-shayg]
fish hal [hol]
fork villa [villo]
glass pohár [po-har]
knife kés [kaysh]
main course főétel [furaytel]
meat hús [hoosh]
menu étlap [aytlop]
pepper bors [borsh]
plate tányér [ta-nyayr]
salad saláta [sholato]
salt só [shaw]
set menu napi menü [nopi menew]
soup leves [levesh]
spoon kanál [konal]
starter előétel [eluraytel]
table asztal [ostol]

another ..., please még egy ... kérek [mayg edj ... kayrek]
waiter! legyen szíves! [ledjen seevesh]
waitress! kisasszony! [kishosso^{nyuh}], legyen szíves! [ledjen seevesh]
could I have the bill, please? megkaphatnám a számlámat, kérem? [megkop-hotnam o samlamot kayrem]

áfonyamártás [afo-nyomartash] cranberry sauce
alföldi marharostélyos [olfuhldi morhorosh-tay-yosh] steak with a rich sauce and stewed vegetables
alföldi saláta [sholato] 'Great Plain Salad' – sliced sausage in vinaigrette dressing
alma [olmo] apple
almamártásban [olmo-martashbon] in an apple sauce
almás [olmash] with apple
almás cékla [tsayklo] apple and beetroot slices in salad dressing
almás rétes [raytesh] apple strudel
almával párolt káposzta [olmavol parolt kaposto] braised cabbage with apple
amerikai mogyoró [omeriko-ee modjoraw] peanuts
ananász [ononas] pineapple
ananásztorta [ononas-torto] pineapple cake
angolos marhahús [ongolosh morho-hoosh] rare steak
aprósütemény [opraw-shewtemay^{nyuh}] shortcake biscuit
apró tengeri rák [opraw] shrimps
aranygaluska [oro^{nyuh}golooshko] walnut and raisin cake

bab [bob] beans
babérlevél [bobayr-levayl] bayleaves
bableves [boblevesh] bean soup
bácskai rostélyos tarhonyával [bachko-ee roshtay-yosh torho-nyavol] braised steak with bacon and pasta
badacsonyi fogas [bodocho-nyi fogosh] giant pikeperch fillets with green pepper and tomato sauce
bajai halászlé [boyo-ee holaslay] fish and tomato soup
bakonyi betyárleves [boko-nyi beh-tyarlevesh] 'Outlaw Soup' – spicy soup made with chicken, beef, noodles and vegetables
bakonyi csirke galuskával [chirkeh golooshkavol] fried chicken in paprika and sour cream sauce with dumplings
balatoni zöldbabpaprikás [bolotoni zuhldbob-poprikash] green bean, paprika and sour cream stew
banán [bonan] banana
barack [borotsk] apricot
barackosfánk [borotskoshfank] apricot doughnut
barackos gombóc [borotskosh gombawts] large dumpling containing half an apricot and rolled in fried breadcrumbs
bárány [bara^{nyuh}] lamb
báránycomb pékné módra [bara^{nyuh}tsomb payknay mawdro] roast leg of lamb with onions and potatoes
barna kenyér [borno keh-nyayr]

brown bread; wholemeal bread
baromfi [boromfi] poultry
bécsi hering-saláta [baychi hering-sholato] rollmop herring containing pickled onion, whole black peppers and hard-boiled egg slices
becsinált csirke [bechinalt chirkeh] pieces of chicken in thick garlic sauce
bécsi szelet [baychi selet] veal chop in breadcrumbs
beigli [beh-igli] sweet roll with walnut or poppy-seed filling
békacomb rántva [bayko-tsomb rantvo] frogs' legs in breadcrumbs
bélszínérmék gombával [baylseen-ayrmayk gombavol] tenderloin steak with mushrooms
bélszínfilé [baylseen-filay] boneless tenderloin steak
besamelmártás [beshomel-martash] white sauce
betyárfogas [betyarfogosh] pikeperch fillets with mushrooms in sour cream sauce
betyárleves [betyarlevesh] thick spicy broth with vegetables and cubes of beef or pork
birka [birko] mutton
birkacomb kapormártással [birko-tsomb kopor-martash-shol] roast leg of mutton in dill and sour cream sauce
birkagulyás [birkogoo-yash] mutton goulash soup
birkaszelet vadász módra [birkoselet vodas mawdro] mutton chops in wine and parsley sauce
bográcsgulyás [bograchgoo-yash] thick spicy goulash soup made with diced meat, vegetables and paprika
borjú(hús) [bor-yoo(hoosh)] veal
borjúkotlett kertészné módra [bor-yookotlet kertaysnay mawdro] veal chops with mixed vegetables
borjúmirigy és velő [bor-yoomiridj aysh velur] veal sweetbreads and brains
borjúpörkölt [bor-yoopurkuhlt] veal stew in paprika and onion sauce
borjútokány [bor-yootoka[nyuh]] veal casserole with onions, mushrooms and sour cream
borjúvelő [bor-yoovelur] calves' brains
bormártásban [bormartashbon] in wine sauce
bors [borsh] pepper
borsó [borshaw] peas
borsostokány [borshosh-toka[nyuh]] beef casserole with pepper and onions
boszorkányhab [bosorka[nyuh]hob] 'Witches' Froth' – apple and rum mousse
buggyantott tojás [boog-djontot toyash] poached eggs
bukta [bookto] sweet roll filled

with jam
bundás alma [boondash olmo] apple fritter
bundás kelbimbó [kelbimbaw] Brussels sprout fritter
burgonya [boorgo-nyo] potatoes
burgonyaleves [boorgo-nyo-levesh] potato, onion and paprika soup
burgonyapüré [boorgo-nyo-pewray] mashed potatoes
burgonyasaláta [boorgo-nyo-sholato] potato salad
burgonyásnudli [boorgo-nya-shnoodli] potato gnocchi in breadcrumbs

cékla [tsayklo] beetroot
cigány marhasült [tsiga^{nyuh} morhoshewlt] braised beef with bacon and vegetables
cigánypecsenye [tsiga^{nyuh}pecheh-nyeh] pork chops roasted on a spit
cigányrostélyos [tsiga^{nyuh}roshtay-yosh] 'Gypsy-style' steak with brown sauce made of stock, spices, sour cream and flour
citrancs [tsitronch] grapefruit
citrom [tsitrom] lemon
citrom fagylalt [fodjlolt] lemon ice cream
citromos vajas pulykamell [tsitromosh voyosh poo^{yuh}komel] fried turkey breast in lemon sauce
comb [tsomb] leg
cukkini [tsookkini] courgettes, zucchini
cukor [tsookor] sugar

csabai szarvascomb [chobo-ee sorvosh-tsomb] venison stuffed with spicy sausage
csángó gulyás [changaw goo-yash] sauerkraut and beef stew with paprika and sour cream
császármorzsa [chasarmorJo] semolina pudding with jam and raisins
császárszelet [chasarselet] veal chops in lemon and sour cream sauce
cseresznye [cheres-nyeh] cherry
cseresznyés rétes [cheres-nyaysh raytesh] cherry strudel
csiga házába töltve [chigo hazabo tuhltveh] snails served in their shells
csikóstokány [chikawsh-toka^{nyuh}] braised strips of beef and bacon in onion, mushroom and tomato sauce with slices of green pepper, served with potatoes or rice
csipetke [chipetkeh] small noodles, usually in soups
csirke [chirkeh] chicken
csirke-aprólék leves [chirkeh-oprawlayk levesh] vegetable and giblet soup
csirke becsinált [chirkeh bechinalt] chicken stew with garlic sauce
csirkecomb roston gyömbéreslével [chirkeh-tsomb

roshton djuhm-bayresh-layvel] grilled chicken drumsticks with ginger sauce
csirke nyárson [chirkeh nyarshon] chicken roasted on a spit
csirke roston [chirkeh roshton] grilled chicken
csokoládé [chokoladay] chocolate
csokoládé fagylalt [fodjlolt] chocolate ice cream
csokoládémáz [chokoladay-maz] chocolate icing
csokoládétorta [chokoladay-torto] chocolate gâteau
csontleves [chontlevesh] clear meat soup, usually with long thin pasta
csőrögefánk [churruhgefank] crisp fried twists of thin pastry served hot with vanilla icing sugar
csuka [chooko] pike
csuka tejfölben sütve [tayfuhlben shewtveh] fried pike with sour cream

daragaluska [dorogolooshko] semolina dumplings
daragombóc [dorogombawts] semolina dumpling
darált hús [doralt hoosh] minced meat
daramorzsa [doromorJo] baked semolina crumbs, eggs and raisins
darázsfészek [doraJfaysek] 'Wasps' Nests' – pinwheel-shaped cake with chocolate and nut filling
datolya [doto-yo] dates
debreceni [debretseni] thick, spicy sausage for cooking or frying
debreceni rostélyos [roshtay-yosh] braised steak with spicy sausages
debreceni tokány [toka[nyuh]] beef casserole with onions, bacon and spicy sausages
derelye [dereh-yeh] ravioli-type pasta filled with jam, usually served with poppy seeds and sugar
dinnye [din-nyeh] melon
dinsztelt marhahús [dinstelt morho-hoosh] braised beef
dinsztelt vöröskáposzta [vuruhsh-kaposto] braised red cabbage
dió [di-aw] walnuts; nuts
diós metélt [di-awsh metaylt] sweet pasta with walnuts
diós rétes [raytesh] walnut strudel
diótorta [di-awtorto] walnut gâteau
disznócsülök káposztával [disnaw-chewluhk kapostavol] smoked knuckle of pork with sauerkraut
disznóhús [disnaw-hoosh] pork
disznósajt [disnaw-shoyt] brawn
disznótoros vacsora [disnawtorosh vochoro] pig-killing dinner – two or three kinds of grilled or roast meats, a variety of grilled or

cooked sausages with potatoes, sauerkraut and pickles

Dobostorta [doboshtorto] chocolate cream cake topped with caramel

ebéd [ebayd] lunch

ecet [etset] vinegar

ecetes torma [etsetesh tormo] horseradish in vinegar

ecetes uborka [etsetesh ooborko] gherkin pickled in vinegar

édes [aydesh] sweet

édes paprika [popriko] sweet pepper

édességek [aydesh-shaygek] sweets, desserts

édes tészták [aydesh taystak] pastry desserts

egres [egresh] gooseberries

egresfelfújt [egresh-felfoo^{yuh}t] gooseberry fool

egres mártás [egresh martash] gooseberry sauce

előételek [eluraytelek] starters, appetizers

eper strawberries

eperhab [eperhob] strawberry mousse

erdélyi fatányéros [erday-yi fota-nyayrosh] mixed grill of beef, pork, veal and goose liver

erdélyi rakottkáposzta [rokot-kaposto] layers of cabbage, rice and ground pork baked in sour cream

erdélyi tokány [toka^{nyuh}] beef casserole with bacon

erőleves [erurlevesh] clear meat soup, consommé

erőleves fürjtojással [erurlevesh fewr^{yuh}to-yash-shol] consommé with a quail's egg yolk

erőleves húsgombóccal [hoosh-gombawts-tsol] consommé with meat dumplings

erős paprika [erursh popriko] hot pepper

Eszterházy rostélyos [esterhazi roshtay-yosh] braised steak with vegetables and sour cream

étel [aytel] food

éti kagyló [ayti kodjlaw] mussels

étkezés [aytkezaysh] meal

étlap [aytlop] menu

fácán [fatsan] pheasant

fagylalt [fodjlolt] ice cream

fahéj [fohay^{yuh}], **fahéjas** [fohay-yosh] cinnamon

fánk doughnut

farsangi fánk [forshongi] apricot jam doughnut

fasírozott [fosheerozot] oven-baked beef or pork minced meat loaf with hard-boiled eggs baked inside the loaf; type of hamburger made from minced beef or pork

fatörzs [foturJ] jelly roll filled with apricot jam

fehérbab [fehayrbob] dried white beans

fehérbors [fehayrborsh] white pepper

fehérhagyma mártásban [fehayr-

hodjmo martashbon] in an onion sauce
fehér kenyér [fehayr keh-nyayr] white bread
fejes saláta [fayesh sholato] lettuce
feketebors [feketeborsh] black pepper
felfújt [felfoo^{yuh}t] soufflé
felvágott [felvagot] cold cuts
filézett rántott csirke [filayzet rantot chirkeh] boneless chicken in breadcrumbs
finomfőzelék [finom-furzelayk] mixed carrots, peas and kohlrabi in thick sour cream sauce
finommetélt [finom-metaylt] thin egg noodles
fogas [fogosh] Lake Balaton giant pikeperch
fogasfilé Bakony módra [fogoshfilay boko^{nyuh} mawdro] fillets of pikeperch in paprika and sour cream sauce
fogasszeletek Gundel modra [fogosseletek goondel modro] pikeperch fillet in breadcrumbs
fogolypecsenye [fogoypecheh-nyeh] larded roast partridge
fokhagyma [fokhodjmo] garlic
fokhagymás mártásban [fokhodjmash martashbon] in garlic sauce
folyami rák [foyomi rak] freshwater crayfish
főételek [furaytelek] main courses
főtt [furt] boiled
főtt kukorica [furt kookoritso] corn on the cob
főtt tészta pasta; gnocchi
főve [furveh] boiled
főzelék [furzelayk] vegetable dish served with meat, in thick flour-based sauce
franciakrémes [frontsio-kraymesh] custard cream sandwiched between flaky pastry, with chocolate icing and whipped egg white on top
franciasaláta [frontsio-sholato] peas, carrots and turnips in mayonnaise
füge [fewgeh] figs
fürjtojás [fewr^{yuh}toyash] quail's egg
füstölt főtt csülök tormával [fewshtuhlt furt chewluhk tormavol] smoked, boiled knuckle of pork with horseradish
füstölt marhanyelv [morho-nyelv] smoked ox tongue
füstölt sajt [shoyt] smoked cheese

galuska [golooshko] small soft dumplings
garnéla rák [gornaylo] prawns
gesztenye [gesteh-nyeh] chestnuts
gesztenyepüré [gesteh-nyeh-pewray] sweet chestnut purée flavoured with rum, served with whipped cream

gofri waffle
gomba [gombo] mushrooms
gombakrémleves [gombokraym-levesh] cream of mushroom soup
gombaleves [gombo-levesh] mushroom soup
gombamártásban [gombo-martashbon] in mushroom sauce
gombásrizs [gombashriJ] mushrooms, rice and peas
gombástokány [gombash-toka[nyuh]] beef casserole with mushrooms and onions
gomba tojással [gombo toyash-shol] mushroom omelette
gombóc [gombawts] scoop of ice cream; dumpling
göngyölt felsál [guhndjuhlt felshal] larded and braised beef olive
görögdinnye [guruhg-din-nyeh] watermelon
gránátoskocka [granatoshkotsko] potatoes with pepper and paprika, served with egg noodles
grízgaluska [greezgolooshko] semolina dumplings
gulyásleves [gooyash-levesh] goulash soup – meat, vegetable and paprika soup
Gundel palacsinta [goondel polochinto] pancakes filled with nuts, raisins and cream paste and chocolate sauce, sprinkled with rum and flambéed
gyömbér [djuhmbayr] ginger
gyuvecs [djoovech] spicy summer vegetable casserole with beef or pork
gyümölcs [djewmuhlch] fruit
gyümölcshab [djewmuhlch-hob] fruit mousse
gyümölcssaláta [djewmuhlch-sholato] fruit salad
gyümölcstorta [djewmuhlch-torto] fruit gâteau

hab [hob] type of mousse
habcsók [hobchawk] cream puff
habosszilva [hobossilvo] plum and chocolate mousse
hagyma [hodjmo] onions
hagymásrostélyos [hodjmash-roshtay-yosh] steak with onions
hagymástokány [hodjmash-toka[nyuh]] beef casserole with onions, marjoram and sour cream
hajdúsági csirketokány [hoydooshagi chirketoka[nyuh]] chicken fricassee with smoked bacon, peppers and onions
hal [hol] fish
halászlé [holaslay] spicy fish soup with paprika and vegetables
halételek [holaytelek] fish dishes
halfilé roston [holfilay roshton] grilled fillets of fish
halikrával töltött palacsinta [holikravol tuhltuht polochinto] pancakes filled with roe

halkocsonya [holkocho-nyo] jellied fish
halmajonéz [holmoyonayz] fish with mayonnaise
harcsa [horcho] catfish
harcsa roston [roshton] grilled catfish fillets
harcsaszeletek rántva [horchoseletek rantvo] catfish fillets in breadcrumbs
hasábburgonya [hoshabboorgo-nyo] chips, French fries
hátszínszelet makói módra [hatseenselet mokawi mawdro] grilled rump steak
hentestokány [hentesh-toka[nyuh]] beef stew and sliced frankfurters
hét vezér tokány [hayt vezayr toka[nyuh]] 'Seven Chieftains' – pork, veal and beef casserole with smoked bacon
hideg almaleves [olmolevesh] cold apple soup with cinnamon
hideg előételek [eluraytelek] cold starters/appetizers
hideg gyümölcsleves [djewmuhlch-levesh] cold fruit soup with cinnamon
hideg libamáj zsírjában [hideg libomī Jeer-yabon] cold goose liver served in its fat
hideg meggyleves [megdjlevesh] cold morello cherry soup with cinnamon
hollandi mártás [hollondi martash] hollandaise sauce
homár lobster
hortobágyi húsospalacsinta [hortobadji hooshosh-polochinto] minced meat pancakes with sour cream dressing
hortobágyi rostélyos [roshtay-yosh] braised steak with a large dumpling
hortobágyi rostélyos galuskával [golooshkavol] braised steak with dumplings in paprika and sour cream sauce
hurka [hoorko] type of sausage filled with rice and pork liver or rice and black pudding
hús [hoosh] meat
húsételek [hoosh-aytelek] meat dishes
húsleves [hoosh-levesh] beef or chicken soup
húspástétom [hoosh-pashtaytom] meat pie
hússaláta [hoosh-sholato] meat salad

indiáner sphere-shaped gâteau with chocolate icing and whipped cream between the half spheres
ínyencségek [ee-nyenchaygek] delicacies
ízestekercs [eezesh-tekerch] jam roll

joghurt [yoghoort] yoghurt
Jókai bableves [yawko-ee boblevesh] bean soup with smoked knuckle of pork and sour cream

juhtúró [yooH-tooraw] ewes' milk cheese, similar to cottage cheese

kacsa [kocho] duck
kacsapecsenye [kocho-pecheh-nyeh] roast duck
kalocsai halászleves [kolocho-ee holaslevesh] spicy fish soup with red wine
kapor [kopor] dill
kaporleves [kopor-levesh] fresh dill soup with cream
kapormártásban [kopor-martashbon] in dill sauce
káposzta [kaposto] cabbage
káposztásgombóc [kapostash-gombawts] dumplings stuffed with cabbage
káposztáskocka [kapostash-kotsko] square-shaped gnocchi with cabbage and paprika
káposztás palacsinta [kapostash polochinto] pancakes filled with cabbage
káposztás rétes [raytesh] cabbage strudel
kapros túrós rétes [koprosh toorawsh] strudel made with curds and dill
kapucineres felfújt [kopootsineresh felfoo^{yuh}t] coffee soufflé
karalábé [korolabay] kohlrabi
karaván [korovan] smoked cheese
karfiol [korfiol] cauliflower
karfiol krémleves [kraym-levesh] cream of cauliflower soup
kaszínótojás [koseenaw-toyash] hard-boiled eggs in mayonnaise and sour cream
kávé fagylalt [kavay fodjlolt] coffee ice cream
kecsege [kechegeh] sterlet, small sturgeon
kecskeméti hírös palacsinta [kechkemayti heeruhsh polochinto] pancakes filled with apricot jam, flambéed with apricot brandy
keksz [keks] biscuit
kelbimbó [kelbimbaw] Brussels sprouts
kelbimbó kontinentál baked Brussels sprouts
kelkáposztafőzelék [kelkaposto-furzelayk] Savoy cabbage in white sauce
keménytojás [kemay^{nyuh}toyash] hard-boiled egg
kenyér [keh-nyayr] bread
képviselőfánk [kayp-vishelur-fank] custard doughnut
keszeg [keseg] bream
kifli croissant
kijevi pulykamell [ki-yevi poo^{yuh}komel] cheese-filled turkey breast in breadcrumbs
kocsonya [kocho-nyo] jellied meat and haslet
kókusz [kawkoos] coconut
kókusztekercs [kawkoos-tekerch] coconut roll
kolbász [kolbas] spicy paprika sausage

kolozsvári gulyás [koloJvari goo-yash] goulash stew with cabbage
kolozsvári rakottkáposzta [rokot-kaposto] baked sauerkraut
kolozsvári töltöttkáposzta [tuhltuht-kaposto] cabbage stuffed with meat and rice
konyhafőnök ajánlata [ko^{nyuh}hofurnuhk oyanloto] chef's special
korhelyleves [korha^{yuh}levesh] 'Tippler's Soup' – sauerkraut soup with bacon, smoked sausage and pasta
kovászos uborka [kovasosh ooborko] pickled gherkins
kömény [kuhmay^{nyuh}] caraway seeds
köretek [kuretek] vegetable side dishes
körítések [kureetayshek] garnishes for soup
körömpörkölt [kuruhm-purkuhlt] knuckle of pork casserole
kőrözött [korruhzuht] ewes' milk cheese spread with caraway seeds and paprika
körte [kurteh] pear
krém [kraym] mousse
krémes [kraymesh] thick layer of custard cream sandwiched between two thin layers of flaky pastry, with powdered sugar on the top layer
krumpli [kroompli] potatoes
krumplistészta [kroomplish-taysto] pastry made from mashed potatoes and flour
kukorica [kookoritso] sweet corn; corn on the cob
kunsági pandúrleves [koonshagi pondoorlevesh] chicken or pigeon soup seasoned with nutmeg, paprika, ginger and garlic

lágy sajt [ladj shoyt] soft cheese
lágytojás [ladjtoyash] soft-boiled egg
lángos [langosh] savoury doughnuts
lazac [lozots] salmon
lé [lay] juice; gravy
lecsó [lechaw] green pepper and tomato stew
lekvár jam
lencse [lencheh] lentils
lencseleves [lencheh-levesh] lentil soup
lepény [lepay^{nyuh}] pie
leves [levesh] soup
levesek [leveshek] soups
liba [libo] goose
libaaprólékos rizottó [libo-oprawlaykosh rizottaw] goose-giblet risotto
libamáj [libomī] goose liver
libamájjal töltött borjújava kapros túrógombóccal [libomī-yol tuhltuht bor-yoo-yovo koprosh tooraw-gombawtstsol] veal chops stuffed with goose liver, with paprika and mushroom sauce, served with dill-flavoured curd dumplings

libamájpástétom [libomī-pashtaytom] goose-liver pâté
libamáj rántva [libomī rantvo] goose liver fried in breadcrumbs
libapecsenye [libopecheh-nyeh] roast goose
libatepertő [liboteh-pertur] goose crackling
linzer shortcake
liptói sajt [liptawi shoyt] cream cheese
liszt [list] flour
lucskoskáposzta [loochkosh-kaposto] cabbage stew

maceszgombóc [motses-gombawts] matzo ball (dumpling made from unleavened bread) in beef or chicken soup
madártej [modartay] 'floating island' – custard with poached meringues on top
máglyarakás [mag-yorokash] apple, nuts and raisins on a rum-flavoured sponge, topped with apricot jam meringue
magyaros burgonyaleves [modjorosh boorgo-nyo-levesh] potato soup with paprika and sour cream
magyaros hidegtál [modjorosh] assorted cold meats
máj [mī] liver
májas hurka [mī-osh hoorko] type of sausage filled with rice, pigs' liver and spices
májgaluska [mīgolooshko] small liver dumplings
májgombóc [mīgombawts] liver dumpling, usually in beef soup
majonézes burgonyasaláta [moyonayzesh boorgo-nyo-sholato] potato salad
majonézes kukorica [moyonayzesh kookoritso] sweet corn with mayonnaise
majonézmártás [moyonayz-martash] mayonnaise
majorannás krumpli [moyoronnash kroompli] sautéed potatoes with marjoram
mák poppy seeds
mákos [makosh] poppy-seed
mákos metélt [metaylt] sweet noodles with ground poppy seeds
mákos rétes [raytesh] strudel with poppy-seed paste filling
malac [molots] sucking pig
malacpecsenye [molotspecheh-nyeh], **malacsült** [molots-shewlt] roast sucking pig
málna [malno] raspberries
mandula [mondoolo] almonds
margarin [morgorin] margarine
marhahús [morho-hoosh] beef
marhahús angolosan [ongoloshon] rare steak
marhahús cigányosan [tsiga^{nyuh}oshon] steak with bacon
marhahús vadasan [vodoshon]

steak in game sauce

marhapörkölt [morho-purkuhlt] beef casserole

mártás [martash] sauce

mártásban [martashbon] in sauce

márványsajt [marva^{nyuh}shoyt] Stilton-like blue cheese

mazsola [moJolo] raisins

mazsolás kalács [moJolash kolach] milk bread with raisins

megfőzve [megfurzveh] boiled

meggy [megdj] morello cherries

meggyes rétes [megdjesh raytesh] morello cherry strudel

meggyleves [megdj-levesh] chilled sour cherry soup

meggymártásban [megdj-martashbon] in morello cherry sauce

megsütve [megshewtveh] fried or roasted

meleg előételek [eluraytelek] hot starters/appetizers

melegszendvics [melegsendvich] toasted sandwich

menü [menew] menu

metélt [metaylt] sweet noodle dessert with poppy seeds or other topping

méz [mayz] honey

milánói makaróni [milanawi mokorawni] pasta with ham and mushroom sauce

mogyoró [modjoraw] hazelnuts

mogyorótorta [modjoraw-torto] hazelnut gâteau

mustár [mooshtar] mustard

napi ajánlatunk [nopi oyanlotoonk] today's special

napi menü [menew] set menu

narancs [noronch] orange

narancslekvár [noronch-lekvar] marmalade

natúrszelet [notoorselet] sautéed pork chops

női szeszély [nuh-i sesay^{yuh}] 'Lady's Whim' – rich cake with raspberry jam and nut meringue

nyárson sült [nyarshon shewlt] roasted on a spit

nyelv tongue

nyelvhal [nyelvhol] sole

nyúl [nyool] rabbit; hare

nyúlpörkölt [nyool-purkuhlt] hare casserole

nyúlragu [nyool-rogoo] hare stew

olaj [oloy] oil

olajbogyó [oloybodjaw] olives

omlett omelette

orjaleves [or-yolevesh] pork chitterlings soup

orosz kaviár vajjal citrommal [oros koviar voy-yol tsitrommol] Russian caviar with butter and lemon

oroszkrém torta [oroskraym torto] rum-flavoured cream gâteau

őszibarack [ursiborotsk] peach

őzhúsleves [urzhoosh-levesh] venison soup

őznyak [urz-nyok] neck of venison

pacal [potsol] tripe
pacalpörkölt [potsol-purkuhlt] tripe casserole
padlizsán [podliJan] aubergine, eggplant
padlizsánpástétom [podliJan-pashtaytom] aubergine/eggplant purée
palacsinta [polochinto] pancakes
palócgulyás [polawts-goo-yash] lamb goulash stew
palócleves [polawts-levesh] mutton, bean and sour cream soup
paprika [popriko] pepper, bell pepper; chilli pepper
paprikás [poprikash] diced meat in paprika and sour cream sauce
paprikás burgonya [poprikash boorgo-nyo] potatoes cooked with paprika and served with sausages
paprikás csirke [chirkeh] chicken in paprika and sour cream sauce
paprikás csirke galuskával [golooshkavol] chicken fricassee in paprika and sour cream sauce with dumplings
paprikás mártásban [martashbon] in paprika and sour cream sauce
paprikás ponty [pon^{tyuh}] carp in paprika and sour cream sauce
paprikásszelet [poprikasselet] pork chops with potatoes in paprika and sour cream sauce
paradicsom [porodichom] tomatoes
paradicsomleves [porodichom-levesh] tomato soup
paradicsomos káposzta [porodichomosh kaposto] cabbage in tomato sauce
paradicsomos tökfőzelék [tuhkfurzelayk] marrow in tomato sauce
paradicsomsaláta [porodichom-sholato] tomato salad
paraj [poroy] spinach
parajos palacsinta [poro-yosh polochinto] pancakes filled with spinach
parfé [porfay] layers of ice cream and fruit
párizsi szelet [pariJi selet] pork chops fried in batter
párolt braised; steamed
párolt káposzta [kaposto] steamed or braised cabbage
párolt marhasült [morhoshewlt] braised beef
pászkagombóc [pasko-gombawts] matzo ball – dumpling made of unleavened bread
péksütemeny [paykshew-temeh^{nyuh}] bread rolls
petrezselyem [petreJeh-yem] parsley
petrezselymes burgonya [petreJeh^{yuh}mesh boorgo-nyo] potatoes with parsley
pirítós [pireetawsh] toast
pirított burgonya [pireetot boorgo-

nyo] roast potatoes
pirított libamáj [libomī] sautéed goose liver
pirított máj [mī] sautéed liver
pirított májas sertésjava [mī-osh shertaysh-yovo] sautéed pork and liver
pirított zsemlekocka [ʒemlekotsko] croûtons
pirospaprika [pirosh-popriko] paprika
piskóta [pishkawto] sponge cake
piskótatekercs [pishkawto-tekerch] jam roll
pisztráng egészben [pistrang egaysben] fried whole trout
pisztráng tejszínes mártásban [tayseenesh martashbon] trout baked in cream
pogácsa [pogacho] savoury scone
ponty [pon^{tyuh}] carp
ponty filé gombával [filay gombavol] carp fillet in mushroom sauce
pontypaprikás galuskával [pon^{tyuh}poprikash golooshkavol] carp fillets in paprika and sour cream sauce with dumplings
pörkölt [purkuhlt] meat casserole with paprika and sour cream
pörkölt rostélyos [roshtay-yosh] stewed steak
puliszka [poolisko] corn meal porridge
pulyka [poo^{yuh}ko] turkey
pulykamell [poo^{yuh}komel] turkey breast
pulykapecsenye [poo^{yuh}kopecheh-nyeh] roast turkey
puncs fagylalt [poonch fodjlolt] fruit-punch flavour ice cream
puncstorta [poonchtorto] rum and chocolate gâteau

rablóhús [roblaw-hoosh] assorted meat and vegetable kebab
rablóhús nyárson [nyarshon] pork, veal and bacon kebab
rácponty [ratspon^{tyuh}] roast carp with onions, paprika and sour cream
raguleves [rogoolevesh] chicken and vegetable soup
rák crab; lobster
rakott [rokot] layered
rakott burgonya [boorgo-nyo] boiled potatoes and hard-boiled eggs, sliced and baked with sliced sausages and sour cream
rakott kelkáposzta [kelkaposto] Savoy cabbage bake with minced meat
rakott kelvirág [kelvirag] cauliflower bake with minced meat
rakott metélt [metaylt] baked sweet noodles with ground walnuts or poppy seeds
rakott padlizsán [podliʒan] aubergine/eggplant and minced meat bake
rakott palacsinta [polochinto]

layers of pancakes with sweet fillings
rák rizottó [rizottaw] shellfish risotto
rántott in breadcrumbs
rántott csirke [chirkeh] chicken in breadcrumbs
rántott gomba [gombo] mushrooms in breadcrumbs
rántott gombafejek tartármártással [gombofayek tortar-martash-shol] mushrooms in breadcrumbs with tartar sauce
rántott hal [hol] fish fillets in breadcrumbs
rántott hús [hoosh] pork or veal chops in breadcrumbs
rántott ponty mártással [pon[tyuh] martash-shol] fillets of carp in breadcrumbs with a sauce
rántott pulykamell [poo[yuh]komel] turkey breast in breadcrumbs
rántott sertésborda [shertayshbordo], **rántottszelet** [rantot-selet] pork chops in breadcrumbs
rántott velő [velur] calves' brains in breadcrumbs
retek radish
rétes [raytesh] strudel
ribizli redcurrants
Rigó Jancsi [rigaw yonchi] chocolate gâteau with whipped cream
ringló [ringlaw] greengages
rizibizi rice with peas
rizs [riJ] rice
rizsfelfújt [riJfelfoo[yuh]t] rice soufflé
rizsköret [riJkuret] rice garnish
rókagomba [rawkogombo] chanterelle (mushroom)
rostélyos [roshtay-yosh] braised steak
rostélyos töltött ponty [tuhltuht pon[tyuh]] carp stuffed with bread, egg, herbs and fish liver or roe
roston [roshton], **rostonsült** [roshtonshewlt], **roston sütve** [shewtveh] grilled
rozmaring [rozmoring] rosemary
rozs [roJ] rye
rozskenyér [roJkeh-nyayr] rye bread

sajt [shoyt] cheese
sajtos omlett [shoytosh] cheese omelette
sajtos pogácsa [shoytosh pogacho] cheese-filled pastry cone
sajtos-rollo [shoytosh-rollo] cheese-filled roll
sajttál zöldkörettel [shoyttal zuhldkuh-rettel] cheese board with salad
saláta [sholato] salad
saláták [sholatak] salads
sampinyongomba [shompi-nyongombo] champignon (mushroom)
sárgabarack [shargo-borotsk] apricot
sárgaborsó [shargo-borshaw] dried peas

sárgadinnye [shargo-din-nyeh] honeydew melon
sárgarépa [shargo-raypo] carrots
savanyú káposzta [shovo-nyoo kaposto] sauerkraut
savanyúság [shovo-nyooshag] pickles
savanyú uborka [shovo-nyoo ooborko] pickled cucumbers; gherkins
serpenyős rostélyos [sherpeh-nyursh roshtay-yosh] braised beef and vegetables
sertés [shertaysh] pork
sertésborda [shertaysh-bordo] pork chop
sertéscsülök pékné módra [shertaysh-chewluhk payknay mawdro] knuckle of pork with onions and potatoes
sertéshús [shertaysh-hoosh] pork
sertéshúspogácsa [shertaysh-hoosh-pogacho] minced pork balls
sertéskocsonya [shertaysh-kocho-nyo] jellied pork
sertésoldalas [shertaysh-oldolosh] pork ribs
sertéspörkölt galuskával [shertaysh-purkuhlt golooshkavol] pork casserole with dumplings
só [shaw] salt
sólet [shawlet] oven-baked beans and barley with goose
sólet füstölt tarjával [fewshtuhlt tor-yavol] beans with smoked spare ribs
somlói galuska [shomlawi golooshko] rum-flavoured sponge cubes with chocolate sauce and cream
sonka [shonko] ham
sonkás fánk [shonkash] ham-filled doughnuts with grated cheese on top
sonkás karfioltorta [korfioltorto] cauliflower bake with ham
sonkáskocka [shonkash-kotsko] egg noodles with ham
sonkás palacsinta [polochinto] pancakes filled with diced ham
sóska [shawshko] sorrel
sós sütemény [shawsh shewtemay[nyuh]] small savoury cakes made with flaky pastry
spárga [shpargo] asparagus
spárga krémleves [kraymlevesh] cream of asparagus soup
spárga vajas morzsával [voyosh morJavol] asparagus au gratin
specialitások [shpetsiol-itashok] specialities
spenót [shpenawt] spinach
spenótbomba [shpenawt-bombo] spinach fritters
Stefánia marhasült [shtefanio morhoshewlt] meat loaf filled with hard-boiled eggs
Stefániatekercs [shtefanio-tekerch] pot roast beef roll filled with hard-boiled eggs
Stefániatorta [shtefanio-torto] chocolate gâteau
stíriai metélt [shteerio-ee metaylt] sweet pasta dessert with

raisins, ground walnuts and jam
süllő [shewllur] pikeperch
sült [shewlt] fried; roast
sült burgonya [boorgo-nyo] chips, French fries; baked potatoes
sült csirke [chirkeh] roast chicken
sült hal [hol] fried fish
sült krumpli [kroompli] chips, French fries; baked potatoes
sült tök [tuhk] baked pumpkin (dessert)
sülve [shewlveh] roasted
sütemény [shewteh-may[nyuh]] cake
sütemények [shewteh-may-nyek] pastry
sütve [shewtveh] fried
svájci sajtfondue [shvītsi shoytfondew] cheese fondue
svéd gombasaláta [shvayd gombo-sholato] mushroom salad
szalámi [solami] salami
szalmakrumpli [solmokroompli] crisps
szalonna [solonno] fat bacon
szalontüdő [solontewdur] lung casserole with sour cream
szamóca [somawtso] wild strawberries
szárazbableves [sarozbob-levesh] haricot bean soup
szárnyas [sar-nyosh] poultry, fowl
szárnyasaprólék-kocsonya [sar-nyosho-prawlayk-kocho-nyo] jellied giblets
szárnyaskrémleves [sar-nyosh-kraymlevesh] cream of fowl soup
szarvasgomba [sorvosh-gombo] truffles
szarvashúsleves [sorvosh-hoosh-levesh] venison consommé
szarvas magyarosan [sorvosh modjoroshon] haunch of venison
szeder [seder] blackberries
szegedi gulyás [segedi goo-yash] beef goulash with bacon and sauerkraut
szegedi halászlé [holaslay] mixed fish soup with onions and paprika
szegfűszeg [segfewseg] cloves
székelygulyás [saykeh[yuh]ygoo-yash] sauerkraut and pork stew with sour cream
szelet [selet] chop
szendvics [sendvich] sandwich
szerb gulyás [serb goo-yash] pork or beef stew with cabbage, tomatoes, onion and green pepper
szerecsendió [serechendi-aw] nutmeg
szilva [silvo] plums
szilvásgombóc [silvash-gombawts] plum dumplings
szilvás rétes [silvash raytesh] plum strudel
szósz [saws] sauce
szőlő [surlur] grapes
szűzpecsenye [sewzpecheh-nyeh] roast tenderloin of pork

tarhonya [torho-nyo] pellets of pasta
tarkabableves [torko-boblevesh] bean soup
tárkony [tarko^{nyuh}] tarragon
tárkonyos mártásban [tarko-nyosh martashbon] in tarragon sauce
tartár bifsztek [tortar bifstek] raw minced beef with a raw egg and spices
tartármártás [tortar-martash] tartar sauce
tavaszi saláta [tovosi sholato] salad of cucumbers, tomatoes, turnips, radishes and lettuce in vinaigrette dressing
tej [tay] milk
tejberizs [tayberiJ] rice pudding
tejföl [tayfuhl] sour cream
tejfölös bableves [tayfuhl-uhsh boblevesh] green bean soup with sour cream
tejszín [tayseen] cream
tejszínes paprikás mártásban [tayseenesh poprikash martashbon] in cream and paprika sauce
tejszínhab [tayseen-hob] whipped cream
tejszínhabbal [tayseen-hobbol] with whipped cream
téliszalámi [taylisolami] Hungarian salami
temesvári sertésborda zöldbabbal [temeshvari shertayshbordo zuhldbobbol] pork chops with green beans
tengeri hal [hol] saltwater fish; seafood
tepertő [tepertur] pork or goose crackling
tepertős pogácsa [tepertursh pogacho] savoury scone with pork crackling inside
tészta [taysto] pasta; dessert of chopped sweet noodles, with poppy seeds or other topping
tészták [taystak] pastry; sweet pasta dish
tojás [toyash] egg
tojásos borjúvelő [toyashosh bor-yoovelur] calves' brains with scrambled eggs
tojásrántotta [toyashrantotto] scrambled eggs
tokány [toka^{nyuh}] meat and onion casserole
tonhal [ton-hol] tuna
tonhal Orly módra [or^{yuh} mawdro] tuna fried in batter and served with tomato sauce
torta [torto] gâteau
tök [tuhk] marrow; pumpkin
tőkehal [turkehol] cod
tökfőzelék [tuhkfurzelayk] marrow in sour cream sauce with dill
töltött [tuhltuht] stuffed
töltött alma [olmo] baked apple with vanilla, raisins and cream
töltött borjúhús [bor-yoo-hoosh] stuffed roast veal

töltött csirke [chirkeh] stuffed chicken
töltött fasírozott [fosheerozot] meat loaf containing hard-boiled eggs
töltött káposzta [kaposto] soured cabbage stuffed with meat and rice, in tomato sauce with sauerkraut, usually cooked with pork
töltött paprika [popriko] peppers stuffed with meat and rice, in tomato sauce
töpörtyű [tuhpur-tyew] pork or goose crackling
trappista [troppishto] Edam-like cheese
túró [tooraw] cottage cheese
túróscsusza tepertővel [toorawsh-chooso teperturvel] noodles with cottage cheese, pork crackling and sour cream
túrós metélt [toorawsh metaylt] noodles with soft white cheese, bacon and sour cream
túrós palacsinta [toorawsh polochinto] pancakes with cottage cheese and raisin filling
túrós pite [toorawsh piteh] sweet cottage cheese pie
túróspogácsa [toorawsh-pogacho] soft white cheese scone
túrós puliszka [toorawsh poolisko] corn meal porridge with cottage cheese
túrós rétes [toorawsh raytesh] cheese strudel
túrós táska [toorawsh tashko] pastry envelope filled with soft white cheese
tüdő [tewdur] cows' lungs
tükörtojás [tewkur-toyash] fried eggs
tűzdelt fehérpecsenye [tewzdelt fehayrpecheh-nyeh] larded tenderloin steak
tűzdelt nyúlgerinc [nyoolgerints] larded saddle of hare

tyúkhúsleves [tyook-hooshlevesh] chicken broth

uborka [ooborko] cucumbers; gherkins
uborkasaláta [ooborko-sholato] cucumber salad
Újházy tyúkhúsleves [oo[yuh]hazi tyook-hoosh-levesh] chicken soup with noodles and dumplings

ürü [ewrew] mutton
ürüborda [ewrew-bordo] mutton chop
ürücomb [ewrew-tsomb] leg of mutton
ürügerinc [ewrew-gerints] saddle of mutton
ürügulyás [ewrew-goo-yash] mutton goulash

vadas [vodosh] sauce made from lemon juice, mustard, sour cream and diced vegetables
vadasan [vodoshon] meat and vegetables in lemon juice,

mustard and sour cream sauce
vadasmártásban [vodosh-martashbon] in mushroom, almond, herb and brandy sauce
vaddisznó borókamártással [voddisnaw borawko-martash-shol] wild boar in juniper sauce
vaddisznó erdész módra [erdays mawdro] haunch of wild boar with mushrooms, bacon and potatoes
vaddisznósült borosmártással [voddisnaw-shewlt borosh-martash-shol] roast wild boar chops in wine sauce
vadszárnyas [vodsar-nyosh] fowl
vagdalt libamelle [vogdolt libomelleh] goose-meat loaf
vaj [voy] butter
vanília [voneelio] vanilla
vanília fagylalt [fodjlolt] vanilla ice cream
vargabéles [vorgobaylesh] vanilla and raisin sponge cake
vegetariánus [vegetorianoosh] vegetarian
vegyes saláta [vedjesh sholato] mixed salad
velő [velur] brains
velő tojással [toyash-shol] scrambled eggs with brains
véres hurka [vayresh hoorko] type of sausage filled with rice and black pudding
vese [vesheh] kidney
vesepecsenye [vesheh-pecheh-nyeh] kidneys in mustard sauce
vesepörkölt [vesheh-purkuhlt] kidney and liver casserole
vese velővel [velurvel] kidney and brains casserole
virsli [virshli] frankfurters
vitaminsaláta [vitomin-sholato] grated cabbage, carrot, radish and onion salad
vöröshagyma [vuruhsh-hodjmo] red onions

zabpehely [zob-peheh[yuh]] oat flakes
zeller celery
zellerkrémleves [zeller-kraym-levesh] cream of celery soup
zöldbab [zuhldbob] green beans
zöldborsó [zuhldborshaw] peas
zöldpaprika [zuhldpopriko] green pepper
zöldség [zuhldshayg] vegetables
zöldségleves [zuhldshayg-levesh] vegetable soup

zsemle [Jemleh] bread roll
zsemlegombóc [Jemleh-gombawts] potato dumplings with croûtons inside
zserbószelet [Jerbawselet] apricot jam, nut and chocolate cream layer cake
zsíros pirítós [Jeerosh pireetawsh] fried bread with garlic
zsiványpecsenye [Jiva[nyuh]pecheh-nyeh] assorted roast meats

Menu Reader:

Drink

ESSENTIAL TERMS

beer sör [shur]
bottle üveg [ewveg]
brandy konyak [ko-nyok]
black coffee fekete [feketeh]
coffee kávé [kavay]
cup csésze [chayseh]
  a cup of ... egy csésze ... [edj chayseh]
fruit juice gyümölcslé [djewmuhlchlay]
gin gin [jin]
  a gin and tonic gint és tonicot [jint aysh tonikot]
glass pohár [po-har]
  a glass of ... egy pohár ... [edj po-har]
milk tej [tay]
mineral water ásványvíz [ashva^{nyuh}veez]
red wine vörösbor [vuruhshbor]
soda (water) szódavíz [sawdoveez]
soft drink üdítő [ewdeetur]
sugar cukor [tsookor]
tea (drink) tea [teh-o]
tonic (water) 'tonic'
vodka 'vodka'
water víz [veez]
whisky viski
white wine fehérbor [fehayrbor]
wine bor
wine list borlista [borlishto], itallap [itollop]

another ... még egy ... [mayg edj]

Akali zöldszilváni [okoli zuhld-silvani] sweet white wine
alkohol [olkohol] alcohol
alkoholmentes ital [olkohol-mentesh itol] soft drink
almabor [olmobor] cider
Arany Ászok® [oro^{nyuh} asok] brand of light bottled lager
ásványvíz [ashva^{nyuh}veez] mineral water
asztali bor [ostoli] table wine
azonnal oldódó kávépor [ozonnol oldawdaw kavaypor] instant coffee

Badacsonyi Szürkebarát [bodocho-nyi sewrkeborat] 'Grey Friar of Badacsony' – a medium-dry white wine
Balatonfüredi szemelt [boloton-fewredi semelt] sweet white wine
barackpálinka [borotsk-palinko] apricot brandy
barna sör [borno shur] brown ale
bor wine
borkóstoló [borkawsh-tolaw] special wine-sampling meal – the meal is served with different wines, starting with the driest and working through to the sweetest
borlista [borlishto] wine list

citromos tea [tsitromosh teh-o] lemon tea
cukor [tsookor] sugar

csapolt sör [chopolt shur] draught beer
cseresznyepálinka [cheres-nyeh-palinko] cherry brandy

Dreher® brand of bottled lager

édes [aydesh] sweet
édes bor sweet wine
Egri bikavér [bikovayr] 'Bulls' Blood of Eger' – full-bodied red wine
Egri Leányka [leh-a^{nyuh}ko] 'Little Girl of Eger' – medium-dry white wine
Egri pinot noir light red wine
étvágygerjesztő [aytvadj-ger-yestur] aperitif

fehérbor [fehayr-bor] white wine
fekete(kávé) [feketeh(-kavay)] black coffee, espresso
féldeci [fayldetsi] 1/20th of a litre – measure for spirits
félédes bor [faylaydesh] medium-sweet wine
fél liter [fayl] half a litre
forralt bor [forrolt] mulled wine
friss csapolás [frish-sh chopolash] beer from a newly tapped barrel
fröccs [fruhtsch] wine with soda water
furmint [foormint] dry

gyomorkeserű [djomor-kesherew] bitter-sweet alcoholic herbal drink
gyümölcslé [djewmuhlchlay] fruit juice

házi bor house wine

hosszú lépés [hossoo laypaysh] spritzer made with one part wine to two parts soda water
Hubertus [hoobertoosh] strong, bitter-sweet, alcoholic herbal drink

ital [itol] drink
itallap [itollop] wine list

jég [yayg] ice
jeges kávé [yegesh kavay] iced coffee
jégkocka [yaygkotsko] ice cube

kakaó [koko-aw] cocoa
kávé [kavay] coffee
kisüsti [kishewshti] 'small cauldron' brandy – brandy made in small quantities (often at home or as cottage industry)
koffeinmentes [koffeh-inmentesh] decaffeinated
konyak [ko-nyok] cognac
korsó [korshaw] half-litre mug
Kőbányai® [kurba-nyo-ee] brand of bottled lager
körtepálinka [kurteh-palinko] pear brandy

lé [lay] juice
likőr [likur] liqueur
limonádé [limonaday] lemonade
lógatós tea [lawgotawsh teh-o] teabag
lopó [lopaw] glass instrument used in wine cellars to take a sample of wine from the barrel

málnaszörp [malnosurp] raspberry juice with soda water
meleg hot
meleg csokoládé [chokoladay] hot chocolate
meleg tej [tay] hot milk
minőségi bor [minurshaygi] quality wine

narancslé [noronchlay] orange juice
narancsszörp [noronch-surp] orangeade

óbarack [awborotsk] 'old' apricot brandy – a better quality version of barackpálinka
Olasz riszling [olos risling] sweet white wine

őszibarackpálinka [ursiborotsk-palinko] peach brandy

pálinka [palinko] Hungarian fruit brandy
Pannonia [ponnonio] sparkling wine
Pannonia Sör® [shur] brand of bottled beer
paradicsomlé [porodichomlay] tomato juice
pezsgő [peJgur] fizzy; champagne
pohár [po-har] glass

rózsaszín bor [rawJoseen] rosé
rumos tea [roomosh teh-o] tea with rum

Soproni Kékfrankos [shoproni

kaykfronkosh] full-bodied red wine
sör [shur] beer

száraz [saroz] dry
szárazbor [sarozbor] dry wine
szárítani [sareetoni] dry
szilvapálinka [silvo-palinko] plum brandy
szódával [sawdavol] with soda water
szódavíz [sawdoveez] soda water
szörp [surp] fruit squash, fruit cordial
szürkebarát [sewrkeborat] dry white wine

tea [teh-o] tea
tea citrommal [teh-o tsitrommol] tea with lemon
tej [tay] milk
tejeskávé [tayesh-kavay] coffee with milk
tejes tea [tayesh teh-o] tea with milk
tejjel [tay-yel] with milk
tejszín [tayseen] cream
tejszínhab [tayseen-hob] whipped cream
tejszínhabbal [tayseen-hobbol] with whipped cream
Tihanyi merlot [tiho-nyi] full-bodied red wine
Tokaji [tokoyi] very sweet white wine
Tokaji Aszú [osoo] very sweet white wine
Tokaji Furmint [foormint] medium-dry white wine
Tokaji Szamorodni [somorodni] dry white wine
törköly [turkuh^{yuh}] brandy made from various fruits

Unicum [oonitsoom] strong, bitter-sweet alcoholic herbal drink to help digestion

üdítőital [ewdeetur-itol] soft drink
üdítők [ewdeeturk] refreshments
üveg [ewveg] bottle

Vaskúti kadarka [voshkooti kodorko] light red wine
világos sör [vilagosh shur] lager
villányi burgundi [villa-nyi boorgoondi] light red wine
Villányi medoc noir full-bodied red wine
viszki [viski] whisky
vörösbor [vuruhsh-bor] red wine

zöldszilváni [zuhld-silvani] dry white wine

I would like to receive ROUGH*NEWS*: please put me on your free mailing list.

NAME . . . .

ADDRESS . . . .

Please clip or photocopy and send to: Rough Guides, 1 Mercer Street, London WC2H 9QJ, England

or Rough Guides, 375 Hudson Street, New York, NY 10014, USA.

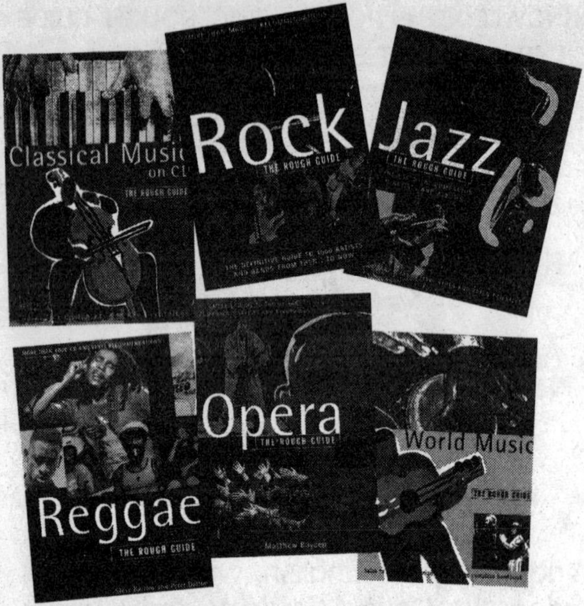